Praise for *The Land R*

"Of all the agrarian scholar-activists in America, Neil Hamilton has played the most pivotal role in pioneering good policy and stewardship practices than any other individual. He is beloved by farmers, seed savers, agricultural land trusts, and the thousands of students whom he has influenced with his brilliant lectures and compassionate mentoring. Now, with a profound and enlivening prose, he weaves together all the strands of agricultural stewardship into a compelling 'crazy quilt' vision for what healthy lands and rural communities ought to be in a just and prosperous future. But unlike other chroniclers of farm country history, Hamilton not only give us hope because of what is in his head, but also because of what he has held in his hands and in his heart."—**Gary Paul Nabhan, author of *Coming Home to Eat, Renewing America's Food Traditions, Food from the Radical Center, and Jesus for Farmers and Fishers***

"*The Land Remains* is the perfect book at the perfect time: a vivid, engaging and thoroughly insightful treatise on land and agriculture. On every page, Neil Hamilton masterfully translates the challenges inherent in our food system—quite literally from the ground up—but then goes beyond the limitations to find solutions and hope. But the real win here is Hamilton's unique perspective that so accurately sums up what many of us already suspect when it comes to caring for the land that feeds and sustains us: whether we come to our actions by understanding the nature of the world, or the world of nature, both must intersect in order to effect positive and everlasting change."—**Tracey Ryder, Co-Founder & CEO, Edible Communities**

"Neil Hamilton is a Lorax for the land—if the Lorax had the insights of a lawyer, the wisdom of an agrarian philosopher, the acumen of a policymaker, and the lived experience of an Iowa farm kid. As we consider what it will take to build an agriculture that nourishes both humans and the land, we are lucky to have Hamilton's wisdom to guide us. *The Land Remains* is a powerful reminder that a better future for food and farming is possible— one that advances social and racial justice, holds the soil in place, and gives our people and communities the nourishment they need to thrive. *The Land Remains* is more than a memoir; it's a stirring call to action to all of us— farmers and voters alike—to protect the soil as if our life depended on it. Because it does."—**Curt Ellis, co-founder and CEO of FoodCorps, and co-creator of the Peabody-winning documentary, *King Corn***

"Anyone interested in exploring how to have a more inspiring, practical way to relate to land sustainably will want to read this book!" —**Dr Frederick Kirschenmann; Retired, former director of the Leopold Center**

"It is clear we need clarion voices like Neil Hamilton's to speak for the land. To this former Iowa farm boy become Emeritus Professor of Law, the soil is an animate being worthy of reverence and a duty of care. Across the nation, and all over the planet, we've allowed our agricultural top soils to erode and lose fertility at an alarming rate. As the substrate for food and agriculture, the land is our most precious natural resource; continued maltreatment sullies our future prospects as a species. At heart, *The Land Remains* is a hopeful book filled with practical advice about soil and water conservation and commonsense solutions within our ken. Let us all join in the chorus and pivot to the future!"—**Amy Goldman, author of *The Melon***

"*The Land Remains* explores our most valuable natural resources—soil, water, air and biodiversity—in Iowa, one of the most altered landscapes on Earth. Neil couples his agriculture law and policy expertise with his deep personal connection to his family's Iowa farm to question how we can work in partnership with the land to build a truly sustainable ecosystem and future. Connecting current land issues to economic inequality, racism and environmental degradation. *The Land Remains* offers an ultimately hopeful outlook for the future, should we all recognize the land as the cornerstone of our lives." —**Paul Willis, Niman Ranch Pork Co., Director/Founder**

"Neil Hamilton has spent decades working the ground where agriculture, conservation, the law, policy, and ethics intersect. In *The Land Remains*, he brings that experience together in stories about and from the Iowa landscape that he knows best—and that has been such a proving ground for our successes and failures in land stewardship. Hamilton combines his personal insights and professional expertise, yielding a compelling commentary on our responsibilities as caretakers of the land.—**Curt Meine, Author, *Aldo Leopold: His Life and Work***

"We all depend on the land. Our basic needs of food, clothing, and shelter all come from the land. The air we breathe, the water we drink, all depend on the land and the biodiversity it wants to support. One would think stewardship of this precious resource would be our highest priority. But instead of listening to the land we ignore it. We see this with unsustainable soil loss, polluted water, and vanishing biodiversity. As the land suffers so, do we. Yet, Mother Nature is both benevolent and forgiving. If we simply listen to her and apply her wisdom the land responds in wonderful ways. In *The Land Remains* Professor Neil Hamilton writes from the land's perspective. Allowing us to hear its story firsthand. Helping us understand what we're doing to it, and to understand how we can help. In this wonderful book the land shares the wisdom we need to work with it, advocate for it, and help others to do the same. Allowing all of us to serve the land that has served us all so well."—**Seth Watkins, Pinhook Farm, Page County Iowa cattleman**

"Professor Hamilton skillfully weaves together a narrative of his personal connection to the land with sound policy advice—grounded not only in years of research, but also in his deep experience. His forthright critique of our current approach to issues from soil conservation to water quality is balanced by an essential optimism in the future of our relationship to the land."—**Jerry L. Anderson, Dean and Richard M. and Anita Calkins Distinguished Professor of Law, Drake University Law School**

"There is a rhythm to *The Land Remains* that reminds me of the rhythms embedded deep in the land that Professor Hamilton reverences. I noticed this same rhythm the first time I sat in Professor Hamilton's food policy class: a pattern of blending midwestern, unpretentious moral sensibilities with an endless intellectual curiosity and new ideas about relationships between people, land, law, and agriculture. These inflections have steadily marked Hamilton's work over the years and loom large in this personal memoir. They also fuse perfectly with his practical legal and policy recommendations which make the book a substantive read as well as interesting, engaging, and reflective. In short, the book does what Hamilton did for me in the classroom: it invites the reader–to quote a line from a page–'to stop and think.'" —**Michael T. Roberts, Executive Director, University of California, Los Angeles, School of Law Resnick Center for Food Law and Policy**

"This book is from the land and for the land. Professor Hamilton lays out the legal underpinnings of property in Iowa, the most cultivated patch on Earth. The law defines how we approach the land, and it can provide the moral rationale for a conservation ethic that can protect world food production threatened by ecological catastrophe. Answers to our most existential problem lies in the Back 40 of an Adams County farm: How do we live with the land?"—**Art Cullen, editor of *The Storm Lake Times* and Pulitzer Prize-winning author of *Storm Lake: Change, Resilience, and Hope in America's Heartland***

"The stars aligned just right to tug a farm kid from the fields of Iowa to a degree in economics and forestry at ISU and through law school and a distinguished professorship in agricultural law. His hands-on experience with the land, nature, history, and the law come together in this highly readable and valuable work. It's ripe with wisdom, and should be well-thumbed, and in a highly visible place on every land owner and policy maker's desk."—**Robert Leonard, author of *Deep Midwest*, and radio host KNIA/KRLS**

"If this land could talk, ah, the stories it would tell! Neil Hamilton hears the compelling voice of his historic Back 40. He translates its tales into constructive dialogue of how to preserve and protect all Iowa's priceless land and water resources. A read like no other."—**Pat Boddy, former deputy and interim director of Iowa DNR**

"No one is more qualified than Neil Hamilton to teach us about the land and its continuing impact on our lives and our world. From personal experience as an Iowa farm boy, he has a rare and profound understanding of the pleasures and pain of life on the farm, and as a noted scholar and professor of agricultural law, he has a deep knowledge of where we have gone wrong in our stewardship of the land and what we must do to correct these wrongs. Hamilton is not an alarmist but he does a good job of making us understand that the story of the land is our story as well."—**James A. Autry, author of** *The White Man Who Stayed*

"This book will make a major contribution to the discussion of the direction of Iowa's agriculture."—**Dennis Keeney, first director of the Leopold Center for Sustainable Agriculture**

"Neil Hamilton's book is a love song to the earth, informed by deep family bonds, as well as extensive knowledge of the ecological, agricultural, legal and political nature of the land that sustains us all. There is warning here, but also hope, found in Neil's portrayal of heroic environmental voices in Iowa's past and in his inspiring (and practical) advice for those of us who want to make a positive difference today. An essential read for all Iowans—and all Americans."—**John T. Price, author of** *Man Killed by Pheasant* **and** *editor of The Tallgrass Prairie Reader*

"A excellent read from cover to cover. The impacts of Midwestern agricultural and environmental policies, woven with the traditions and ideas of the past make this an ideal addition to understanding the Midwest heartland!"—**Liz Garst, Farmer and Banker**

"Neil Hamilton blends Iowa history, family history, and current farm and land policy into a provocative discussion on the future of land in Iowa and the United States. You may not agree with him on every topic but the narrative features important figures in Iowa and US history, and is worthy of additional reflection by all."—**Leo Landis, Iowa Historian**

"Professor Hamilton has a unique background for the subject matter in his book, *The Land Remains*. He grew up on a farm in Iowa with an outdoor hand pump for a water source. He studied forestry before studying law as it applies to agriculture. He headed up the Drake University Agricultural Law Center. He has lived at the center of the Iowa storm over agricultural practice and water quality. His appreciation of Leopold's Land Ethic, Lacey's public lands legislation and Ding Darling's poignant conservation cartoons are beautifully expressed in *The Land Remains*. This is a must read for all who care about our Soil, Air, Water, Woods, and Wildlife. His knowledge must be put to use for the benefit of our children and their children."—**Mike Delaney, Conservation Director, Iowa Izaak Walton League**

"In *The Land Remains* Iowa treasure Neil Hamilton is hopeful for the land and the people who care for it. He uses his powerful intellect and extensive experience to articulate ways to address climate change and our other challenges on land and make a more livable and sustainable world for all of us."—**Teresa Opheim, Climate Land Leaders**

"Hamilton is a masterful story-teller, weaving history seamlessly into current events and using his personal story to showcase our public interest in caring for the land. Rich historical references bring together the writings of great agriculturalists from the early days of soil conservation with the current writings of the present day. This book is a delightful read that is both entertaining and provocative. His innovative use of the first-person narrative from the "back forty" tract of farm land gives the land its voice and perspective, showcasing the land as life, past present, and future. *The Land Remains* unique approach combines personal story with in depth analysis, introducing and discussing many of the most important figures in the development of US land and conservation policies and providing powerful lessons regarding soil loss, soil health, and the impact of both on our world—all with the personal touch of the life story of one of the greatest agricultural law leaders of our time."—**Susan A. Schneider, William H. Enfield Professor of Law; Director, LLM Program in Agricultural & Food Law, University of Arkansas School of Law**

"This book will give the reader a better understanding of Neil Hamilton's legacy. His love of life and land. There are so many wonderful references to other prominent conservationists and their writings. *The Land Remains* is a reminder and an inspiration that we must never give up on our land and conservation efforts."—**Mark C. Ackelson, President Emeritus, Iowa Natural Heritage Foundation**

"A keeper for the 'movement.'"—**Wes Jackson, President Emeritus, The Land Institute**

"*The Land Remains* is an engaging exploration of our relationship with land. It tells an honest story of how we have treated our most fundamental natural resource and the author's efforts to provide it a voice. He literally does so here by personifying land as carrying on through our legal institution of property. Professor Hamilton simultaneously tells his own story as a farm kid, a forestry major, a law professor, a farmer, and an advocate. Part memoir, part legal history, part policy analysis, and part caricature, this book provides a rich understanding of midwestern land and our best hopes for its future. The land is our heritage, our livelihood, and our legacy. *As we pass through, the land remains.*"—**Anthony Schutz Associate Dean for Faculty & Associate Professor of Law, Nebraska College of Law**

"*The Land Remains* gives great insight into the complexity of land tenure in Iowa, past, and present. In addition to sharing his own lineage of cultural memories of farm life in rural Iowa, Hamilton courageously addresses the issues of inequity and past failures of land policy in the Midwest, which can often be an elephant in the room in the field of land conservation in the United States. Rooted in a comprehensive historical context, Hamilton has gifted the reader an invitation to reimagine what the future of land stewardship can look like in the Midwest with a lens that holds a diversity of stakeholders essential. Hamilton boldly encourages readers to unpack the many layers of impacts of settler colonialism and to lean into ways that all Midwesterners can reconcile their relationships to the land that sustains them. Uniquely weaving in narratives from the land itself from his childhood farm, Hamilton unearths the depth of connection that he himself, and those in his lineage have to the fertile fields of the heartland, and tends the possibility of new visions of stewardship of these lands for future generations."—**Rowen White, Mohawk Farmer/Seedkeeper**

"If a sign of a good book is that you have to constantly put it down because what you read spurs you to action, then you'll find this an almost impossible book to finish. Neil Hamilton's deep and practical knowledge will activate you! Hamilton's unique ability to persuade us that, for all of 'modernity,' humanity remains utterly contingent upon the land and on the ways we interact with it, is a result of who he is. Raised on some of the planet's best agricultural land, an Iowa farm, Hamilton was educated at an agricultural university but—improbably—emerged a committed environmentalist, became a leading agricultural law expert, advised non-profit organizations and governments from local to federal, and continues to be active in illumined land management and policy as a farmer and elected official. If you doubt that given the existential crises we currently confront as a species—climate change, pandemics, economic inequality and the threat to democracy—you need to spare a moment to think about land management and policy, just give Hamilton the opportunity to demonstrate that land is the keystone we're all seeking for the arch of harmonious human wellbeing on the planet."
—**Ricardo Salvador, Director and Senior Scientist, Food & Environment Program, Union of Concerned Scientists**

"What if a parcel of land could speak? What would it tell of its past, present, and future and interactions with the people and institutions which impact it? Neil Hamilton lays this out in an engaging and perceptive manner that requires the reader to stop thinking about the land as just dirt."
—**Dr. Cornelia Butler Flora, Charles F. Curtiss Distinguished Professor of Agriculture and Sociology, Iowa State University and Research Professor, Kansas State University**

The Land Remains

Listen to the Land

Neil D. Hamilton

Ice Cube Press. LLC (Est. 1991)
North Liberty, Iowa, USA

Dedicated to the memory of my parents, Lowell and Zella Mae Hamilton, and to the lifetimes they spent caring for their land and their boys.

"The social lesson of soil waste is that no man has the right to destroy soil even if he does own it in fee simple. The soil requires a duty of man which we have been slow to recognize."
— Henry A. Wallace

"When the logic of history hungers for bread and we hand out a stone, we are at pains to explain how much the stone resembles bread."
—Aldo Leopold

"People who imagine that history flatters them…are impaled on their history like a butterfly on a pin and become incapable of seeing or changing themselves, or the world."
—James Baldwin

Contents

Hamilton Prairie in Adams County, Iowa, an INHF project

Preface—
The Land Remains

This book is about the Land, mainly about farmland but not entirely.

A good deal of the story takes place in Iowa but not all of it – because to understand our land you must consider the nation.

Many of the stories are told through the reflections of my life growing up on our Iowa farm and over forty years of teaching about the law of the land, but not all.

Much of the book is told by the people who own and use the land and who shape our thinking about it – but not everything. Any book about the land needs to hear from the land itself, so we will hear from the Back Forty on my family's farm.

You may be one of the millions of fortunate Americans who own a tract of land. Perhaps it is a quarter section, 160 acres of fertile Midwestern farmland. If so congratulations for holding this ticket to our future. If you don't have the good fortune or family history to own farmland you most likely do own your home and the land on which it sits. You may also be among the over 40 million Americans who tend a garden of vegetables or flowers, and you probably mow your yard. If so, you know the joy of putting your hands in the soil, of watching seeds and plants grow, bloom, and ripen on your land.

Even if you do not own a home or tend a garden, as an American you are still a landowner because we all share ownership in our rich stock of public lands – the over 1 billion acres we own together.

As Americans we are all landowners! The lands we share include our National Forests and Grasslands, National Parks and wildlife refuges, state and local parks, trails and play grounds – thousands of different tracts in all shapes, sizes, and types found all across the nation. America is rich in land and as Americans we are beneficiaries of this richness, directly and indirectly. Whether we care to acknowledge it or not, we are shaped by our land.

This book tells the story of our land, both the private land families may cherish and the public lands we share. But it is about more than just the land in a physical sense, it is really about the people who have shaped our land and about how history has determined who among us owns what and what it means to be a landowner. Some of our history of land ownership is bloody and bitter, leaving a residue of inequality in wealth and opportunity still haunting us today.

The stories of our land are also filled with hope, with family legacies, with fulfillment and enjoyment - important stories. Important because land provides the foundations for our lives. The food that sustains us; the water, air and wildlife that create our environment; the wealth and income that drives large segments of our economy – all find their origin in the land. Yet the story of our land, both its history and future, is not without conflict and risk. Whether it is in family land disputes threatening to tear apart generations; or in the abusive farming practices seen etched on Midwestern hillsides, abuse that continues a century after our recognition of the dangers of soil erosion; or in the ideological battles between those who deny the public interest in land, not just in lands owned by the public but in ideas of stewardship to restrain the rights of private owners to abuse the land. The truth is if you scratch deeply enough land is at the heart of many of the most fundamental conflicts shaping society's future. These stories are told against a backdrop of individuals – some who may be familiar – people like Aldo Leopold, the Roosevelts - FDR and TR, and Gifford Pinchot. Others, though less well known, are of equal importance – John Lacey, Ding Darling, Russell Lord, Louis Bromfield. You will meet other people unique to my story – grandmother Anna Wray Hamilton, the Icarians of Adams County, and friends and fellow landowners, farmers, neighbors and colleagues. This diverse cast of characters helps put flesh and blood into the story of our land.

Before turning to the story of the land I want to take a moment and address two questions, why I wrote this book and what readers should understand about the land. There are two types of reasons for writing a book – the personal and the political. As to the personal, my recent retirement gave me time to focus on issues that have bubbled in my mind and writing for years but I never had an opportunity to address comprehensively. Having spent my life working on and with the land, personally and legally, I feel a need to share the insights and understanding gained. As to the political reasons for writing, there are many. First, the COVID pandemic helped bring the role of land and nature into sharper relief for many citizens, especially the value of our public lands. Second, the Trump Administration was anti-environment and anti-public lands to an extent previously unseen. This means the damage done by their actions must be confronted and corrected by the new Biden-Harris Administration. Third, the challenge of climate change presents new threats and new opportunities for the land, for farmers and for landowners. Our answers to climate change will come largely from the land, making questions of who owns and controls the land very important. Fourth, our history of farm production has and continues to adversely impact the land. Our historical approach to soil conservation is one policy issue helping mediate this reality, meaning it will be foundational for our future. Fifth, a growing body of organizations working with land and farmers, from land trusts like the Iowa Natural Heritage Foundation to farmer-led organizations like Practical Farmers of Iowa, will shape our land future making it vital to understand their work. Finally, the role of millions of citizens and individual owners make land issues inherently democratic. Even with our legacy of wealth inequality and conflict, the land will continue to be the foundation we rely on going forward as a society – meaning we need to appreciate the land and hear from it.

Whenever I began a new course, I liked to present my students with some idea of our goals – where we were headed and what they could expect to learn. Assuming this same approach may be valuable for you as a reader, the following ideas reflect what I hope you will "take-away" from the book:

> Our history with the land is long and complicated, and parts are soaked in racism as well as opportunity, but the role of land in reflecting wealth is central to our society.

> Our relation to the land shapes the economy and our lives, but what we value in the land evolves over time as new land features come to have value, such as storing carbon, and new dimensions of land are recognized as socially important, for example, historic properties.

> Concepts of private property are deeply embedded in society, in politics and in our economy; however, property is not one-dimensional, all land also has a public dimension influencing how it can be used.

Public land policy played a unique role in our nation's history and public land issues still present some of our most vexing and significant challenges in the human to land relation.

All citizens have a stake in land policy, whether in how regulations are used to conserve soil and protect water quality, in expanding the use of public lands, or in promoting land access, ownership, and equity.

Land issues are too important to be left to a small group of vested interests, the farmers, landowners, and investors who control much of the land. Instead the voices and perspectives of all citizens need to be included in deciding how we use the land.

It is critical to see land issues not just in the abstract but as specific places, because what happens on any tract of land ultimately contributes to our collective land health and future.

The assignment may seem ambitious, but I promise it will be fun.

Fan and Dan — my parent's last team of draft horses.

Chapter One - Grandmother Anna Saves the Farm

Land is the foundation on which we construct our lives, it is the sun-driven factory producing our food and fiber, it is the natural playground where we recreate and connect with nature. Land defines our nation, reflects our history – good and bad – and contains our future. The land is something we consider stable and can take for granted. We do so at our peril.

Yes, the land appears eternal but looks can be deceiving. The truth is the health of our land and from it our own health is troubled. Trouble can be seen in the tons of soil we let erode off each acre of Iowa farmland every year we plant and harvest a crop. Trouble can be seen in conflicts over the "public lands" some people want to privatize for energy, mining, timber, and grazing, denying all citizens the rightful heritage to the bounty in "our" lands. Trouble can be seen in the evolving patterns of ownership and land tenure determining not just who makes the decisions for how it is used, but who benefits from the land and shares in the wealth it creates. Even as our nation experiences an emerging consensus of the need to address climate change and recognizes the vital role land will play in the effort, trouble can be found in deciding whether farmers and landowners will guide these efforts and benefit from so doing, or if the land and landowners will simply become pawns in the latest corporate schemes devised by Silicon Valley investors hoping to squeeze one more payment from the land.

Enough about troubles, this book is really not about them. The real subjects are hope and the land. For each of the troubles listed there is reason for hope, found in the people working on the land constructing brighter stories to drive our future. Understanding our history on the land can shape our future history with the land. There will be a future, for us it won't be eternal because we all must pass, but the land does not die, unless we take active steps to kill it. No, the land remains.

I spent the last forty years working with the land, how it is shaped by the law and how it in turn has shaped the law. My life has never been far from the land – from my childhood on our small farm in southwest Iowa, to forestry school at Iowa State and law school at Iowa, then a turn as an Assistant Attorney General for Iowa, and finally for the last forty years as a law professor – first at the University of Arkansas and for over three decades directing the Agricultural Law Center at Drake University in Des Moines. During these years I served on the boards of various non-profits like the Iowa Natural Heritage Foundation, Seed Savers Exchange, the National Gardening Association, and the Food Corps to name a few, each with a direct connection to the land and food. My public service included over twenty years on the advisory board of the Leopold Center for Sustainable Agriculture at Iowa State, seven years chairing the Iowa Food Policy Council, and co-chairing a USDA subcommittee on land tenure and beginning farmers Secretary of Agriculture Tom Vilsack created at my urging. These activities kept me busy but also gave me a front row seat to observe how law and policy impact our land. In its own way, each effort focused on the land and our relation to it – whether raising better food, protecting land, conserving soil, improving how we farm, or helping pass land to a new generation of farmers.

At home our lives revolve around Sunstead Farm, the market garden my wife Khanh and I have spent twenty-five years building as a showplace for local foods to sell and to share with our friends. More than a large garden, Sunstead has evolved into a beautiful mix of heirloom vegetables, flowers, art, and nature, framed by a 320-year old oak and bordered by Sugar Creek. Planting our fields each spring, harvesting what we grow, and sharing the bounty and beauty of Sunstead has come to define our lives and gives us purpose. All these things we draw from the land.

As you can see, these activities – my work, if you can call what you love doing work – are grounded on the land. This book is the product of these experiences. It uses history to frame the issues and draws on my experiences to tell the story about America's land. The story is not just about a personal journey – by itself that would hold little interest. No, the story is much bigger and more important, touching on issues of how the land impacts all citizens. It begins on the farm where I grew up.

The Hamilton Farm

When it comes to our farm – the one my parents farmed for over 50 years – the most important person in the story of its existence is my grandmother – Anna Wray Hamilton, my Dad's mom. She acquired the farm from her father Mankin Wray who died in 1946 two days shy of his 100th birthday. Mankin and his brother Dan had moved to southwest Iowa in 1872, coming from West Virginia after the Civil War. By the turn of the century they had acquired over 1,000 acres, the tally made famous a century later by Jane Smiley in her book by that name. Mankin's goal in life was to have a farm to leave each of his three children – and he did. The home place with the big house and three-story show barn visible for miles went to his son – Uncle Charlie. The farm next to the family church (more on it later) went to Aunt Jessie, and Grandmother Anna got our home place. Once Mankin had assembled his wealth in land and passed it on to his family his part in the story was pretty much over, but the role of my grandmother loomed large.

She returned to Iowa in the fall of 1935 after twenty years living in southern California, first in National City then Santa Anna. She came home in part to flee a failing marriage to Mel Hamilton, a talented stockman but a hard, mean man – if my father's stories are to be believed. She brought along three of her boys – my father Lowell and his brothers Linn and Warren, to help claim her farm. Her daughters Glee and Bonnie, and the oldest son Dwight, all stayed in California. Dad had been born nearby in Lenox in 1911, but the family moved West in 1916 so he was essentially a southern California kid. Of their return, you can imagine the sight made by the "California fools" as they were known by the tight knit and pious locals, learning to farm with horses and scratching out a living in the depth of the Depression. My father was a sticker, as fellow Iowan, author Wallace Stegner, describes and he would spend the rest of his life in many ways chained to the farm. After two years, his brother Linn fled back West, spurred by a run-in with authorities over an under-age girl, to spend his somewhat dissolute bachelor life as a merchant marine, drinking, wenching, and sailing the seas. Warren, the other son who returned to Iowa was accompanied by his wife Jeanette who had never experienced an Iowa winter. The winter of 1936 was brutal and she soon announced that once the snows melted enough to make it to the rail station in

Creston 15 miles away she was on the next train to California with or without him. Wisely he soon joined her in the exodus back west.

My father stayed and took to farming, at least enough to stay at it, taking care of his mother and no doubt dreaming of his earlier California days as a life guard at Balboa Beach or his stint as a stage hand at MGM Studios. My mother Zella Mae entered the scene near the end of the decade, a farm girl from Shannon City in the Southern Iowa hill country, land nothing like the fertile fields 30 miles to the west in Adams County. She was born in 1919 of a Danish mother Carrie Jensen and a hard drinking, card playing, tenant farmer named Asa Blakesly, Ace as he was fittingly known. Mom found her escape from the poverty of a Depression era tenant farm by working as a "domestic" (Americans never have servants) for a "wealthy" family in Creston. She met my Dad at one of the weekly big band dances at Lake McKinley park in Creston. Pictures of her show a beautiful, petite 95-pound girl who resembled Katherine Hepburn. No doubt my father was smitten. A courtship ensued and marriage followed in November 1941 just weeks before Pearl Harbor and the war that changed life for everyone, even the land.

Marrying my father, a farmer and future landowner, was an important step up in my mom's life. In many ways, it marked her elevation to a life much different than the blue-collar futures of her sisters. Aunt Lois married a tractor mechanic who spent his whole life in Lenox, working hourly wages for the same I-H implement dealer. Her oldest sister Lola married a man who can best be described as a hillbilly. Uncle Tom hunted, fished, worked the road crew, and kept a small farm where they raised their four children. The oldest boy had my mom's maiden name Blakesly for a last name and when I was old enough to notice and ask about this anomaly, she told me a bad man took advantage of my aunt and he was the result. You can guess the rest – his parentage lingered as a cloud in the family story. My strongest memory of visiting Aunt Lola and Uncle Tom's farm was the pail of fresh raw milk in the fridge and its taste - unpasteurized and non-homogenized, straight from the cow. How different from the bottled milk Lyle Bush the AE milkman dropped off at our farm twice a week! But Aunt Lola was another sticker, an entrepreneur for her day though the term was not widely used then. She spent her life working the line at a local factory, squirreling away her wages to buy houses in her small town of Afton. By the time she was in her 70s – and still working – she was a real estate mogul renting houses to highway and railroad workers, supporting her extended family with the proceeds.

Even though ours was a small farm of only 200 acres, my mother moved up in the world as a farm wife. By becoming a landowner, she stepped into a new class. Class is another reality we don't like to talk about in the US but believe me it is real, even in rural farm country. If my mother was here to testify she would say the land made her life more stable and secure than her sisters. She may not have had "running water" in her house until the early 1960s, and of course there were hard times on a small farm, but the land made all the difference.

After my parents married Grandmother Anna continued to live with them for several years in the 1940s, pity my mother under the same roof cooking and cleaning for her mother-in-law. In some ways Mom joined my father, imprisoned each in their own way, on the farm. But their reward was coming. On her death in 1956 Grandmother Anna did something that for the time, and even still today, was remarkable. Rather than divide her land into equal portions for her six children, the other five wise enough to live in southern California, she left one half of the farm to my parents and divided the second half into five shares for the others. And she included a provision requiring them to sell their shares to my father! Her decision was based, I believe, on two considerations. She recognized the years of effort my father and mother had invested in the farm and in her care should be rewarded. She also knew if the farm was to continue as our family farm the land needed to stay intact. That is why she is central to my story.

As you can only imagine, news of her "plan" for the farm was not received warmly by the west coast Hamiltons. They felt it unfair and the result of undue influence exerted by my parents. A lawsuit was even threatened. I know this because fifty years later when cleaning out my Dad's safe deposit box in the Prescott Bank I found the letters from the attorneys. I can only imagine the pain and fear the letter from the high-powered Santa Anna law firm, hired by his oldest brother a wealthy trust officer, must have caused my parents. Other letters indicate there was talk of a settlement, even a proposal my parents disavow their half of the farm and instead accept a 1/6 portion as fair. But that didn't happen and even though I wasn't around to know the details, later events lead me to believe it was only due to my mother's fierce determination and passion forcing my father to stand firm and fight it out with his siblings. She was not going to give up on the land and slip back into poverty – just like Grandmother Anna had not given up on this land. They both saw something in my father he couldn't see in himself. With the help of a county seat lawyer from Corning they resisted and eventually with a loan from the Federal

Land Bank they purchased the other half of our farm. It would take years to pay off the loan and it was a decade before any of the West coast Hamiltons returned for a visit and reunion. I was twelve before I met any of these relatives and can still remember the 1966 summer visit when Uncles Warren and Linn and others came back to visit.

Fifty years later I worked with Iowa lawyers to address the burgeoning number of court cases and litigation involving intra-family fights over who gets what part of the farm. Blood may be thicker than water but it is not thicker than money and the willingness of family members to fight one another over what they believe is rightfully theirs might surprise you. The wisdom my Grandmother showed in deciding to make an "unequal" division made it possible for my family to continue farming our land for the next sixty years, even though my parents had to lawyer up to save it. Now is a good time to learn more about the history of the land that became our farm. There is no better voice to tell the story than the land itself.

The Back Forty Explains Land History[1]

If I have a formal name it is the NW ¼ of the SE ¼ of section 13, Mercer Township, R 33 W, T 71 N in Adams County, Iowa, USA. There are other names as well – the county recorder knows me as Parcel 7515100 and my GPS coordinates are 40 degrees, 57 Minutes and 26 seconds North, by 94 degrees, 36 Minutes and 4 Seconds West, at an elevation of 1250 feet, valuable information if you want to locate me from space. My real friends and loved ones, especially the Hamiltons who owned me and farmed me for nearly 100 years, knew me as the "Back Forty."

---

[1] Author's note – The Back Forty, refers to a part of the farm where I was raised. To understand the story of the land, it helps to actually hear from the land – that is why the Back Forty will appear throughout the book.

I am a forty-acre field of rich fertile class 1 soils [classified by the USDA soil scientists in the 1940s as mostly Winterset and Macksburg types] near the middle of the 640-acre section. I measure a quarter mile on each side and am attached on the west – for purposes of legal descriptions - to the NW ¼ of section 13. I, and all my neighbors, got our formal names from the Northwest Ordinance and the General Land Survey. These 1820s laws set out the manner for measuring, surveying, and bringing into legal ownership the millions of acres brought under the nation's control by the Louisiana Purchase and the other methods of "acquisition" – the treaties and cessations negotiated – if you can call it that – with the native American tribes occupying the land when the settlers arrived. With this act of surveying and identifying each tract of land in a unique manner, the power of the federal government was stamped indelibly on this part of the continent. Almost all the over 400 million acres of cropland in the nation and all of Iowa's 35 million acres have similar formal names.

In contrast to the formal name used for legal purposes, my more friendly and common nickname, the Back Forty, was given me by the people who owned and farmed me the longest. Being the field farthest away from the farmstead where they lived meant I was also the hardest to reach. Being in the middle of section and touched by no roads I was nearly out of sight from passersby and even neighbors – thus my name the Back Forty. This is my story – but before we go further let me tell you more about my origins.

We will skip the geologic and historic parts other than to say it was over 300,000 years ago the last glacier passed over me heading back north to gather more rocks. Since then my surface has been covered by a sea of grass and prairie plants. These deep rooted "natives," grasses like big and little blue stem, side oats gramma and flowers like compass plant and false indigo and their many colleagues produced annual growths of leaves, stems, and seeds. Some were consumed by the bison, deer, and elk periodically sweeping over me, headed for water and protection in the wooded bottomlands of the Nodaway River four miles to the north. Occasionally the rich vegetation was consumed by the prairie fires lit when lightning flashed from the thunderstorms racing in from the west. The storms also brought the steady rains to feed what people came to call the prairie – another name used to describe my historic condition. Each winter as the seasons turned the vegetation would die and be buried under the deep blankets of snow that came to mark the end of one year and beginning of the next. As the centuries passed the grasses grew and died, feeding the rich black soils building on top of me. So much humus and fertility accumulated by the time your ancestors, the "settlers," arrived in the 1850s my topsoil was six feet deep in places before you even got down to what the people who study soil geology later labeled the B horizon of subsoil and clay.

For much of these thousands of years my only company was the animals and birds, the reptiles and others who found their homes nestled in my grasses or burrowed into my soils. Periodically the tranquility they found would be interrupted by the footsteps of humans. The first to visit with any regularity were those known today as Native Americans though at the time we just knew them as the people. In the 1800s when this modern story really begins, the tribe most identified with what became my part of Iowa was the Potawatomi. At least this is the "official" version of my ownership, the history told by white European descendants at the time legal claims of ownership to the Iowa land were "obtained." The Louisiana Purchase in 1803 began this formal process. When President Jefferson negotiated the acquisition from the French of all the lands draining from the west into the Mississippi River, you acquired what today are parts or all of 16 states, for around 3 cents an acre. The next step was to resolve any "legal" claims the native tribes occupying the lands might have. The idea of acquiring something legally from a people who did not recognize your legal concept of "owning property" and who did not understand your reliance on legally binding contracts, by definition lent the whole exercise a certain fictional quality. Even if it were in fact part fiction, it worked for your purposes and resolved in your view any legal or political disputes the previous "owners" might raise later. All the better because these steps were the necessary prerequisites for your real goal, being able to provide documented legal ownership to the coming settlers who knew full well the power and legitimacy associated with these claims.

The manner used by the Americans to acquire land from the Native peoples is a sad but formative part of all that follows. Books have been written about this process but Jedediah Purdy in *After Nature* best crystallizes your treatment of Native Americans when he writes, "The land claims of these first and continuing inhabitants were erased ideologically even as traces of those inhabitants were being wiped out on the ground. Providential imagination reworked conquest, expulsion, and genocide into a benign account of necessary and lawful progress."

It took a series of nine so called "treaties" and cessations with Iowa's various native tribes, all completed in less than 50 years, to fulfill the takeover – or acquisition of the state. The legal claim of ownership to me and the rest of Adams County appears to have taken place in June 1846 when the tribal leaders of the Potawatomi meeting near Council Bluffs signed a treaty selling all the lands they held in the Iowa territory (roughly the western 1/3 of the state) for the price of $850,000 as well as some debt relief and moving expenses. The year 1846 also happens to be when Iowa was accepted into the Union as the 26th state, an action setting in motion the next phase of my formal ownership. In 1851 the Iowa government approved creating Adams County (named after the nation's second President) by withdrawing land from the larger Potawatomi County to the west. Two years later Adams County was reduced in size to a third, as Union County was carved off the eastside and Montgomery County off the west (a county structure still present 170 years later). Creating these counties coincided roughly with the official surveying or platting out of the lands as provided by the US Land Survey. Once an official legal description was created it could be used by the General Land Office to "officially" dispose of the land, meaning it was transferred into private legal ownership. This step happened in May of 1855 when a fellow by the name of Isiah Case obtained title from the government as the "Original Entry" – more on him and those who followed later.

As noted, this is the story of how I came to be, what my life has been (mostly growing hay, corn, and soybeans but with a few other adventures) and more importantly the forces, people, and events shaping my role in American agriculture (and culture) and determining my future. I want to tell you my story, because it is one you never hear. In all the writing and discussion about agriculture, food, farming, and history – from farm bills to food safety, from international trade to ethanol, the focus is always on the crops, the technology, the economics, the policy – and the people – but few ever ask or even think to ask about me – the land. We like to say among ourselves – it seems you treat us like dirt and take us for granted. Aldo Leopold, of him you will hear much more, once said typically when you Americans talk about "the land" you really are talking about the people on the land – not the land itself.

Judging by the news stories, people are more interested in

how much I am worth – my price per acre – than about my health, my happiness, or my real value. I can hear you now – "happiness" – how can a farm field be happy – and even if it could be happy how would we humans even know?! Trust me, farm fields can be happy – or sad, well cared for or abused. We can be stewarded by those with an eye to the future or driven to produce the most at all costs by those who only thirst for profits without caring about the long-term impacts on our productivity.

You may realize or already know not all land is created equal but you should also know neither are all landowners. Some treat us with care and we are grateful, while others do not. What you often fail to consider is what reasons explain the difference, what shapes your attitude to the land? No, you don't often think of the land or hear my voice, but I hope to change that. I want you to hear from me - the land – and hear from my friends and counterparts across the state and nation. Listen to what we have to say, about our history, our treatment, the machines and technologies displayed across our acres, the seeds and the poisons sprayed and planted in our skin – and the people who farm us - the owners, tenants, bankers, and lawyers, all those who claim a legal right to determine our fate. This is my opportunity to tell my story – and your opportunity to think about me, to think about the land, in a new way. I may consist of what you call soil – or dirt, but I am really about life – and your future.

THE BACK FORTY WAS MY FAVORITE FIELD

Well you just heard from the Back Forty, a voice perfectly suited to tell the story and history of the land, and of our farm. Even though it was only forty of our 200-acres in many ways the Back Forty was my favorite part of the farm. In the summer, I raced my bike along the packed earthen lane Dad used to drive the tractor there. Reaching it was a landmark so seemingly far away to an eight-year old streaming through the rows of corn. One of my favorite summer "jobs" was taking my father his mid-afternoon break, usually a cold bottle of Coke and maybe some of the Mom's famous raisin spice bars with the glazed sugar frosting. The first task was to scan the horizon to the south and east, perhaps cocking my ear as well, to spot where he was working. The steady growl of the WD-45 Allis laboring away was a good locater especially if he was hidden by a hill. Then I would set off on my bike if it made sense, or walking if the field was too hard to reach by bike. Arriving at the end of the field with his refreshments always gave me a sense of importance as if I was helping out in this family task of farming. Sure, it was a small thing but the memories are fresh today. I can still see the relief on his face being able to shut the tractor down, dismount to stretch his legs and maybe even recline in the shade of the big tractor tire. Once the Coke was downed – usually I got a swig – he was back on the tractor for several more hours circling the field and back to the house for me. When I think of the countless hours he spent over his fifty years of farming – driving back and forth, back and forth, 4 rows at a time to disc or plant or cultivate I can't help but wonder how he occupied his mind. Was it planning our next summer camping trip out west, or dreaming of his youth in Southern California and what might have been if he hadn't come back to Iowa? Or was he thinking about the future of his boys – my older brother Nate or me, the one he called the Professor? Driving a tractor for hours on end is a bit like taking a long walk – they both give you plenty of time to think.

Life on the farm is an experience I share with thousands of others from my era. It was filled with experiences and memories and regardless of the season or even the time of day, there was always something to do. Invariably these tasks involved working with the land or animals. But this is not a book about the good times down on the farm. If farm kids are truthful the reality is for every good time there was an equally sad or scary time – of weather hardships and sick animals, of worry seen on your parents faces and heard in the tense conversations late at night, the ones you strained to hear from the upstairs bedroom. No this is a book about the land, how it shaped me and how it shapes life for all of us. Stepping forward in time, the decision where to go to college and what to study opened the door to my future working with the land.

WHY FORESTRY?

Looking back at my history on the land, I sometimes wonder why did I go to forestry school and how did it impact my career and thinking about the land? The second answer is easy, it made all the difference, as this book hopefully will make clear. As to the first question, there are several explanations for why I ended up in forestry school. From junior high on, each summer we made trips out west, visiting relatives and former neighbors and camping in national parks and forests. The trips exposed me to the public lands and the great outdoors. Growing up I enjoyed helping work the land and growing things, like my Mom's prized collection of hybrid iris. However, following Dad to return to the farm was never part of the plan and in fact was something both my parents were set against. Much of my boyhood was filled with time outdoors, fishing on summer weekends, and fall days tromping our fields hunting pheasants and small game. The real clincher in this process came in summer 1971 and being selected to attend Trees for Tomorrow Environmental Education camp in Eagle River, Wisconsin.

The opportunity was early in the emerging national environmental movement, at a time of new energy and excitement in the natural resource community. After getting to the camp I realized it was really a recruiting ploy by the Universities of Michigan, Wisconsin, and Iowa State forestry schools, but I didn't mind. The camp brought together twenty soon to be high school seniors from each state for a week touring paper mills and sawmills, hiking in nearby national forests, and attending lectures on ecology and forest management. It was a heady experience, exposing us to a range of forestry careers and opportunities. Studying the issues was very satisfying and even coming from a small school, I was able to hold my own in discussions with other students. The environmental focus was quite new for the time and made the camp a progressive experiment, planting seeds of future activism. Returning home for my senior year of high school, my mind was set, studying forestry at Iowa State was going to be my path into the universe of environmental issues.

Once there several opportunities opened up. Early on a position as research assistant for Prof. Henry Webster the department chair changed my education and future. He took a forward-looking approach to interdisciplinary education and believed foresters needed a broader range of insights than just growing trees. With his encouragement, I entered the Honors program, and essentially designed my own curriculum. Over the next three years my classes combined economics, rural sociology, political science, and land use planning in what today would be a major in environmental sciences, which didn't exist then. The program required pruning several technical core forestry classes from my schedule. The highlight was when Dr. Webster asked me to help him write a book review of *The Taking Issue: An Analysis of the Constitutional Limits of Land Use Control*, by Bosselman, Callies, and Banta, published in 1973 by the White House Council on Environmental Quality. The seminal book examines the Fifth Amendment of the US Constitution protection for private property and judicial interpretations for when compensation must to be paid if government regulations go too far in restricting how land is used. I couldn't know it then, but helping write the book review for the *Journal of Forestry*, changed the course of my education and my life, and led me to law school.

Crafting an interdisciplinary approach to forestry studies worked well until my senior year when Dr. Webster returned to Michigan to run the forestry section of the Department of Natural Resources. He was replaced by Dr. George Thompson an old-school forester – much loved but a bit of a curmudgeon. Meeting with him to review my senior transcript, and receive his final blessing to graduate, he noted all my interdisciplinary course work and all the forestry classes left out. To my dismay he wondered aloud if they could in good faith even allow me to graduate with a degree in forestry? I explained my plan to attend law school and use my forestry studies as the foundation for working on environmental law. I even went so far as to promise to never pass myself off as a forester – if he would just let me graduate with the degree, something I wanted very much. The fact I had enough credits for a second degree in economics made his threat a bit less dire – but I thought of myself as a forester, just a new type of one, a forester in the Leopoldian mold! Ironically my forestry degree came in handy a few years later in a second-year clerkship for a law firm in

Omaha. One assignment was working on a municipal bond project to build a power plant in Michigan's Upper Peninsula to be fueled with timber slash, the material left over from improving timber stands.

Put these things together and you can see how ending up in Forestry at the ISU College of Agriculture seemed predestined. When I enrolled though, the plan for how to use the degree was more uncertain. Trips out west and talking with park rangers had planted the idea of joining the Forest Service or the National Park Service – as many of my classmates did. The political times, the war in Viet Nam ending, the emerging environmental movement, and my work for the Campus Young Democrats, plus *The Taking Issue* review, all moved me toward law school. A summer in Washington DC in 1975 as an intern working on agricultural policy for then newly elected Congressman Tom Harkin, solidified the idea. As time would show, it helped pull me back to my farming roots and ground my career in agricultural law and policy. My thinking was combining a degree in forestry with legal training could serve me well as an environmental lawyer. Eventually running for political office in Iowa was in the back of my mind as well. This led me to choosing between the University of Iowa or my other option of Georgetown. A conversation with Prof. Neil Harl, a legendary agricultural economist, lawyer, and professor at Iowa State, who would become a mentor, helped seal my decision. He explained how classmates at Iowa would be government leaders in the decades to come and important allies for any budding politician. My political campaign never came to be, but his observation about how friends from law school would help run the state proved true.

As to the question of how going to forestry school shaped my career, there are several observations. A science degree involves time, discipline, and thinking, all ingredients and skills needed in law school and teaching. The key ideas of US forest management, a long-term perspective of sustainable harvesting and a multi-use focus for the public lands, are essential to a healthy environmental policy and to a healthier vision for agriculture. Both principles contrast to the production-oriented education and mentality so common at land grant agricultural colleges like ISU, then and now. This difference in orientation to education played out in law students coming from land-grant colleges. Most lacked any appreciation or exposure to ideas of environmental sustainability. One of my favorite roles as a law professor was exposing students to new ideas. For thirty years Aldo Leopold and his essay "The Land Ethic" were a favored vehicle for doing so, though sharing John Steinbeck's *Grapes of Wrath* was a close second. I always asked students in Agricultural Law if they had read *Grapes of Wrath*, and anyone who said no was provided a copy if they promised to read it and report back.

In my Environmental Regulation of Agriculture seminar, I provided all students a copy of Leopold's *Sand County Almanac* and assigned "The Land Ethic" for discussion. Invariably, students with agriculture degrees from Iowa State would say they had never heard of the good doctor Leopold. In recent years, it has become harder for land grant agronomy departments to avoid discussing environmental issues, so student familiarity with Leopold began to change. Conversely, students with a natural resources background or strong liberal arts training, were usually familiar with Leopold's writings. To me, the idea you can go to college for four years learning how to farm the land, and expecting the land to provide for you, but never be exposed to the ethical issues embodied in being a landowner is almost criminal.

Unfortunately given where we are in society's debates over agriculture and the environment, this reality is not surprising. The failure to consider the moral dimension of land ownership helps explain a great deal about the "tensions" in our policy debates over issues like duties of stewardship, water quality, or public lands. If never asked to think differently about how to treat the land why would you embrace ideas of stewardship and conservation?

My career teaching law and my approach to natural resource topics has been informed by my training in forestry. Serving for over 20 years on the advisory board of the Leopold Center for Sustainable Agriculture at Iowa State was an opportunity to put this training into practice. My writing and scholarship on ideas of land stewardship, soil and water conservation, and sustainability have all been directly influenced by my forestry studies. Managing and sustaining soil health and water quality aren't that much different from managing a forest or tract of land – it is all about having a long-term vision, taking a community approach to the resources, and being sensitive to the needs of the land. Over the years I have noticed how many people contributing to conservation began training as foresters.

LAND MANIPULATORS

One aspect of owning land many people find most satisfying is the ability to manipulate its features to reflect our desires and fulfill our needs. Perhaps it is planting trees, or cutting some down, or plowing a field to plant crops, or building a pond to store water and having a place to fish. Being a landowner opens a world of possibilities and ways to leave your mark on the land. Anyone who owns a tractor with a front-end loader knows how working the land can bring satisfaction. It explains America's love affair with mowing the lawn. If we believe the desire to manipulate the land distinguishes modern landowners from the indigenous people who preceded us, we are wrong.

Though they lived centuries ago and lacked the mechanized tools we employ today our forerunners were drawn to manipulating the land in their own ways. Some of the best evidence is found at the Effigy Mounds National Monument in the bluffs above the Mississippi River just north of Marquette in northeast Iowa. Thousands of acres of preserved woodland forests contain dozens of burial mounds created between 800 and 1400 AD by those we today call the late Woodlands people. The mounds, typically 3-4 feet above the surface, range from lines of small conical mounds to the much larger and more elaborate effigies. Rows of bears marching up a hill or birds in flight are among the most spectacular reminders of these people. Some of the effigies are hundreds of feet long tracking the rise of the slopes on the bluff tops. Excavations show the mounds were used as burial sites and for ceremonies over extended periods. Clearly their purposes were greater and more mysterious than we will ever know. Who were the intended viewers of these land-based forms whose beauty and meaning appear most accessible only from far above? Why would a society expend the immense labor and time required to carry countless baskets of soil, clamshells, and other materials to the tops of the bluffs to build these mounds? Was the satisfaction and fulfillment in the doing? Were the various sites and series of effigies a competitive endeavor demonstrating clan fealty to ancestors and the capacity to organize communal efforts?

The glory of mysteries like these we can never know but our imaginations can help us consider reasons why. A recent visit to Effigy Mounds led me to think how these people really weren't that different than my forbearers – Mankin, Dan, and their kin. Their lives were spent tied to the land, using it to provide their sustenance and seeking their own forms of salvation from the efforts. Even in death their actions were much the same. How different are the effigies mounded on the hilltops from the elaborate gravestones and monuments my ancestors ceremoniously placed in the cemetery behind our family church? The church is gone now and someday may be forgotten but the grave markers remain. Two hundred years from now will people find this archaic spot of eroded stones and wonder who were these people who left them and what did they intend to communicate across the eons? This is a good place to learn more about my ancestors and how religion shaped their lives on the land. For that story and a historical perspective, we will return to the Back Forty.

The Back Forty on Religion

Now is a good time to talk about my early history during your "civilized" period. Life continued much as before even once I was officially owned. Some years my grasses were grazed by livestock and in some years my thick stand of prairie grass was cut and stacked as native hay for winter feeding. It was several decades before I felt the sting of the plowshare dragging my surface, cutting the deep prairie roots and turning the sod to open my black soul of soil. The moldboard plow with its self-cleaning plowshare, developed by young blacksmith John Deere one state to the east, changed my life and that of millions of other fields like me across our nation.

Now I want to talk about three odd, or at least unusual occurrences that happened nearby within a few decades. All involved what you refer to as "religion" or at least some version of it. You might be surprised the land doesn't recognize religion, at least not in the way you do. Our religion is nature – the sun, rain, wind, plants, and animals living in us. That is all we know or even care to know. No theocratic debates or need to read H.L. Mencken's *Treatise on the Gods* to plunge the mystery of our origin. Our fate is here on earth and if the geologic record is any guide – it will be eternal. But I digress, back to your religions.

The first event occurred in the winter and spring of 1846, the year Iowa became a state. It started in the far southeastern corner when hundreds, then thousands of people crossed the Mississippi River in the frozen winter to begin a trip west – an exodus they hoped would lead to their promised land. They were the Mormons, or Latter-day Saints, followers of their recently martyred Joseph Smith who had fallen to an angry mob at the jailhouse in Carthage, Illinois. The Mormons were fleeing west under the leadership of their new prophet Brigham Young. The journey would take them from the paradise they had tried to build in Nauvoo, Illinois, over 1,000 miles west to the desert land near the Great Salt Lake in what is now Utah. There they hoped to build their new kingdom of Deseret – hopefully though not actually as events would prove – beyond the reach of the US government and the other gentiles – the Americans who persecuted them for adhering to their new cult-like religion. The journey would be filled with trials and tribulations – death and hunger – epic stories to feed the very creation myth they would turn to in the years to come to inspire and bind, some might say blind, their believers. The trail they followed took them 20 miles to the north of me. In fact, they had a winter quarters named Mt. Pisgah in Union County just miles to the east on the banks of the Grand River. Little is left today other than the graves and memorials to the dozens who died of cold, hunger, and disease as they began the trek west. It is remarkable but today almost 175 years later you can still see ruts their wagon wheels carved in the hillsides near Bridgewater in Cass County. This visible reminder attests not just to their history but to how man's actions can change the face and fate of land forever.

You can read about the Mormons and their journey west in *The Gathering of Zion* by Wallace Stegner, himself a son of the Iowa soil and one of America's most eloquent spokesmen for people and the land. Once they passed, the Mormons left little impact on Iowa in their hurry west. The routes they followed are marked, first across southern Iowa in the exodus of 1846 and then later west from the railhead in Iowa City where trainloads of converts from England and other parts of Europe embarked on "handcart" expeditions plodding west with their possessions and dreams of salvation piled behind them. In a somewhat unusual twist of fate, the city the Mormon's abandoned in Nauvoo with its stone temple and hundreds of houses, played a key role in a "second" quasi-religious incident that happened even nearer to me, just five miles to the northwest.

In the 1800s, turbulent times perhaps not unlike yours of today, society faced the changing fortunes of peasants and workers in relation to the power of kings, landlords, and industrialists who laid claim to their labor. One response found by many was searching for another path, whether based on faith or optimism or a well-spoken vision of a better world. They were found in one of the hundreds of examples you could cite, people seeking refuge and a future through a different way to order life. This history includes bizarre Midwestern examples, like King Strang, a would-be Mormon leader who founded his own variant and moved hundreds of followers to Beaver Island in Lake Michigan to establish a separate nation. His beginnings and end – are richly detailed by Miles Harvey in *King of Confidence: A Tale of Utopian Dreamers, Frontier Schemers, True Believers, False Prophets, and the Murder of an American Monarch.*

41

Today your scholars describe many of this constellation of movements as Utopian societies – people who believed they could create on earth more equitable, caring, and harmonious social structures to guide their lives. This is where our story next unfolds.

In the 1840s in France, one of the most successful of these social dreamers was the philosopher Etienne Cabet who proposed an egalitarian society based on equality of the sexes, common ownership of property, and a related set of beliefs. His movement took the name Icarians from his popular book *Voyage de Icaŕie*. Cabet eventually gathered thousands of followers in France, and he came to believe the place to build their Utopia was on the fertile (and largely unoccupied) lands of the new nation emerging on this continent. Cabet and his followers began an exodus west, first to New Orleans and then on to land purchased in Texas. But the land and climate, both weather and political, proved less than receptive. Once in Texas, Cabet learned of the recently vacated town of Nauvoo and purchased it. The Icarians moved up the great river to Nauvoo, replacing one set of dreamers with another, both who fell outside the existing social bounds.

You may be getting impatient wondering how this story, as interesting as it may be, relates to me, the Back Forty here in Mercer Township, Adams County, Iowa. Well here is the connection. After the Icarians relocated to Nauvoo they determined their best hope for a future, and for peace and freedom to exercise their beliefs, was to send small groups of believers out to scout locations for new colonies. As fate would have it in 1855 the Icarians acquired 3,000 acres of Adams County land along the Nodaway River about five miles northwest of me, to plant a new settlement. They went to work in the timbers and soon had constructed a large barn for the livestock, a communal dining hall, and separate dormitories for the men and women – and a school for the children. The colony was never large, around 60 people, but in the 1860s in this part of Iowa, very much on the edge of the frontier, it was formidable.

Like many religious and political sects of the day the Icarian's views of property, relations between the sexes, and other themes of modern life, were non-traditional and difficult to maintain in the context of surrounding settlements. You can guess what came next. The colony existed until the 1890s, but like most of the 400 plus Utopian experiments in existence in the US during this period, it eventually succumbed to internal strife, desires of younger members for a different life, and the realities of survival. In the 1880s twenty younger Icarians moved to Sonoma County in California and found success raising grapes. One difficulty the Icarians faced was the lack of a theistic creed to discipline and bind the members in the fear of the kingdom come and eternal salvation, as other groups possessed - the Mennonites, Mormons, and Methodists. I wish we could hear from the neighbors who farmed near Icaria to learn how they felt. No doubt they found them a curiosity, as well as a source of gossip and conjecture. The development of Adams County including the settlement of Corning, the soon to be county seat three miles to the west, no doubt became a seductive pull to members who may have wanted out. Their French culture and language would have distinguished them, but perhaps no more so than the Swedes settling 20 miles to the west near Stanton or the Danes who congregated 50 miles to the north near Elk Horn and Kimballton. Eventually the colony came to an end and the few survivors sold the land and buildings, dividing the spoils equally as was their way. Today what remains – beyond some Francophile surnames among long-time residents of the area, like the Bovards who farm to my north, is a historical marker on the north side of US 34.

Being land bound, so to speak, I never got to visit the Icarians or see how they treated their land. I long to have listened in to Mankin and Dan Wray, the brothers who came to own me during this period, to hear what they thought of the Icarians. Were they welcoming or suspicious –or even envious? Did they think they were an oddity to scorn or free-thinkers to tolerate? We can only guess but one thing is clear, the Wrays were religious in their own more traditional way.

This brings us to the third part of the story – the church – or more accurately the three churches you can see from where I rest. The Wray's as Scotch-Irish were not just followers of the plow but also pious disciples of their Lord. Not unlike the thousands of other families who settled the prairies of the Midwest, once the farmsteads were built attention turned to more eternal matters of salvation – the need to build a church to practice their beliefs. Building a church often came before building a school, though that history is one we will address on another day.

It wasn't long until the neighbors built a church near what became known as Stringtown – about three miles to my northeast. This crossroads junction of Highway 34 and Iowa 49 has disappeared from most maps but the church is still there and the cemetery across the highway to the north. At some point in the first decade of the new century the Wray brothers decided they needed their own church. I don't know why and there is no one left to ask, but it may be safe to assume the conflicts, whether theological or personal, were petty but divisive. Whatever the cause, in 1908 the Wray brothers proceeded to build their own church in the section just to my east. Once the church was built a few years later the Wray's decided to dig up their kin and move them and their gravestones, from the Stringtown cemetery. On the move south, a large granite base from the tombstone of their mother fell off the wagon. Rather than reload it, the stone was moved to the front yard of the

Mankin's big house, and used as a stepping-stone for people getting out of their buggies. The stone is still there a century later. To complete the picture, another group built their own church at Mercer Center three miles west, but they don't really figure in my story other than to complete the church building trifecta.

The church at Salem is the important one for our story. It rests on 80 acres of rich fertile land, a portion of the over 1000 acres Mankin and Dan had assembled by the 1890s. The denomination the Wray's adhered to was the Brethren, a pacifist variant of the Anabaptists. In 1908 when the church was built, the 80-acre tract was deeded to the Brethren along with a parsonage for the preacher. The farm work was done by the men-folk of the congregation with the proceeds used to pay the preacher's salary. The Salem Church of the Brethren lasted for over one hundred years. It has since been torn down but the cemetery behind it contains dozens of graves and stone markers, including three generations of the Wray's who settled me. All the important players are there – Mankin and Dan, and Mankin's wife Nancy. Two of their children are there as well, Uncle Charlie and his wife Aunt Minnie, and Aunt Jesse and her husband Henry Walters, all laying in repose hopefully enjoying their heavenly reward. The only child not there is someone you have met, Anna Wray Hamilton, the daughter of Mankin, who would one day be my owner. She is buried in a cemetery in Santa Anna in her adopted California.

Yes, the church is gone, but the gravestones remain and so does the 80 acres of land. Another story for us to consider involves Iowa property law, a subject the boy who grew up on me to become a professor of agricultural law spent his career studying. When Mankin deeded the 80 acres to the church, he included what lawyers call a right of reversion. The deed said the Brethren owned the land as long as a church existed but if the church ever ceased operation then title to the land would revert to Mankin's living heirs. This type of statement creating a reversionary interest is not uncommon, and was often used to project the morality of the sellers, for example, "this building shall never be used as a tavern selling intoxicants." Another American usage was less admirable but also common, to promote the racial animus and xenophobic views coursing through American society. Many American cities and suburbs built before and after WWII include restrictive covenants and homeowner agreements preventing the land from being owned by blacks or Asians. These provisions and related restraints on housing loans like red lining helped create the racial divides, wealth disparities, and housing inequality you can see on the maps of American cities. Even though these covenants may still remain in older property documents, in the 1940s your nation's courts ruled them unconstitutional and unenforceable. This tragic part of America's "property" history is well told in *The Color of Law: A Forgotten History of How Our Government Segregated America,* by Richard Rothstein.

You may be wondering what happened to the 80 acres Mankin tried to restrict, now that the church is gone? Here is a lesson about the development of property law, not unlike lessons the boy professor taught his students. Lawyers will tell you the main goal of the law for interpreting contracts – like a real estate deed – is to carry out the wishes of the drafter. This is why "intent of the drafter" is often described as the "polestar" for courts to follow. But lawyers will also tell you the main goal of property law is the ability to have clear and stable titles to property, including the ability to know everyone who might claim an interest in it. For this reason, states enacted what are known as "marketable title" laws to require potential claims to interests in real property, or even limits on using land such as a homeowner's restrictive covenant, be recorded periodically, typically every 21 years, to remain valid. The idea is if someone checks the property records they will be aware of any potential claims and not be surprised later.

Property law thrives on predictability so you can see how a springing reversionary interest like Mankin penned can create future problems. How can you have stable land titles if someone can make a claim decades or generations later? Predictably the Iowa courts faced just this issue in a case involving facts like what happened with the Salem church. The case involved an Iowa family trying to reclaim land after a local Presbyterian church ceased to exist. Title to the land was claimed by the national church organization as successor to the local congregation. The claim was buttressed by the fact, when Iowa enacted the marketable title, or "stale uses" law in the early 1960s, potential beneficiaries of reversionary interests were given a one-year grace period to file a claim to continue their legal interests. If nothing was filed, any claim arising from a deed provision written more than 21 years before, was extinguished as stale and title to the land passed to whoever was next in line to be owner. It doesn't take a legal scholar to recognize the Iowa courts faced a real dilemma, which rule should control – the goal of contract law to satisfy the intent of the drafter, or the goal of property law to have predictable land records and titles? The vote was close, but in a 5-4 ruling the Iowa Supreme Court sided with the church and ruled the right of reversion had been lost when the beneficiaries did not file a claim to extend its validity.

The result and the reasoning may seem harsh, especially since most people are not lawyers and few knew about the new law or the one-year window to act. Some people might not have even known they were potential beneficiaries of a reversionary interest. Perhaps this proves the logic for the Court's ruling. If you don't even know you have a property right how can you claim to be negatively affected if it is extinguished? It is certain Mankin's kin did not know about the new law because no effort was made to preserve their potential claim. If you go to the Adams County recorder's office the land records for the eighty acres lists the Church of the Brethren, headquartered in Elgin, Illinois as the owner. The land is worth around $640,000 so this "act of providence" was a nice "boost" for their coffers, even if it wasn't Mankin's intention. Remember, I told you the land itself doesn't go anywhere. The eighty acres is still there and in a somewhat interesting twist of fate, today it is leased and farmed by the same man who owns me!

PRIVATE PROPERTY AND PUBLIC RIGHTS

Regardless of the language there is perhaps no more powerful statement than "I own this land." Our farm, like most is "private property". You see this in its history – who owned it, how they acquired it, who it was passed to in an estate, and who sold it and how. All these legal transactions are done privately, some more so than others. Selling a farm through a private negotiation is much different than selling it at a public auction. When we sold the last part of my family's home place to a young neighbor, no one else was involved or even aware the land was for sale. We knew what we wanted to happen to the land and acted accordingly. Could we have received more if the land was put up for auction? Possibly, but then we would have had no control over who purchased it. For us, it was more important to see a young farmer have the opportunity to buy his first piece of property than to have a large landowner swallow it up to increase their holdings. The action we took, a private sale, is not unusual, this type of land transaction happens every day in farm country. The private and secretive nature of many land transactions makes it difficult to track and understand what happens on the land. Even though "deeds" for the transfers are ultimately recorded, there is no state database of landownership or transfers, all land records are with the county.

Given this history is it any wonder why concepts of "private property" and a landowner's ability to do as they wish, unrestrained, are so engrained in our concept of owning land? Even so, the idea land is simply private property is only part of the story. All land has another side, its public dimension. Property begins with the very existence of government and a legal system to create and recognize the concept of privately-owned land, setting out the procedures for "ownership." Once the land is "owned" it still retains a public dimension, subject to the control and regulation by government. If you don't believe it, try not paying your property taxes to the county and see what happens. If you don't know, when property taxes go unpaid the county can eventually sell the land to cover what it is owed. The public dimension of land can be seen in laws regulating its use such as zoning ordinances directing what can be built where, environmental rules requiring sources of air and water pollution be controlled, and nuisance laws used by courts to protect neighbors and even the public from unreasonable interferences caused by how others use their land. The public dimension of private property is at the very heart of efforts to promote soil conservation discussed in Chapter Three and in protecting water quality as discussed in Chapter Five.

The idea all land has a "public" dimension is most fully realized in what we consider to be "public lands," where the legal title and ownership rests with the public, held in trust by the government. Public lands include over 900 hundred million acres of federal land like the national forests; thousands of state-owned parks and wildlife refuges;

local lands like county bike trails; and countless city parks. Public lands play a critical role in creating the spaces where we live and in maintaining the connection between people and the land. The public lands help set the standards of care we expect from landowners and influence what can happen on private lands. Issues shaping our public lands are the focus of the next chapter.

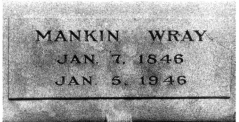

Mankin's tombstone.

What is left of the Salem Church of the Brethren.

Uncle Linn with his mother Anna.

Mankin and Dan Wray, early 1940s.

Chapter Two – America's Public Lands and a Forgotten Conservation Hero

PUBLIC LANDS DAY

On a picture-perfect September afternoon, a dozen of us volunteered for a seed harvest at Snyder Prairie in northeast Polk County. It was National Public Lands Day, an event started in 1996 by the National Environmental Education Foundation, to connect citizens with the bounty in the nation's public lands. We spent the afternoon harvesting prairie seeds, one of over 2,000 outdoor activities around the country involving tens of thousands. Our event was co-sponsored by the Des Moines Parks Department and Iowa Natural Heritage Foundation, owner of the 156 acre Snyder farm. It received the farm 30 years ago as a donation from an elderly couple, and has restored the prairie, established wetlands, and opened the oak-hickory savanna making the property an oasis of nature in an ocean of cornfields. The vital land protection work carried out by the INHF and the nation's many other land trusts is the subject of Chapter Eight. Across the nation these groups are cooperating with public agencies to increase access to nature and to enhance the public lands. Prairie seeds we harvested: Blazing Star, Yellow-headed Cone-flower, Purple Prairie Clover, and Rattlesnake Master, will be used to create new prairies on public lands.

The idea of "public lands" has played a remarkable role in our nation's land story. In states like Iowa most of the newly "acquired" land was quickly disposed of into private ownership, so by the 1860s little was left to set aside for public use. The Homestead Act of 1862 did much the same for land in Nebraska, the Dakotas and other Great Plain states as 160-acre quarter sections were made available to people who would farm them. As you travel further west and cross the Rockies, the story was different. The geology and climate presented new and different obstacles to privatizing the public domain, at least if economic success was a goal. The reality of aridity born by climate and the lack of water placed serious restraints on turning the dry, rocky, and often desert-like land into productive private property, but that didn't stop us from trying. This reality was well documented by John Wesley Powell in his landmark *1878 Report on the Lands of the Arid Region*. Powell argued the Nation needed a different approach to the system of allocating small lots of land to individuals with the goal of farming. When dealing with the arid West, small farms were unsustainable and irrigation projects to make the land bloom were beyond the means of individual farmers, requiring coordination and public funding at a larger scale. Powell's report was largely ignored for many decades, an unfortunate history eloquently told by Wallace Stegner in *Beyond the Hundredth Meridian: John Wesley Powell and the Second Opening of the West* (1954). The effect of ignoring Powell's wisdom is etched as scars seen on millions of acres of abused land in the West. As physical reality slowed efforts to distribute lands to individuals, a political recognition emerged of the inherent value of retaining a portion of the timbered western lands as a resource for the nation. Beginning with Yellowstone, later to become our first national park, tracts of forested lands were "reserved" and a new chapter of America's relation with the land was born. How and where the public domain was retained as "public land" was shaped by geography, aridity, and the politics of the day, and the story has influenced national political debates ever since. Today, public lands are the fulcrum balancing the goals of citizens against the economic needs of the communities where the lands are located. Understanding America's public lands is central to considering our future as a nation and as citizens, and for the land.

It was no coincidence the weekend of National Public Lands Day, PBS rebroadcast the Ken Burns documentary "National Parks: America's Best Idea." One episode details the tireless efforts of Steven Mather, first head of what became the National Park Service, and his ally Horace Albrecht, to create a network of national parks and outline the vision for what they could mean for all citizens. The key was not just saving lands as places to camp, hike, and see the sights. More importantly, national parks embodied the ideal of public lands as a resource for all citizens to share, regardless of proximity. The story of our public lands, then and now, has never been free of conflict. It is hard to imagine there being no Great Smoky Mountains National Park but Congress resisted acquiring the land, as did the over 5,000 people living in the hollows who faced being uprooted by its creation. Nor can we imagine there being no Grand Teton National Park near Jackson Hole, but neither of these national treasures would exist today if not for the beneficence of John D. Rockefeller who stepped in to buy the land when national politics threatened their creation. As we think about the story of public lands today, this history of overcoming expected voices of local opposition must inform our actions.

DESTRUCTIVE POLICIES BRING NEW ATTENTION TO PUBLIC LANDS

In 2020 public lands had a cultural moment of renewal in public awareness and controversy, much of it due to the actions of the Trump Administration to open the lands for exploitation and use. Perhaps no action was more symbolic or emblematic of the Administration's disregard for the public interest and nature, not to mention legal precedent or tribal sovereignty, than the drastic reduction of two national monuments Bears Ears and the Grand Staircase Escalante in Utah. The unprecedented 2018 action removed protections from over one million acres in Bears Ears alone, exposing hundreds of square miles of sacred tribal lands to energy extraction. The attack on the public interest was repeated when the Northeast Canyons and Seamounts Marine National Monument was opened to commercial fishing. The abuses of the Antiquities Act were challenged in court and thankfully have been reversed by President Biden. The Trump Administration's goal was to elevate private interests and profits over the public interest and our common good, especially by increasing extraction of natural resources from the public lands. How ironic at a time when COVID-19 magnified the benefits of being outdoors and having open spaces to enjoy, the Administration raced to open the public lands for private use. In 2020, then Secretary of Agriculture Perdue directed the Forest Service to expand logging in National Forests and Grasslands, and the Administration reversed earlier findings to renew mining permits next to the Boundary Waters. Renewable energy sources of wind and solar continue to grow and evidence of climate change shows the need to move away from fossil fuels, yet the Trump administration was committed to the idea of "energy dominance." This explains their rush to open the

Arctic National Wildlife Refuge to oil exploration, disregarding threats to the calving grounds of the caribou herds relied on by the indigenous Gwich'in people.

The threats to public lands were vividly portrayed in the film "Public Trust," produced by the outdoor equipment maker Patagonia. Watching the film, you can't help but see the current "crisis" on the public lands as a continuation of conflicts fought at the turn of the last century over the public lands. The renewed attention and boost in cultural awareness of America's public lands is reflected in many recent books. Consider these titles:

Christopher Ketcham, *This Land: How Cowboys, Capitalism, and Corruption are Ruining the American West*, (Viking 2019)

Anthony McCain, *Shadowlands: Fear and Freedom at the Oregon Standoff*, (Bloomsbury 2019)

Jedediah Purdy, *This Land is Our Land: The Struggle for a New Commonwealth*, (Princeton University Press 2019)

David Gessner, *Leave It as It Is: A Journey Through Theodore Roosevelt's American Wilderness*, (Simon and Shuster 2020) and

Terry Tempest Williams, *Erosion: Essays on Undoing* (Sarah Crichton Books 2020)

Reading these authors helps shape our understanding of the role public lands play in the national dialogue. Your own experiences with nature may be just as important as any writings explaining the significance of the public lands. As our nation faced the COVID-19 pandemic, Americans found relief and respite being outside on the land, perhaps more than any period in our lifetimes. Taking a walk in the neighborhood, visiting a national forest, and camping in a local park, these were the activities many people sought. We turned to public lands to find the peace, safety, and even the therapy we yearned for to help weather the troubled times. When we look back through the lens of history on the national tragedies we lived through in 2020, certainly the COVID-19 crisis, but on a larger scale the aftermath of four disastrous years of the Trump Administration, using and enjoying public lands will stand as a bright spot in our survival. In turn, the growing reliance on "our" lands fueled recognition of the threats they face, not just from the now defeated Administration hell bent on reversing the certainty of public lands but other threats as well. Thankfully the Trump Administration is gone, hopefully to a well-deserved home in the dustbin of history, but other threats are more engrained, linked historically to the creation of public lands. These threats are reflected in the mindset and actions of politicians, landowners, and industry leaders who see "public lands" as obstacles to exploiting the natural resources the lands may hold. Whether traditional uses like grazing, timber, and mining – or a new generation of energy extraction like hydraulic fracturing, aka fracking, or large-scale solar facilities, greed and a sense of personal entitlement drive many who see the public lands as just one more place to stake their claim and chase a fortune.

These attitudes are most common in the West where a significant portion of land is owned by the federal government. But the West does not have an exclusive lock on opposing new public lands. Even in Iowa a conservative farm group driven by an anti-public ideology in 2019 proposed a bill to prohibit new land acquisitions by state and county agencies. This in a state ranking 49th in the percent of land owned by the public, a state where less than 3% of the land is permanently protected and 60% of that is estimated to be road ditches! The exciting end to the story is how on short notice, hundreds of Iowans flooded the Capitol to oppose the outrageous proposal, leading to its quick demise. The lesson though is how citizens need to remain vigilant in protecting the public domain wherever it is found.

The public lands play an essential role in mediating the relation between the public and all citizens with the land. Thankfully, even with the stress and threats, the trajectory of public lands policy is on the ascent, as we saw in Iowa. Before looking to the future, it is vital to understand more about the history of public lands and how the foundation we build on today was laid. For that story, we turn to an Iowan whose legacy has faded toward obscurity but who deserves much greater appreciation from the Nation he served.

Who is John F. Lacey?

When people think of public lands several important figures come to mind. Foremost is President Teddy Roosevelt or TR, undoubtedly a champion in the pantheon of land protectors who set a pattern for those who followed. His cousin President Franklin Roosevelt or FDR, did as much or more than TR when measured in lands protected. New wildlife refuges, national parks, and national forests totaling hundreds of million acres owe their existence to FDR. The legacies of these giants of America's environmental history are beautifully told by historian Douglas Brinkley, in a pair of biographies: *The Wilderness Warrior: Theodore Roosevelt and the Crusade for America* (Harper 2009) and *Rightful Heritage: Franklin D. Roosevelt and the Land of America* (Harper 2016). Other figures from that formative era come to mind, people like Gifford Pinchot, the nation's first forester who created the Forest Service to manage the millions of acres of what became our national forests and whose "wise use" philosophy still guides these lands, for good and ill. John Muir looms large as the intellectual father of public lands and the romantic spokesman for the role wilderness plays in our conscience, as explained by Donald Worster in *A Passion for Nature: The Life of John Muir*, (Oxford 2008). George Bird Grinnell may be less well known, but he played a pivotal role as a writer and politician in the public land effort, as detailed in a recent biography, *Grinnell: America's Environmental Pioneer and His Restless Drive to Save the West* (2019) by John Taliaferrois.

Few readers know of the one person who arguably did more than anyone else as the pioneering lawmaker responsible for laying the foundation for an array of public land and environmental protections we enjoy today as our national patrimony. This politician was responsible for protecting the wildlife in what became Yellowstone National Park, authored the first federal wildlife protection law to end the commercial slaughter of plumed birds in Florida, created the Wichita Mountain wildlife refuge in Oklahoma saving the American Bison from extinction, and authored the law used by every President since 1906 to protect priceless federal lands as national monuments. You are excused for thinking the references are to Teddy Roosevelt, but you are wrong. The man leading these efforts and more, was an Iowan whose legacy is now largely forgotten. Congressman John F. Lacey from Oskaloosa, was regarded at the turn of the last century as the "shrewdest, pro-conservation legislator of his time." His friend Teddy Roosevelt referred to him as "the man" when it came to passing legislation to protect wildlife and natural lands. Sadly, Lacey-Keosauqua State Park in Lee County on the south bank of the Des Moines River, is one of the few monuments in Iowa or the nation honoring the legacy of this pioneer of American conservation. John Lacey would not be troubled by the lack of notoriety or public memorials, he didn't lead the effort for the glory. What motivated Lacey was his belief Congressional actions to protect wildlife and our nation's natural treasures would be his enduring monument and they are.

John Lacey's career grew from years as a county seat lawyer in Oskaloosa and as a Civil War veteran, one of the thousands of Iowans who served in Iowa's deep and blood-soaked contribution. Lacey was born in Virginia but grew up near Oskaloosa, and saw distinguished service in the Civil War, enlisting twice and ending his service as a major. He returned to Oskaloosa, finished his legal studies and served a term in the Iowa House of Representatives. He devoted the next decade to the legal issues of the growing railroad industry, the most significant development in the national economy. After years of practicing law, he was drawn back to politics and elected to Congress, ultimately serving nine terms until his defeat in 1906. It was during the 1890s and the early 20th century Lacey left his mark, and when his commitment to wildlife and natural lands found expression.

From today's perspective, it is clear Lacey was not a typical member of Congress for the time. Rather than occupy himself with the parochial issues of his constituents in rural southern Iowa, Lacey saw his work as being a representative of the nation and its larger public interests. It appears this view grew from his service in the Army fighting across the South and from his frequent travels and work with railroad clients. As the railroads emerged they were a critical national matter shaped largely by federal policy and legal issues of interstate commerce. Lacey's work in Congress covered a variety of other national issues such as miner safety in the federal territories (miner safety in states was left to state law) and education of Native American children, who Lacey felt should be educated on their reservations rather than in federal boarding schools. But the hallmark of Lacey's career and the source of the rich legacy he left, still resonating today, was conservation in its broadest sense. Much of his pioneering work was done as chair of the House Committee on Public Lands. Today the posting would be a backwater spot of little influence. In the 1890s, as the nation struggled with how to balance using what was left of the public domain against the need to preserve our natural heritage, these issues gave his committee sweeping influence.

Lacey's reputation as a mild-mannered but shrewd politician led to him being known as the "velvet hammer" of the US conservation movement. In 1900 his hammer fell on the commercial hunters decimating Florida's plume birds like snowy egrets, to fuel the fashion for feathered hats. The Lacey Act of 1900 makes it illegal to transport protected birds across state lines, and is now considered the first federal game protection law. It triggered the "feather wars," as newly authorized game wardens battled the poachers and hunters profiting from the slaughter. Several wardens were murdered but eventually the law and the birds won out, and today we see their beauty across our land.

Lacey's most enduring legislative triumph is the Antiquities Act. The law is short and simple, it authorizes the President, without need for Congressional approval, to designate on federal land, historic landmarks and lands with scientific and scenic value as "national monuments." When enacted in 1906, those who came to rue the law considered it minor, to be used to protect small tracts of federal land. But Lacey's friend TR knew different, the law is unbridled in its reach. Over the next few years he used it to create 18 national monuments, protecting such treasured sites as the Grand Canyon, Devil's Tower,

Muir Woods, and the Petrified Forest, protections in many cases buying time for Congress to designate the sites as National Parks. The Antiquities Act is recognized as giving unprecedented power to the President to act unilaterally. It has since been used many times by every President to create national monuments now covering tens of millions of acres. Some designations are controversial, especially to state officials, who fear the lands are being "locked up" and made unavailable for the extractive pursuits still possible on much of the federal domain.

If he were alive John Lacey would be heartened to see how his law is still central to protecting natural lands and wildlife for all citizens to enjoy their beauty. As an Iowan, I am proud of the legacy Lacey left us and hope our new interest in public lands might restore his deeds and lift him from obscurity. To appreciate the role John Lacey played, it is worth noting Iowa had essentially no public lands left when he served in Congress. In speeches, he acknowledged this arguing it made him a "neutral" player on the economic aspects, unlike the Western politicians who stood to gain, often personally or through powerful political constituents. To these people he must have seemed an even bigger threat because "what did he know or care" about their unique needs when Iowa had no federal lands left. How convenient for someone from a state where the public domain had been entirely privatized and exploited, to be setting policy for other states seeking the same opportunity! This is how and why Lacey's service as a "national" citizen looking out for the public interest was unique for its time. But if the Westerners didn't appreciate this work, his Iowa constituents didn't either, as seen by his loss of re-election in 1906! Thankfully he was in Congress when, as history shows, the nation and our lands needed him most.

Examining Lacey' legislative career and legacy show without question he is one of the most important pioneers in America's conservation and environmental history. His leadership cut across the range of natural resource issues – forest reserves, wildlife refuges, national parks, bird and game protection, and protecting unique public lands. His work on any one of these issues should have cemented his legacy. Considered together his achievements across such a broad front of critical issues mark him as truly deserving of recognition and appreciation, much greater than exists today.

In a 1901 talk Lacey crystallized his commitment to conservation saying, "The immensity of man's power to destroy imposes a responsibility to preserve." Lacey's role in setting the foundation of American conservation marks him as America's Forgotten Conservation Hero. His leadership on the forest reserves was critical in helping articulate the federal role in conserving public lands. His work wasn't just pioneering and foundational in the laws he penned, it changed the nation's understanding of the role of the federal government, helping create the context for what would come in the decades to follow. His ideas about using the interstate commerce clause as the basis for federal authority, over federal lands and in relation to the states, helped develop the context for progressive ideas on conservation.

Lacey understood the foundational role of public lands for the nation. His view of how the expanding public domain influenced the Nation's founding is reflected in this quote on the relation of public lands to the Constitution:

> The Constitution did not prepare the way for our public domain. It was that domain which prepared the way for the Constitution.... The cession of the great Western Empire to the nation was essential to the adoption of the Constitution itself.

The Back Forty on Lines, Boundaries, and Names

This chapter is about public land, a topic you might think doesn't interest me that much. True, I am not public land today but at one time I was. Before the white settlers came we were all "public land" - unfenced, unclaimed, and wide open to be used by anyone who desired. Even after the surveyors came in 1851 and marked my boundaries, for a few more years I was still in the "public domain" claimed by the federal government but not yet patented or sold. That happened in 1855 when my new life got started – at least in your eyes. Today my public features are found largely in the laws designed to influence how I am used – like conserving the soil as discussed in the next chapter. There is one habit of the people that amuses me and shows how "the public land" may be based as much on lines drawn on maps as on anything more concrete.

Even though they call me the Back Forty, from my perspective there are really no lines on the land. No real boundaries separate one field from another. When I was young and new the only line you saw was the horizon, even then, we knew if we could head towards it, it would move and there would just be more of us, more land. Sure, there were rivers and streams to cross, the Nodaway and Nisnabotna, and then the bigger ones, the Missouri and Platte but on the other side there was still more land.

It wasn't until the people came, the white folks, then lines and boundaries began to appear and boy did they ever! People seemed to make a hobby out of drawing lines. Most of them don't appear on the land physically, unless you consider the roads, fences, and tile ditches. Their lines are drawn on paper and on maps. There are maps for the section, for the township, for the county and even for the state. In fact, the first thing people did when they landed on me, what they like to call settling, a term even the most restless of them used, was to draw lines. The surveyor came with compass and chain and measured off portions of me in rods. That is how I came to be a 40 – and a Back Forty at that, meaning I am in the middle of a 640-acre section.

In the early 19th century the federal government knew if it was going to sell off and dispose the millions of acres it was in the process of "acquiring" from the native tribes it needed a way to know what was what – and especially who had legal title and owned what land. This meant land could be sold or granted away and the government could receive the income. Plus, it created a way to "legalize" the claims people made to the land and minimized potential conflicts or disputes over ownership. The government set out on the experiment of the General Land Survey. Beginning on a river bank in southeast Ohio, it marked off the straight lines and 640 acre sections eventually covering hundreds of thousands of square miles all across the nation. You can read about this fascinating history in Andro Linklater's 2002 book, *Measuring America: How an Untamed Wilderness Shaped the United States and Fulfilled the Promise of Democracy*. In many ways, he explains how I was born, though not conceived, man didn't play any role in that! Because his book tells how the lines came to be and how the people came to own me, in some ways it is like their Bible!

The survey platting me out as Mercer Township Section 13 was just the start of the line drawing. Soon other lines showed up. There were roads, running north and south and east and west, each with some land set off for the ditches. This explains why there is never 640 acres of farmable land in a section. The section lines meet in the middle of the road but you can't plant corn there, instead you must deduct several acres for the roads and ditches.

Other lines and boundaries came after the roads. There were school district lines to determine where youngsters went to school. In the early years there was a network of one-room country schools. The nearest one was Mercer Center #2 at the southwest corner of my section. One of the great things about the people, they loved education. They loved it so much the federal law for disposing of the land from the public domain required the proceeds from the sale of the 16th section in each township be set aside for use in education. The "16th section law" is how America came to have a network of country schools and how the hallmark of free public education and rural history was funded. In fact, the boy who grew up on me to be a professor went to a one-room school for the 1959-60 school year, the last year Mercer Center #2 existed. When they closed the rural schools a 100-year experiment in public education came to an end.

As for me, the lines don't mean much except for the one relating to who owns me, but this status only changes every generation or two. The economists describe the market for farmland as thin, because any particular tract of land may only come on the market once every 50 years. If your time horizon is long enough, as is mine, this is still a short period of time. The fact land doesn't come up for sale very often though can lead people who live next to it or who crave more land to spend huge sums to secure the right to "own" it, even spending more than the land can reasonably be expected to earn. The story of land fever fuels periodic "farm crisis" when land prices drop.

As for people, the lines have a real impact on how they lead their lives: which school the kids attend, the bus route coming by, the town where you get mail, and your official "address" sanctioned by the federal government. My mail is addressed to Prescott, a small hamlet, four miles to the north, but the school district is Lenox, a town seven miles to the southeast

– and Corning, the Adams county seat is eight miles to the west. So many lines, but the people don't seem to have trouble keeping them straight. Even though the lines are "artificial" they influence who is considered a neighbor and the people to socialize with. The lines determine the parents sitting in the seats at the ball game as well as who is on the team. There was a family living ¾ of a mile north when the boy grew up and he barely knew the kids, because they went to school in Corning. If the bus had come to the next corner south, they might have been his classmates and best friends.

All these lines, jurisdictions as lawyers call them, have a political origin and purpose, in fact they add a public dimension to the land. There is one more line, a natural line or boundary people are coming to recognize out of necessity, the watershed. My natural topography determines where the water falling on me will flow. Gravity moves it down slope where it collects in natural channels to eventually become streams and then rivers – flowing toward the sea. The watershed is the area of land draining into a particular stream or river. Even though watersheds exist, my experience is most landowners can't draw a map of the one they live in! Why? Because the lines don't follow any of the political lines people use to organize their actions. When you look at a map of Iowa you see a network of rivers etched across the state, draining fields like me down to the Gulf, taking along with the water whatever else you might have added to the soil. In recent years concern has grown over how excess nutrients like N and P can pollute the water, along with the silt the rivers carry. It all means the land is helping pollute the Gulf, creating a Hypoxia zone, a story you will hear in Chapter Five.

While I am at it, let me say a few words about how the people loved to name things, like Adams County and Mercer Township where I am located. It was a way to "claim" an area, marking it as civilized I guess. They used names to honor heroes, leaders, and others they felt worthy. This is why the names of Iowa's ninety-nine counties read like a list of Presidents, founding fathers, and war heroes. Not all counties received such a christening though, some were given names left by the Native Americans first here, evocative names like Winneshiek, Poweshiek, and Potawatomie. In the settlement years, new counties were carved out of the original divisions and sometimes original names were swapped out for new and better ones as the politics of settlement evolved. My favorite county name lasted only a few years from 1843 to 1846. What today is Monroe County, sixty miles to my east was originally named Kishkikosh County, now that is a name!

The Back Forty on Property Rights

What is the effect of someone saying they "own" you? No one ever owned me before the settlers came so the concept was new. One thing it meant was if I could be owned then I could also be sold. As later events showed, one beauty of the law is how it developed other recognized forms of "ownership" such as leases and tenancy. The idea of ownership introduced a whole new concern, who owned me and what did they plan to do with me? (i.e., why did they want to own me?) Owners come with all types of motivations for why they want to be owners. As time and a century plus of "being owned" has shown, their main purpose is to use my fertility to grow plants they find useful. This has included pasture for livestock and forage crops like timothy and alfalfa for hay, but for the last 100 years it has been to grow corn or in some years, soybeans.

One of the great things about being able to grow crops is how versatile the owners find me and how many different ways what I produce can be used. For most of the Wray-Hamilton century the corn I produced was used right on the farm to feed the hogs and cattle they raised for market. In the early years there were oats to feed and fuel the draft horses, like Fan and Dan, the team pulling the implements grooming me. In the winter and spring, some of what was left after the hogs and cattle consumed my corn, what you call manure, was brought out and spread on me to nourish the worms and bugs living in my topsoil. This rich pungent material was tilled back into me and gave my fertility a boost, kind of like how you people take vitamins. This replenishment helped me grow more corn the next year. This cycle may seem repetitive, but to me it created a rhythm to life.

In the 1970s I learned much of my corn was being trucked to town and sold. Who knows where it ended up, perhaps on a barge on the Mississippi headed to New Orleans to go on a boat headed to Rotterdam, or in a truck headed to a cattle feedlot in Kansas? All I know is no longer were there any live-stock on the farm and the annual coatings of manure to re-plenish my energy came to an end. I missed these annual vis-its, just as I missed feeling the footsteps of the cattle each fall when they were turned out after harvest to find the ears the picker missed and eat the stalks and shucks left on the land. When they stopped visiting, I knew something had changed in how the people were farming me. They may have felt the change was natural, simply changing with the times to meet evolving markets, but to me the changes had a more perma-nent and unhealthy impact.

More recently I learned of an even newer and different use being made of my corn. Today we are in the "ethanol era" and all the corn I grow is trucked to an industrial site in Nodaway, about 10 miles west. The corn is ground up, placed into large di-gesters, and fermented to produce alcohol. This alcohol, what the people call ethanol, is shipped away and used to mix with gasoline to burn in automobiles! Can you believe it! They take the food I produce then grind it up to make ethanol and then burn it! The part left over, what they call the distiller's grain or DGG, can be used to feed animals, if they can find anyone who wants it. Hearing about this I have to say was a bit of a shock. I always prided myself on the fact people used me to grow food. Perhaps they didn't eat it themselves but they loved to eat the meat it helped produce. Now they don't even eat what I grow, instead they burn it to fuel their cars!! It has taken some time to get my head around this. So much for impassioned cries how Iowa farmers "feed the world!"

Iowa and the Public Domain

In the days of Lacey and Powell, federal officials faced the question what to do with the "Public Domain," how to deal with the millions of acres of land still under control of the General Land Office? Much of the land was slated for disposal and sale to private individuals or for use in land grants to support public projects like building railroads. Thankfully in the 1880s the government began setting aside some timber-covered land as national forest reserves. As years passed, more land was designated as national parks and wildlife refuges and soon our thinking changed about reserving part of the public domain for the public. As a result, by the turn of the century several hundred million acres had been withdrawn from disposal and reserved as "public lands." The legacy Lacey and his cohorts built on created one of our greatest national treasures. Conflicts over who should control the lands and whether the federal government owns "too much" in western states are political questions stalking the halls of Congress, just as in Lacey's days.

Today if you ask what remains of the "public domain" in a state like Iowa the answer is not much if you view the issue as Lacey did. But if you take a broader view of what it means to be in the "public domain" Iowa reflects a mix of real property, and other public interests in land. Here are examples of Iowa's "public domain":

State owned land in parks, preserves, and meandered lakes; county owned land in over 900 parks and wildlife management areas; public college and university campuses; and thousands of municipal parks.

Water surfaces of "non-meandered streams," where the streambanks do not operate as legal boundaries, are public water by law; and for meandered streams and rivers, the waters, beds, and stream banks.

Road ditches and rights of way on thousands of miles of county roads as well as along primary highways.

Land owned by private land trusts like the Iowa Natural Heritage Foundation and the Nature Conservancy, some may even have a "quasi-public" nature, open for public use with permission.

Hundreds of miles of bike trails owned by the counties and cities and dozens of public golf courses, protected for natural uses.

Private lands under long-term easement, like the 20,000 acres of fields and stream banks subject to state use for public hunting and fishing.

Federal wildlife refuges like the Neal Smith, Union Slough, and the Upper Mississippi, administered by US Fish and Wildlife Service, and the National monuments at Effigy Mounds and the Hoover Birthplace Library, under direction of the National Park Service.

Conservation benefits from farmland under contracts and easements with USDA, such as the Conservation Reserve Program, the Wetland Reserve, and Agricultural Land Easements to protect farmland. The lands are permanently protected even if not open for public use.

Some of these lands are "public domain" in the traditional sense with full access and use by the public. Other lands listed are privately owned yet subject to some legal obligation giving the public limited rights to use and enjoy the land, even if only for looking across the scenery. In any case, the list is impressive and represents a significant amount of widely distributed land, and an array of legal interests extending the "public domain."

Just as the list of different land interests is broad, the source and "nature" of the legal claims can vary widely. For a citizen, the variation may limit the public's rights to use the land, such as being physically present on the land or water. For example, if a stream is meandered the public owns not just the water but also the streambed and banks. If a stream is non-meandered the streambed and banks are privately owned and the public's rights are limited to floating on the water.

Vigilance is required to safeguard the "public" interest in the land. For example, most farmers and landowners entering conservation agreements with USDA do not consider the contracts as having a "public" dimension but they do. Articulating the extent and meaning of the public trust doctrine and what it requires of state officials and the courts in protecting public waters is uncertain. Chapter Six explains a case recently before the Iowa courts, alleging state officials violated the public trust by failing to protect the Raccoon River from pollution. There are definitely public attributes associated with all these land and resources. The key is recognizing how robust and diverse Iowa's "public domain" really is, regardless of the nuances or uncertainties in the types of interests involved.

LAND AND LEADERSHIP

If you read Brinkley's *Wilderness Warrior*, the description of Teddy Roosevelt working with Lacey and others to create the national forests and wildlife refuge system, reveals just how committed these leaders were to the idea of conservation – writ large. They felt an obligation to "save" the lands and resources from wasteful exploitation so they would be available in the decades and centuries to come. Their wisdom is noteworthy because today we take for granted the existence of the national forests, parks, and other public lands – the 900 hundred million acres we enjoy and have available for future opportunities. It didn't have to turn out this way and without the efforts of many conservation leaders it would not have. If the governors of the western states and territories or the dominant industries of logging, mining, and grazing, what David Korten in *The Great Turning; From Empire to Earth Community*, labels the forces of Empire, would have their way we would cut every forest and mine every location we can reach, as some are still trying to do. Unique scenic lands and natural features, our national heritage and history of archaeological sites and treasures would be sold off, plundered, developed, and otherwise spoiled and defaced. We need to appreciate how fortunate we are and how thankful we should be for the foresight and courage of these conservation and public land pioneers.

The battle to save public land and protect it from exploitation is not finished with a designation. Instead it is an on-going struggle. The work of historian Bernard DeVoto in his mid-century writing for *Harper's* helped focus national attention on the abuse of public lands, such as over-grazing. His crusading work to protect natural lands is well told in his collection of essays, *The Easy Chair* from 1955, and is further developed in his close friend Wallace Stegner's 1974 biography of DeVoto, *The Uneasy Chair*. This work continues in the fight against the so-called Sagebrush rebellion and the newer iteration of the Bundy's and all those who dream of privatizing the western lands as the books by

Ketcham and McCain demonstrate. What lessons can we draw from this history? First, is a need to appreciate the foresight and vision of the national leaders who created our public lands policy. Second, is how the nation gained by their taking the long view toward resource management, especially goals of long-term sustainability and multiple uses. Third, and most important, the question for today is how lessons from this history should guide our actions in addressing challenges, most notably the policies we design to address climate change.

We may not have many classic examples of "public domain" left to protect from the traditional forces of exploitation, but there are definitely other resources with a public dimension, in need of protection for future generations. The quality of water, the existence of wildlife, the use of the public airwaves, and now, perhaps most significantly, our climate, are all examples of "public" resources. How different is acting to protect the "climate" from assault by $CO2$, from reserving national forest lands? Taking a broader view of public resources raises the question who will be the "leaders" to stand up for these resources? Hopefully our efforts did not end with Al Gore and the US efforts at COP 15 in Copenhagen in 2009. The Obama carbon tax idea can't be the best we can do. These were just preliminary skirmishes, helping illuminate the divides and the battles still to come. The best news is we elected a new Administration aware of the nature of this challenge. As we will see in the final chapter, a new generation of leaders is emerging to engage the challenge of climate change and to continue the necessary work of defending the "public domain."

FDR personified leadership and his incredible work crossed a range of natural resource protection issues building on the foundation TR, Lacey, and their allies laid down. Even though he is not as widely recognized or appreciated for his contributions, FDR took the work much farther in lands protected and conservation laws enacted. His work on conservation and public lands are overlooked in part because the list of social advancements we owe him is so long. FDR's leadership on natural resource conservation is just one facet of his larger political legacy: winning WWII, saving democracy from the forces of fascism, pulling us out of the Depression, and building the framework for the New Deal of social and political reforms we still value today. These were all major tasks, which makes it even more remarkable how in the midst of dealing with these monumental issues, FDR devoted so much of his time and energy to natural resources conservation. He saw himself as a tree farmer from New York. Others may have found his description self-effacing, but he saw land conservation as central to the health and future of the nation. In today's world, it is hard to imagine a president so aware of the natural world and conservation as key national issues! The lack of a shared national vision and leadership on issues of conservation is one of the tragic "losses" we have experienced in our relation to the land. The bright question we can consider now is if a Biden-Harris administration will usher in new thinking, a new generation of leadership, and a new set of ideas to reinvigorate how we approach the land and conservation, driven in part by the necessity of addressing climate change?

The Back Forty on Trespassing

It has come to my attention people who own land, like me, get very concerned about something you call trespassing. Apparently, this means when a person is on another person's land without the owner's permission. The power to restrict anyone coming on the land is part and parcel of the "exclusivity" ideal of private property, so important to Americans. It can be summarized as "I own mine and you can't use it." You see this notion of trespassing, or protecting the privacy and primacy of owners, in signs hanging on fence posts "No Trespassing," "Private Property – Keep Out."

Trespassing is a relatively new idea in the life of the land. Before you "settled" me no one thought in terms of ownership or restricting the movement of others. Certainly, the natives who were here first felt free to come and go as they pleased, as did the deer, fox, bison, and all the other creatures passing over me. It wasn't until you came along with your surveys and lines, deeds and legal titles, any thought was given to ideas like trespassing. Even then, the issue wasn't about someone passing over me heading somewhere else as this was widely accepted. Instead the concern was different, what worried you was "squatting," someone claiming the right to use and possess the land. This is what your land titles are for, deciding who has the best legal claim to me, I can only have one owner at a time!

Matters got a bit more complicated when farmers started raising animals, especially cattle who liked to graze my grass but were just as tempted by a nearby stand of green corn. Then the issue became who had to keep the cows from getting into the corn? Was it the farmer who owned the cows or the fellow growing the corn? Out west where the lands were wide and open, people called it free-range country, meaning cows could come and go as they pleased. If you were a settler, planting crops, then you had to fence your land to keep the cows out. You can imagine there were plenty of conflicts between the range happy cattlemen and the settlers putting up fences. It even led to famous range wars and later, a movie-making fiasco! From a legal perspective, this approach came to be known as a "fence out" law. If there was no fence then there was no legal right to seek damages for whatever mischief the cows caused. In the more settled Eastern states, the law developed in the other direction. If you owned cows then you had a duty to keep them on your land, to fence them in. If they got out and ate the neighbor's corn you were liable for any damages. The law might even let the neighbor keep the cows until you paid up. This approach came to be known as a "fence in" law.

Iowa always had an independent streak, leavened with a dose of common sense. When it came to issues of wandering cows, Iowa took a unique approach. If your cows got loose and ate the neighbor's corn you were liable, that is unless the neighbor had failed to build a partition fence to keep your cows out. Then you were off the hook. Yes, Iowa became both a "fence in" and a "fence out" state, turning the issue of wandering cows into a whole new subject – fence law! As you can imagine in a state with several hundred thousand small farms and even more miles of fences, the Iowa courts had ample opportunities to plumb the nuances of fence law and straying livestock. We need not pursue the topic much further, other than to wonder what the law will be tomorrow? The shift to producing only crops and the disappearance of livestock from most farms, has resulted in many fences disappearing, even along the roads. Today there is little to keep a cow from going wherever it wants and there is hardly a place to hang a "No Trespassing" sign warning people to stay out!

The worry someone might walk across your land is almost amusing if it wasn't such evidence of the state of fear many landowners live in today. Why are you so worried someone might walk across your land – what exactly are you trying to hide? Things are so different in the US where people have no "right to roam" or walk a path across a field to the other side of the mile. In Europe and the UK the right to roam is a cherished and protected public right, as long as people act responsibly. Try doing the same in America and you might end up with a lesson about what trespassing means, and the opportunity for a heated conversation with an armed and angry landowner in a pickup demanding to know "why are you trespassing on my land!" This situation makes me think about old Woody Guthrie and his famous song "This Land is Your Land." Not the verse you learned in school but a later verse, the one that goes:

> As I was walking I saw a sign there
> And on the sign it said "No Trespassing"
> But on the other side it didn't say nothing.
> That side was made for you and me

That verse is discussed in Ken Ilguanas' book, *This Land is Our Land: How We Lost the Right to Roam and How to Take it Back* (Plume 2018). Read his book and you will realize Americans used to have the right to roam the land unhindered by worries of trespassing, and not all that long ago. Speaking for myself, and I think most of the land, we would be happy to give you back the right to roam. Trespassing is an invention of man, not something inherent in the land. All we ask is you respect us and treat us well. Your footsteps cause us no harm.

WHO WAS DING DARLING – AND WHAT WOULD HE SAY TODAY?

Thinking about our future and about the new Administration bringing in a burst of attention to conservation, draws us to another Iowa conservation hero, J. N. "Ding" Darling. Darling was a conservation icon in the first half of the 20th Century, a two-time Pulitzer Prize winning cartoonist and national political figure. His drawings and leadership cut across many fronts, from serving under FDR leading the US Biological Survey (soon to become the Fish and Wildlife Service), to drawing the first Duck Stamp ushering in a national program which has raised over one billion dollars used to acquire hundreds of thousands of acres of wildlife habitat. In Iowa, he led efforts to get politics out of natural resource protection and game management, helping professionalize the administration of Iowa's regulation of game and the outdoors. If you are one of the millions of Americans who enjoy bird watching, you may have visited his namesake, the J. N. "Ding" Darling Wildlife Refuge at Sanibel-Captiva on the Florida Gulf Coast. To learn about Darling's life work in conservation a great place to start is David L. Lendt's 1979 biography, *Ding: The Life of Jay Norwood Darling*.

Asking what Darling can tell us, requires considering Iowa's legacy of leadership. Leopold, Lacey, and Henry A. Wallace, were conservation leaders, who like Darling understood the foundation of our society, economy, and lives are built on soil and water. They believed how we steward these resources is one measure of our morality. This attitude applies to the "public lands" they worked to protect, but also to the much larger share of the Nation's land in private ownership, most being farmed. I like to believe we share many traits, perhaps most important is a willingness to see through the happy talk the public is fed about the great job we do protecting natural resources, and a willingness to step on toes if doing so might help change the discourse. One benefit of teaching at a private university like Drake was the institution's commitment to academic independence. I worked free from the dogma and hegemony pervading and restraining many professors at public institutions involved with agriculture and conservation. Darling used wit, independence, and his talents to challenge the complacency and short sightedness of his day. That is why I think channeling what he might say about our current situation can help inform our understanding.

Darling would agree we have a crisis on our hands in Iowa and the nation when it comes to the land. He would be appalled by the toll we have wrecked on the land, the soil loss and polluted water we tolerate and justify as the price of modern farming, issues examined in chapters to follow. It is clear we need voices like Darling's to illuminate the illogic of our public policy and our unwillingness to address the crisis we've created. Things might be different if we had Darling's cartoons to lampoon Congress's hollow "actions" on climate change and environmental protection, to debunk Iowa politicians' pious resistance to funding protection of soil and water, and to question agriculture's unrelenting fight against phantom regulations to avoid responsibility for stewarding the land and water.

Darling would be proud of the farmers and landowners who protect their land, soil and water, but he would be disheartened by the many who fail to embrace a duty to the soil. He would be critical of the lack of leadership we have for protecting water and land, and would have been merciless in scorning the Iowa legislators and "leaders" who killed the Leopold Center for Sustainable Agriculture. Aldo Leopold was his friend and contemporary, their having served together on a three-member national commission on wildlife, appointed by FDR in 1934. He would be angry we have turned protecting land, soil, and water, the fundamental ideas of conservation, into partisan issues and re-politicized them, something he worked to end in the 1930s. Darling was mindful "as goes the Land so goes Man."

Darling knew how well Nature had stocked our pantry but bemoaned how profligate we are with these resources, mining soil to grow more corn, polluting water to carry away fertility, cutting forests to plant more crops, all the while pretending we do all we can to protect the land. He knew nature can restore itself, if we work with it and give it time. He would be a fan of groups like the Iowa Natural Heritage Foundation and other land trusts, and proud of the thousands of landowners protecting their land. Darling knew it takes organizing people to harness their voices and resources to make progress, as illustrated by his efforts to create the National Wildlife Federation. On water quality Ding knew its causes and impacts, and understood how our efforts to drain the land only lead to more flooding, pollution, soil loss, and destruction of wildlife habitat.

If he were here today, Darling would feel the public discourse has become too one-sided, too anti-government and anti-public, on resource conservation and public lands. He understood the need for wise regulations to assist landowners in meeting their obligation to the land and understood it was lunacy to believe voluntary programs alone can do the job. He would see how our efforts lack context and a vision for what we are trying to achieve. These are the issues Darling would be fighting today, as would DeVoto, Lacey, and the Roosevelts if they were still with us. But they aren't. Instead the work of conservation, of protecting the public lands, and of working with farmers and landowners to safeguard the public interest in the private lands they own, now falls to us. These are the subjects we turn to next, starting with the most fundamental issue of soil conservation.

Chapter Three – Soil Conservation and our History on the Land

I have been studying and writing about US soil conservation for over forty-five years. My major project the last year of law school was a six-credit study on US soil conservation policy. The scale and technology used in farming may have changed but one thing hasn't changed during this period - we continue to lose soil at an alarming rate, on average well over 5 tons/acre/year on the Nation's roughly 400 million acres of crop ground. This rate of soil loss greatly exceeds the rate new soil is being "made" or replaced through natural processes. Most US fields are farmed with intensive agro-chemical systems and the amount of new soil being created on these lands is minimal. This is true even though conventional wisdom in US agriculture, and the official policy of USDA, is even intensively farmed fields replace soil at approximately 5 tons/acre/year. This comforting fiction lets us believe things are just about in balance and our approach to soil management is sustainable. Ask a reputable scientist working on soil conservation if this is true though and you may get a much different answer. Iowa's top soil scientist, Dr. Rick Cruse, an agronomist at Iowa State University, estimates most conventionally farmed Iowa fields reproduce soil at a rate of half a ton per year or $1/10^{th}$ the figure used for official government estimates.

To put the soil loss of 5.5 tons coming off each Iowa acre into perspective, it helps to compare the lost soil to the crops produced on the same land. In 2019 Iowa's average corn yield was a record 198 bushels per acre. A bushel of shelled corn weighs 56 pounds so the weight of the corn produced on an acre is around 11,000 lbs. You can do the math - it roughly equals the weight of the soil lost in growing the corn. Another way to picture it is for each semi-truckload of corn driven off the farm another truck is driven away filled with rich top-soil. This "crop" of soil doesn't go to the elevator in town instead it is dumped into nearby streams, rivers, road ditches, or wherever else the wind and water take it. If instead of corn you grow soybeans the story gets even worse. In 2019 Iowa's average yield for soybeans was 55 bushels per acre and a bushel weighs 60 pounds. This means the field produced about 3,300 pounds of crops but lost over 10,000 pounds of soil. So instead of one truck of soil leaving for each truckload of beans, the picture now shows three truckloads of lost soil! How long can we keep doing this you ask? Apparently as long as we keep fooling ourselves into believing it isn't a problem – or as long as the soil we are mining holds out.

Some observers argue we are making progress on soil conservation because more farmers are using no-till and reduced tillage practices. There is some truth in this but it all depends on where you look. Forty years ago, writing my law school study on soil conservation policy the view was we were losing two trucks of soil for every truckload of corn produced. Are we making progress? Not really because back then corn yields were closer to 100 bushels per acre rather than the 200 bushels today. In the intervening period improved corn genetics, higher rates of fertilizer, increased seed populations, and other cropping practices have doubled yields but when it comes to topsoil lost, not a whole lot has changed. In fact, on more marginal ground intensive row cropping is making soil erosion worse.

Therein lays one of the many obstacles to improving how we treat the soil and one of the contradictions in our attitudes toward farming. The long-term dangers and threats of soil loss, leaving aside the impact of degraded water quality and silt-filled streams, are a long-term, gradual loss of soil fertility, soil health, and crop productivity. Soil scientists, conservation officials, and some politicians have been warning about these dangers for almost one hundred years. Because losses in soil fertility are often masked over by "improved" cropping practices, threats of soil erosion are easy to ignore. As Aldo Leopold put it, most improvements in agriculture have focused on improving the pump but little has been done to take care of the well.

Today, eighty years have passed since the 1930s Dust Bowl made soil erosion a national concern, but the debate has changed very little. Those who fear the threat of soil erosion say Iowa has lost one-half of its topsoil in the last 100 years. People were saying the same thing sixty years ago when I was a boy and the 100-year mark then was measured from when we broke the prairie sod and turned to raising crops. Now we are 160 years down this destructive path and continue to lose more topsoil. Are we now down to one-half of the soil we had left in 1960? Trying to answer this question helps identify a second contradiction fueling our Nation's conflicted attitudes toward soil loss. The existence of soil erosion depends on where you look because croplands across Iowa and the nation vary widely. In the flat region of north central Iowa, the Des Moines Lobe as geologists call it, soil erosion from water runoff is minimal, though winter wind erosion can be a problem. The last glacier 14,000 years ago flattened the land and left it with little slope to speed water run-off causing erosion.

Travel to western Iowa where fields are defined by longer slopes and steeper hills and the answer is much different. There we didn't lose one-half of the topsoil, on many of the ridge tops we have lost it all! You can see for yourself by driving I-80 west from Des Moines toward Nebraska in the late spring after crops have emerged. Driving for miles through the rolling hills reveals spots on the hillsides where lighter colored soils are visible across the landscape. These bald knobs are devoid of the rich black topsoil once present, a reality made clear by the sparse stands of corn and soybeans growing on them. Drive by again in August and the thin spots will seemly have disappeared, as the fields look lush and green, full of tall stalks of corn. Don't let the appearance of fertility fool you, reality is revealed once harvest comes. Farmers in their combines will watch the yield monitors, technology telling them in real time how much crop is being harvested. Then the truth comes out as the digital readouts dip and fall, signaling not just lost productivity but a waste of the high-priced inputs, seed, fertilizers, insecticides, and herbicides, applied to these "bald spots." Data indicates on many Iowa farms as much as 10% of farm fields consistently fail to produce a profit, due largely to long-term effects of soil erosion and how degraded soils have lost fertility, the ability to hold water, and their productive capacity.

The loss in soil health is felt in other ways as well. Spring rains will pour down these hillsides because there is little carbon-rich topsoil to act like a sponge to absorb it. As the water runs downhill it claws and grabs more loosely bound soil particles, channeling into the rivulets and rills gravity draws on the land. When the farmer returns next spring, these lines will be visible, etched like spider webs drawn by nature on the land. One pass with the disk or field cultivator will sweep them away, like a child shaking an etch-a-sketch, to start a fresh drawing with every new crop year. The USDA even has a name for these annual etchings, labeling them "ephemeral gullies," ephemeral because they can be erased each spring. How ironic such a poetic name can capture the contradictory sweep of our conservation policy? If it is called a gully it is bad, but if we change the label to ephemeral it is only temporary, and tomorrow is just another day. If the gullies are ephemeral, we don't even need to worry about them! Soil scientists estimate ephemeral gullies account for 30% of our soil losses, but the USDA does not measure or count them in the official estimates of soil loss. Remember the 5 tons mentioned above, it is really closer to 6.5 when the soil lost to ephemeral gullies is added. We may need to hire another truck to carry away the additional lost soil.

Enough talk about the physical dynamics of soil loss, instead of focusing on why it is happening, a better question to ask is why we have let it continue for generations? It was not always like this. In the early years of federal farm policy beginning in the 1930s soil erosion was seen as a critical issue. Then our attention to soil erosion was crystallized by scenes from the Dust Bowl and images of the destruction and human despair it produced. There was common agreement about the need to fight soil erosion and for direct government action to promote soil conservation all across the farm sector. Books were written, agencies created, laws enacted, and billions of dollars in public funds invested, along with the time and efforts from countless farmers and landowners. Progress was made, soil and water conservation districts were formed all across farm country, conservation plans were written to help farmers know what practices to adopt, and thousands of soil conservation technicians were hired by the USDA and local districts to carry out the work. The results were visible on the land and can still be seen in the seemingly endless miles of terraces built on the sloping lands, the grass waterways slowing the water, the shelterbelts taming the winds, and in the contouring farming and wiser practices used by farmers. These efforts combined to save millions of tons of soil and keep it in place.

Over time, as with many other "great concerns," national attention flagged as more pressing issues demanded our attention. The war came and land was put back into production to help win it and to feed a hungry world. As farming practices improved concern for lands once consider "abused," like the "bleeding hills of southern Iowa," diminished. The idea became we can farm these lands if only we do it the right way. Fears about soil loss were lessened as crop yields grew and worries about "losing" abused land faded. We didn't lose all interest in promoting soil conservation, the issue just lost its immediacy and potency to spur action. Instead, soil conservation became just one part of a larger web, a constellation of government agencies and farm programs, another factor and option for a farmer to consider. That is, to consider while at the same time trying to produce enough crops and income to stay in farming, or expand to compete in the coming age of farm consolidation and crop specialization. The new emerging farm structure left less room on the land for livestock and less reason for diversified crop rotations. The farming mentality of the 1940s and early 50s, the period for which our conservation policy was designed, gave way to a more industrialized and chemical dependent style of farming. In many ways, a farmer's commitment to soil conservation became a personal choice, something you could choose to do or not.

As a boy participating in 4-H in the 1960s, there was one neighbor, Gene Swartz, who farmed about four miles east and was widely known for his commitment to soil conservation. He served for years as an Adams County Soil and Water Conservation District commissioner, installed many conservation practices on the land, and hosted field days and demonstrations. Besides him, I can think of no other farmers in the neighborhood who made a big deal of soil conservation. Come to think of it neither did the 4-H movement. I remember few lectures, classes, or projects designed to instill in us, a crew of budding farmers called the Grant-Go-Getters, the ideals of soil conservation. Don't get me wrong, I am not saying my neighbors did not care about their land. To know that answer you had to walk their fields, instead it just wasn't a priority. I worked on many of those farms each summer as a hired laborer putting up hay, walking beans, or cutting thistles in the pastures. The fact there were still hay fields and pastures tells us something about it being a different era. Today most of those fields have been plowed under, put into crop ground to raise the state's darling crops of corn and soybeans.

If you could choose to be a conservation farmer as neighbor Swartz did, you could also choose not to be one. That was the story throughout the 60s, 70s, and into the early 80s. Federal soil conservation programs offered by the USDA through the Soil Conservation Service (SCS), now the Natural Resources Conservation Service or NRCS, were there if you chose to use them. Only in those years when there was a mandatory set-aside of corn acres was conservation a requirement to be eligible for farm programs payments. Then farmers had to set aside a required percent of their base acres, planting them to conserving crops such as grass. Conservation was only required on the set-aside ground, and typically farmers chose the least productive acres to set aside. How the rest of the land was farmed was entirely up to the farmer and no federal conservation rules applied. Some people had a conservation plan drawn up by a SCS soil technician. Doing so could help secure cost-sharing funds from the USDA to help pay part of the cost of installing soil conservation practices, like terraces and building farm ponds to water the cattle. If a farmer didn't need terraces or didn't feel like farming according to a plan there was no need to worry because soil conservation was entirely voluntary, then and now. Attention to how the other land was farmed didn't become a concern until decades later when passage of the conservation title in the 1985 farm bill brought about the modern era of soil conservation. The 1985 law used conservation to address the financial stress caused by the 1980s farm crisis, repeating how conservation was used during the Great Depression as a way to justify getting federal payments to struggling farmers.

The Back Forty Talks About Conservation

If you think about me in a topographical sense the only way I can be described is flat! My elevation does not vary more than three feet from one corner to the other. This is pretty unusual for Mercer Township, even for the adjacent sections. That condition may be common in the river valley flood plains or in North Central Iowa's flatlands but it is not common in the Southern Iowa uplands. My situation no doubt has something to do with being located near the dividing line between two river watersheds – the 102 River and the Nodaway. The man who farmed me for decades liked to muse if he stood in just the right place to pee, half would flow west to the Missouri and the other half east to the Mississippi. It turns out he was only half right because once his eastern "stream" made it to the

Grand River, the river eventually turns back southwest to flow into the Missouri. Either way you get the point, I am flat. This helps give me another description as "a flat black 40" – this is good thing when it comes to farmland although it does carry one drawback. My lack of slope means surface drainage can be a challenge in wet times. When it rains the water doesn't run-off but instead pools and ponds until it can percolate down into my soil.

For centuries, my main condition was native prairie, and then for a few decades after that pasture and hay ground. Then my tendency to stay wet didn't give anyone much trouble, in fact it just made for lush growths of grass to be cut once the soil dried. When my owners began to turn over my soil to plant crops to harvest each fall – then my wet spots became more of a problem. If the spring was wet it could delay when I got planted. If the weather turned wet with summer rains the farmer might get stuck in the mud trying to cultivate the weeds. Even worse was a wet fall, then my crops might not be harvested until the ground froze and by then the snow might be falling. As the saying goes on the farm – if it isn't one damn thing it's two! It didn't take the folks helping "modernize" agriculture long to come up with the solution for my wet spots, even though I didn't really mind them. The idea was installing drainage tile by digging ditches about three feet deep and burying clay pipes to gather the water from the top layer and drain it down slope to an outlet. The idea was by installing tile, basically a plumbing system for the land, the soil where the crops roots grow would dry out sooner so field work could be done and the roots didn't get water-logged by wet soils. Sure, it took a fair amount of labor and expense to tile a field but the increased profits often quickly paid for the investment. In the early years at the turn of last century the trenches were dug by hand and not as deep, but by the 1930s and certainly after the war powerful trenching machines were used to dig the ditches and lay the clay tile. By the 1970s clay tile was replaced with the huge spools of perforated plastic drainage lines you see today. Plastic is less expensive and requires much less labor to install. The idea of tiling a field by installing an underground plumbing system may seem radical but it is common. In Iowa, over 14 million acres of the 24 million acres of crop ground is tiled and here in Adams County over 100,000 acres of the 140,000 acres of cropland is tiled. Iowa farmers and landowners still install thousands of miles of drainage tile each year, often in lines placed only a few yards apart, called pattern tiling. Today it is estimated over one million miles of tile lines have been buried in the Iowa soil. Tiling isn't without issues, the main one being how tile lines act like direct conduits, taking fertilizers and pesticides applied on the land more quickly to streams and rivers. Speeding the drainage also has had the effect of increasing the amount of water flowing in Iowa's rivers and streams and has made them flashier, rising and falling more quickly after it rains. The issue of water quality is discussed in a Chapter Six. Today my topic is soil conservation and its evil cousin soil erosion.

Once the plants and sod covering me were turned under, my soils were exposed to the forces of nature – rain and wind. It is simple physics when these forces meet bare soil there is going to be trouble. The energy in these "acts of nature" is huge. If you watch raindrops fall on the sidewalk you will notice how they seem to explode on impact. Each raindrop is like a little bomb going off. Now think of what happens when those raindrops strike my bare soil. The energy is transferred to dislodge any soil particles at the surface. As the soil is disturbed, if there is any slope the dislodged soil is carried off by the water as gravity begins moving it downhill. The longer the slope the greater the speed, the greater the speed the more energy it builds. Now it is coming back – you learned all these things in junior high science class! The same thing happens with the wind. If the wind is strong enough you see dust coming off the bare soil. As the wind speed increases it picks up larger soil particles but as they fall back to the ground they dislodge smaller particles and before you know it a dust cloud is roiling across the field. Only when the wind speed drops or is obstructed, such as by a fence, will the soil particles fall out in piles. This is what happens with drifting snow, except here we are talking about my topsoil! In some parts of Iowa, it is not uncommon to see drifts of topsoil in road ditches once snow melts in spring. Now, you understand why I get a little worked up talking about or even thinking about soil erosion!

This may simply be science at work but it can be incredibly destructive to the land. Every photo you have ever seen of a gully washed out of the land began with these simple forces. If left unchecked erosion can, in a matter of years, destroy the very structure of land, making it of little use to man or nature's other beings. Here is the beauty in all this, soil erosion is not hard to prevent or stop! Again, it is simply science. If you cover the soil with vegetation the energy in raindrops is absorbed and loose soil particles are not dislodged to run off. The vegetation serves to slow down and hold the rain once it falls. Vegetation has the same effect for wind erosion, if the energy in the moving air doesn't reach the soil then it can't pull any soil particles aloft! When it comes to moving water and the force of gravity, the answers and solutions are almost as simple. If the erosive force of water depends on its speed or velocity gained moving down slope, the answer is to flatten the slope or make it shorter. This is the basic idea behind planting crops along the contour of the hill rather than up and down the slope. Rather than create a long straight slope for water to course down like a ski slope, the contours break the slope into many shorter sections, slowing the water and dispersing the energy laterally rather than downhill. Field terraces, long earthen berms built on the hillsides, do the same thing as contour planting but on a larger and more permanent scale. As the water moves downhill it naturally funnels and collects into watercourses. The solution is to plant the area as grass waterways, like you see growing on many farm fields.

The point is controlling soil erosion, what you call soil conservation, is not rocket science. It is just basic science and is fundamental to good farming. The issue we should all be concerned about is if soil conservation is so straight forward and relatively simple to correct, why has your nation spent ninety years trying to address it and why are you still losing millions of tons of soil from farm fields every year!!! Personally, soil erosion hasn't been a major issue because I am so flat, but believe me for millions of other acres across Iowa soil loss is a destructive enemy threatening our ability to remain productive and healthy. That is why the people who farm and care about agriculture spent generations developing soil conservation practices.

Early last century a few visionary agriculturalists began to raise the alarm about soil erosion. Folks like Hugh Hammond Bennett of North Carolina, who identified what is now called sheet erosion, the steady loss of a thin sliver off the soil surface, kind of like tearing pages out of a book. This type of erosion is not obvious because it happens gradually and doesn't impact farming yields very much. It is less visible than the rills, small channels of missing soil, you can see etched on the hills after it rains. Over time even the rills can become gullies and the gullies can become ravines. With sheet erosion, the soil just gets thinner and thinner, until eventually all the topsoil is lost. In any case, after the soil is lost, it moves on to clog lakes and streams. One of the best ways to see the cumulative impact of sheet erosion is to stand next to a fence line between farmed ground and a field that hasn't been tilled, like a pasture or perhaps a country cemetery. Then you will see how the farmed field may be several feet lower than the untilled land across the fence! Where did all the soil go? This is what Bennett observed and came to understand.

He came along at a good time as the federal government and USDA were beginning to recognize the threat soil erosion poised and why the nation needed to act. In the 1920s with his leadership the government created the Soil Erosion Service to study erosion problems and to offer education and advice to farmers about how to protect the soil. It wasn't until the 1930s and the Great Depression that things came to a head on soil conservation. At that time, the economic distress in agriculture came face to face with years of extreme drought, especially in the Great Plains. Several decades of wet years had led farmers to plow up millions of acres of grass from the plains and expand farming onto the dry lands. They did so in part under the mistaken belief "rain follows the plow." Well it doesn't and didn't. Instead what developed was the great blow out of the 1930s known as the Dust Bowl. The destructive phenomena, both for humans and the land, was captured in John Steinbeck's classic *Grapes of Wrath*, in the songs of Woody Guthrie like "Dust Bowl Blues," and more recently in Tim Egan's *The Worst Hard Times*. Once you had plowed under the millions of acres of native short grass prairie there was nothing left to hold the soil. When the winds came, the land literally blew away. The social and economic destruction brought on by bad farming and the lack of care for the soil was poignantly documented in Pare Lorenz' 1936 film *The Plow that Broke the Plains*, featuring the classic score by Virgil Thomson.

Fortunately, I got to sit this period out, mostly. It did get hot and dry in southwest Iowa and we had chinch bugs, and the farm economy was bleak but as for me and my soil we did OK. For the Nation's lands this was a time of great turmoil, but also a critical period in the development of state and federal programs to address soil conservation. Many of these programs, led by the USDA, shaped my fortunes and still do today.

The old Soil Erosion Service became the USDA Soil Conservation Service and for the next half century it shaped these efforts, with the assistance of Congress. In 1937 FDR sent a letter to the governors concerning a model state soil and water conservation law. Within a few short years every state had adopted some version of the model law, Iowa included. States enacted the laws in part because doing so was the ante the states had to put in the game to partake in new federal funding for conservation efforts. The most significant part of the law provided for creating locally organized soil and water conservation districts governed by elected five-member commissions. Secretary of Agriculture Wallace's idea was creating a locally run, de-centralized system to promote soil conservation would protect USDA from claims of federal over-reach, and allow conservation efforts to be tailored to the soils and agriculture of the region. Adams County formed its SWCD in the early 1940s meaning the 80th anniversary of the district is near.

The late 1930s was a fertile period for new thinking about land conservation, even as the nation was preparing for the war people knew was coming. The SWCDs were created, USDA hired thousands of soil conservationists to work with farmers developing conservation plans for their farms, and tens of thousands of young men were employed by the Civilian Conservation Corps or CCC to work on conservation projects throughout the Nation. The history of the CCC is a fascinating tale told by Neal Maher in *Nature's New Deal: The Civilian Conservation Corps and the Roots of the American Environmental Movement*. One year there was even a CCC camp near Lenox, just 7 miles south of me, housing a crew working on conservation projects. When America entered the war in late 1941, the nation needed the farming sector to step up to increase food production to help win the war. The good news is by that time, the idea of addressing soil erosion as part of that fight was well engrained in the minds of farmers and landowners, as well as politicians.

OBSERVATIONS AND INTERVIEWS ON SOIL POLICY

In the fall of 2015 my Center hosted the first in what would be a series of conferences called SOIL, for Sustaining Our Iowa Land. The 2015 conference was on the Future of Soil Conservation in Iowa and it brought together over 150 citizens for an engaging and inspiring day. Farmers, professors, public officials, students, and conservationists from across the state recognized the need for action and shared new ideas about what Iowa could do. My notes identified the following ten key observations.

First, the idea of tolerable soil loss needs to be rejected and instead the focus should be a broader focus on soil health. The concept of T or tolerable soil loss is built into most conservation programs but rather than believe there is an "acceptable" level the goal should be to eliminate any soil erosion. Second, the adoption of cover crops and other innovative conservation practices such as field edge buffers, needs to accelerate. Third, keeping livestock on the land to utilize more grass and forage is an opportunity we can't afford to overlook. Fourth, agricultural retailers selling farmers chemicals and fertilizers need to be engaged in reducing nutrient loss and promoting soil health because they are a critical source of advice for farmers. Fifth, more landowners need to talk with their tenants about soil and water conservation.

Sixth, the changing nature of land tenure is creating new audiences of landowners, such as increasing landownership by women, who will be critical to addressing soil and water conservation. Seventh, the main tool for effective conservation projects is using watershed planning to develop collaborative projects neighboring farmers and landowners can support. Eighth, increasing public funds to help share costs and investments made by farmers and landowners on the land is critical to protecting soil and improving water quality. Ninth, Iowa has a rich history of legislative and judicial support for protecting soil and water resources and the laws already on the books need to be enforced, and the soil and water conservation districts need to be more active. Tenth, Federal farm programs need to work in unison and not at cross-purposes, so conservation efforts to protect soil and water aren't defeated by other programs, such as expanded reliance on crop insurance which can encourage farming vulnerable lands and contribute to soil loss and water problems.

WHAT DO THE EXPERTS SAY ABOUT WHERE WE ARE WITH SOIL CONSERVATION?

Several years have passed since the 2015 conference but reflecting on the observations reveals why we need to shake off the inertia of our current thinking and re-energize efforts to protect soil and water. To ground-truth the observations against current reality, I turned to two of the nation's most well-respected experts on soil conservation and soil health. Both have spoken at SOIL conferences, and are friends I trust to give me their honest opinions. My first interview was with Dr. Rick Cruse, a professor of agronomy at Iowa State and head of the Iowa Water Center. Cruse is best known for creating the Iowa

Daily Erosion project, an extensive statewide network of field monitors. The project makes it possible to estimate in real time the soil erosion happening anywhere in the state based on current precipitation events. The effort is remarkable for the complexity of the design and the powerful data it generates. It is helping change understanding about the magnitude and costs of the soils being lost from Iowa farmland. The second interview was with Dr. Jerry Hatfield, the recently retired head of the National Laboratory for Agriculture and the Environment, a USDA Agricultural Research Service facility located on the ISU campus in Ames but not part of the university. Hatfield is a straight shooter known for his candor and honesty in talking to farm audiences, and has long been one of the nation's leading scientists studying soil health. His research on soil carbon and microbial life has improved understanding of how soil structure contributes to the ability to absorb rainfall. His observations are helping farmers understand how soil conservation and soil health are essentially a function of how water is managed on the land. Hatfield believes the key to preventing erosion is improving soil capacity to absorb precipitation, especially the larger rains becoming more common with a changing climate.

To guide the interviews, I posed several questions to the scientists, beginning with: Have we given up on traditional soil conservation goals and instead come to institutionalize soil erosion as the cost of production? There was broad agreement from both we have largely given up on soil conservation in the traditional sense, or at least lost sight of it. Jerry Hatfield commented about our need to look for new approaches to soil conservation, even saying we need an awakening in agriculture and more imagination. He said, "we are going to have to look at agriculture differently going forward," later adding, "we need a revolution in agriculture on how we treat our soil and stabilize productivity." His concerns were best summarized, when he said, "In our era of agriculture we have taken soil for granted which was made possible for corn and soybeans with technology driven increases in productivity and an infrastructure of government support like crop insurance to remove the risk. The result is we have become complacent about soil and don't focus on the role of water or carbon." He concluded by asking whether producers are ready to consider doing things differently and begin treating soil as a living entity, rather than just as a growth medium?

Dr. Cruse made several observations confirming how our attention to soil conservation has waned. As a good scientist, Cruse likes to use the image of a Bell Curve to describe variations in the attitudes of farmers and landowners when it comes to addressing soil conservation and water quality. The reality is people are spread all along the curve and where they are located is a function of economics, education, and even politics. Cruse noted it is important to recognize there is a third dimension we must consider, the role of landowners and their ability to influence what farm tenants can do on the land. Issues such as the length of the lease, the priority owners give to conservation, the nature of the required "investments," and how these factors play out in a competitive land market, can all influence if soil conservation practices are implemented. Cruse answered my question about whether we have the policy capacity to develop innovative conservation ideas by noting he has trouble identifying anyone with the scope and stature of the individuals who developed the landmark conservation programs included in the 1985 farm bill. This lack of capacity is true even for the Soil and Water Conservation Society, now focused less on policy development than a generation ago. The NRCS embrace of policy innovation is limited because the agency is strapped for funding and has reduced staff capacity. In a larger sense, Cruse believes agriculture has come to treat soil erosion and its costs as an "inconvenient truth," an issue to deal with in the future, but not now. He explained this shift by describing how farmers historically used crop diversification to reduce risk and stabilize income, and to address conservation. This approach disappeared with today's corn and soybean monoculture and the lack of livestock on most farms. Instead of crop diversification, Cruse notes we substituted public programs like crop insurance, farm program subsidies, and market facilitation payments, as the way to deal with risk and income instability. The effect, he believes, is we treat agriculture like an industrial system, rather than the biologic system it is. He observed, "we know what we need to do" when it comes to soil conservation, we just need basic rules to level the playing field.

Cruse concluded by admitting he is not optimistic we will change our ways as to the soil, or that newfound interest in soil health will overcome concerns with economics. On reflection, he quickly regained his characteristic optimism, observing how the term "health" adds a new and powerful idea to our thinking about soil. His final comment echoed Dr. Hatfield's, and concerned our need to address the changing rainfall patterns being brought on by climate change. He said we can't build terraces big enough to handle 5-inch rains, instead we have to be able to absorb the water in the soil.

WHAT ARE THE MYTHS WE TELL ABOUT THE LAND?

The late 1930s national movement to address soil conservation led to creation of the Soil Conservation Service, to new USDA conservation programs, and the local soil districts to support conservation efforts on many farms. Over time our efforts lost steam and, perhaps as is human nature, attention to soil conservation needed to be re-invigorated periodically. The last major effort to do so was thirty-five years ago with passage of the conservation title of the 1985 farm bill. Today it is time to reexamine where we are and to re-energize addressing the soil erosion and land abuse threatening the future of US agriculture. Doing so first requires addressing the skeptics who question why such an effort is needed and the doubters who believe everything is just fine with current farming practices, when it comes to the soil. One way to stimulate a new effort is to examine the myths we tell ourselves about the current situation with the soil, the half-truths helping lull us into a sense of complacency. Confronting the beliefs we take for granted and questioning their truth may help us recognize our need for change. Here are what I see as some of the myths:

1. Soil conservation is no longer a problem, at least in Iowa because USDA estimates soil loss is only around 5 tons per acre per year – a 20% improvement from 40 years ago. This is the "we have taken care of it" myth. These numbers are averages and on millions of acres soil loss are much higher than 5 tons. In addition, USDA does not include the soil lost to ephemeral gullies, which would add another 30%. As to the level of change, much of the previous improvements came in the late 1980s when over 25 million acres of erosive cropland was taken out of production under the recently enacted CRP. Since that time there has been little improvement in soil loss rates.

2. The USDA says Iowa soils replace themselves at around

5 tons/year meaning soil losses are tolerable and balanced near a maintenance level. This is the "tolerable soil loss" myth. USDA estimates on the rate of soil replacement are optimistic, and many soil scientists believe the real rate is closer to half a ton per year or one tenth what USDA says, meaning we may be losing soil at 10 times the replacement rate. The truth is no level of soil loss should be "tolerable," because any soil that moves reduces fertility and water absorption capacity, becomes the silt in lakes and streams, increases flooding potential, and degrades water quality.

3. *All farmers have a government designed conservation plan in place so what else is needed?* This is the "all farmers have conservation plans" myth. The truth is most farmers do not have a conservation plan for their land and if one was written in the past it may have been long forgotten. No federal law requires farmers or landowners to have a conservation plan, unless they choose to do so, or are participating in a USDA program requiring one, such as the Conservation Security Program. Iowa law provides county soil districts authority to require conservation plans for all landowners but the districts and state have been reluctant to require them, or to enforce the state law establishing mandatory soil loss limits.

4. *To participate in federal farm programs and crop insurance, farmers and landowners must meet strict soil conservation rules, enforced by USDA, so any past problems have been addressed.* This is the "government conservation rules

are sufficient" myth. The truth is the "mandatory" federal rules are not very rigorous and pose few restrictions on most farming practices. Farm program participants are required to sign a conservation compliance form, AD-1026, but it only requires promising to refrain from draining any new wetlands (swamp busting) or farming highly erodible land not recently cropped (sod busting). If producers are farming Highly Erodible Land like the 10 million acres of HEL being farmed in Iowa, they need to meet any conservation requirements established for those fields. Many studies and government reports indicate USDA efforts to "enforce" these conservation compliance rules are spotty and inconsistent, when efforts at enforcement even exist.

5. *Protecting the soil is a main concern for most farmers and landowners who readily invest in protecting the soil.* This is the "farmers and landowners love the soil" myth. It is true many are concerned about soil losses, but it is certainly not the general rule. Surveys of rural landowners and farmers done by Iowa State indicate most have spent or invested little money in the last decade to improve soil conservation. Surveys also indicate most landowners who rent land are reluctant to make long-term investments in soil conservation and do not discuss conservation with their tenants.

6. *Even if soil losses occur yield trends show they don't impact productivity.* This is the "we have plenty of soil so not to worry" myth. The fact we have deep fertile soils left in some places is not a justification for letting soil continue

to waste away, any more than having money in the bank means it is wise to spend it foolishly. Allowing soils to wash off and erode will gradually and eventually reduce yields, as ISU research shows. Decades of soil neglect are readily apparent in the spring when you drive the countryside and see the bald knobs, and the thin stands of new crops. Lost soil does not disappear, it just becomes a problem for others to address, whether as drainage issues when the neighbor's waterways silt full, water quality issues for nearby towns, or downstream flooding because reservoirs are full of "lost" soil. Allowing soil erosion to pollute others is anti-social behavior and essentially immoral. It is important to remember we all live downstream from someone.

How We Treat the Land Today – Leopold via the Back Forty

One powerful feature of Aldo Leopold's writing was his ability to put into historic and biblical context the issues resonating today. Consider this quote on the understanding landowners have about why we, the lands, exist: "to drip milk and honey into Abraham's mouth ... [a]t present moment, the assurance with which we regard this assumption is inverse to the degree of our education." Your current rush to produce corn-based ethanol and visions of a golden period of agriculture based on ever greater productivity seem reminiscent of Abraham's view of the land, dripping honey into your collective mouths. Leopold's powerful metaphor of agriculture being a pump and my land being your well rings so prophetic:

The ecological fundamentals of agriculture are just as poorly known to the public as in other fields of land-use. For example, few educated people realize that the marvelous advances in technique during recent decades are improvements in the pump, rather than the well. Acre for acre, they have barely sufficed to offset the sinking level of fertility.

New attention to the negative impacts of tenancy and for the opportunities of resilient and regenerative agriculture show concern for me as a well, not just as a pump. Your climb toward anything resembling Leopold's version of a land ethic is steep. Seeing how some owners treat the land is disheartening and it is clear many landowners recognize little semblance of an ethical duty to the land, at least in a Leopoldian sense. To a cynic it appears your land ethic, if the term ethic can be used so casually, is all about economics, maximizing returns, increasing yields, and selling for the highest price. "Get the most you can out of your land now" could be the state motto. If this requires plowing under a hillside pasture or grassland protected for the last fifteen years under a CRP contract, to plant more corn, so be it. If it means recreational fall tillage and leaving soil bare to blow until spring, so be it. If it means running the planter over the stream bank or letting cattle amble in the streambed, so be it. If it means bulldozing the last plum thicket in the fencerow, the one where the quail covey thrived, so be it. Even if it means staking out streets and platting housing lots for the final harvest on a flat fertile forty, whose only crime was being in the way of an annexation hungry town and suburban progress, so be it. As owners, you are legally entitled to do all of this and more to me, and dare anyone say or even hint your doing so is somehow unethical or improper.

You ask little of the land, other than we yield without resistance to your decisions and return the largest sum possible, to drip Abraham's honey into your mouth. In exchange, you expect the land to ask nothing of you, perhaps other than paying the taxes, recording the deed, and cashing the checks. There is no expectation you will care for the land, at least if caring means love, respect, attention, or foregoing a harmful action. What care you do provide is driven by a calculus it will pay off in the near term, or help meet some oppressive government regulation, one obeyed grudgingly, if at all. The truth is you don't expect anyone to ask you to do anything for the land, certainly not the government, neighbors, nosey environmentalists, or do-gooder professors. "If you care so much for the land then buy some of your own" is your answer.

The state may have laws to protect the soil but who is there to enforce the law here on the Back Forty? You are quick to sing paeans to rich Iowa farmland and its bounty but good luck finding a community willing to stay its annexation plans to protect prime farmland. If you feel risky, try telling a dues paying member of a farm organization they cannot sell land for housing lots. Iowa law may make it the duty of every landowner to protect the land from erosion but soil and water conservation districts need to be reminded of the wisdom in enforcing the law. The story is no different with the federal farm program payments and crop insurance subsidies doled out by the billions, with few questions asked. The public's bargain in providing taxpayer support was supposed to be a commitment by landowners to comply with soil conservation rules. Drive down any country road in the spring or check the local USDA office enforcement records to see if the promise of conservation compliance is empty or real?

DOING CONSERVATION SO IT STAYS DONE

A constant challenge in America's battle with soil erosion is once farmers and landowners adopt conservation practices how can we be sure the practices will stay in place on the land? A perfect example is the popular Conservation Reserve Program or CRP, paying landowners annual rental payments under 10 or 15-year contracts to retire the land from crop production and implement basic conservation like planting vegetation. From 1987 when the CRP was introduced until today participation has fluctuated between 20 and 33 million acres, with annual rental payments to landowners averaging over $2 billion each year. But those numbers obscure another truth about the CRP, millions of the acres retired and compensated by the public return to production when the contracts expire, and other lands cycle in. Some farmland has been subject to repeated CRP contract renewals and been retired for over a generation, while owners received annual rent from taxpayers. From a public perspective, the conservation benefits from the land retirement were welcomed but financially the public may have paid enough to purchase the land, it just didn't get a deed transferring the land to public ownership. Instead the land is privately owned and can be taken out of conservation and put back into crops if a new owner decides not to renew the CRP contract. A similar thing can happen with other permanent conservation practices, such as field terraces, if a change of ownership or the scale of farming leads new owners to remove the practice because it no longer fits their style of farming. Cost-sharing contracts used by conservation agencies to help landowners install practices, include requirements to maintain them for up to twenty years, but the provisions are not routinely enforced or regularly checked for compliance.

The critical question is how do we do conservation so it stays done? To answer the question, consider what options might be available to do so. One option is better landowner education so there is a stronger commitment to conservation. Then the challenge is how can the commitment be carried forward to new generations of owners? Public ownership of land could be an answer but the idea is unworkable and unreasonable, not just because of the expense but because it runs counter to America's founding ideal, farmland should be privately owned and kept in production. It is also unnecessary if maintenance agreements and rules for when public funds pay for conservation practices on private land are enforced. Another important step to take is establishing basic standards of stewardship and incorporating them into regulations applying to all land and all landowners so conservation is permanent. A final suggestion is using a property interest held by a third party, such as a land trust, to certify the continuation of conservation practices. This approach, essentially a conservation easement, could compensate the landowner for the property interest, and provide long-term certainty for the public. The role could be filled by a private non-profit land trust like those discussed in Chapter Eight, or the government conservation agencies could enforce the obligations. USDA NRCS already does something similar for the lifetime of CRP contracts, which it treats as legal easements on the land. NRCS does hold permanent easements on land entered into USDA's programs for farmland protection and wetland restoration.

The point is, if we are serious about conservation and land stewardship, there are policy tools available to make sure public investments are not lost due to short-term pressures landowners may experience. One exciting aspect of the growing interest in using farming and farmland to address climate change is how the contractual agreements created to compensate landowners for the benefits may likely incorporate provisions to insure the commitments are long-term.

Did We Give Up on Soil Conservation?

In telling the story about soil conservation and land abuse, one factor making it difficult for people to "see" or accept soil loss as a threat is how yields are increasing. Many facts explain this apparent conflict of how soil erosion and increasing yields can co-exist. Rick Cruse's calculations show the annual yield losses from soil erosion are relatively small making them easier to ignore. But the effects compound over time, meaning while it is hard to see soil loss in the near-term, unless it is observable such as a gully, the longer-term effects on yield are real. Better seeds and higher fertilizer inputs can increase yields even on degrading land. The fact soil losses may not be visible to the naked or untrained eye doesn't mean erosion isn't happening. Areas of low yields raise questions for how the tracts could be farmed going forward, such as planting perennial habitat or taking land out of production?

Remember the question I asked the experts: have we stopped caring about soil conservation and if so, why? Some of the reasons are historical. The 1930s showed how government officials approached soil conservation as a vital public policy concern, a recognition widely shared by farmers, agricultural leaders, and the public. Unfortunately, the same thing can't be said about the food and agricultural community today. It has been many years since a USDA Secretary raised the alarm about soil loss and the same is true for farm and commodity organizations. Admitting we have an erosion problem might focus blame on farmers so major farm groups like the American Farm Bureau choose to ignore soil loss rather than risk the government asking farmers to do something. The most you can expect from farm groups is pressing Congress for more money for "conservation," especially programs paying to retire land or for practices already adopted. Implementing innovative conservation practices or taking permanent steps to protect the soil will require new initiatives and leadership. In recent years more attention has been given to working lands programs to pay farmers for integrating new conservation practices on the land. Notably USDA is now examining methods to improve soil health and promote efforts to sequester carbon. We will see in Chapter Nine how helping farmers lead the nation's fight against climate change may prove to be among the most significant opportunities of this generation.

Several observations can be distilled from this history. One reason attention to soil conservation declined is the proliferation of commodity specific organizations. Issues like conservation are not their main concerns, instead they focus on expanding export markets, supporting crop insurance, and related production issues. Major farm organizations assume conservation is a job for USDA and Congress to address. They have not built staff capacity for policy development on the issue, but instead expect professional groups like the Soil and Water Conservation Society to lead. As a result, no farm organization focuses on land care, conservation, or sustainability. Most environmental organizations don't focus on soil loss either because they view it as an agricultural issue. Unless farming practices and soil erosion impact their main concerns, such as loss of wildlife habitat, degrading water quality, or restricting outdoor recreation, the issue isn't a priority. When groups like the Audubon Society or the Izaak Walton League, do show interest in agricultural practices, the response of most farm groups is to tell them to stay in their own lane, and leave farm policy to the experts. We shouldn't expect USDA to advocate for new policy ideas unless new department or Presidential leadership demands it. The department is hard pressed to enforce the conservation rules now on the books and lacks staff or funding to do much more. When it comes to enforcing or strengthening conservation rules there is little support in Congress or the farm community for doing so because it is apparently never the right time to expect farmers to act if it means spending money or changing practices to care for the land.

If we have stopped caring about soil conservation, is it because no one sees it as their job? Leopold said we made it too easy for farmers to be good conservationists – just join some organizations and adopt a practice or two and you are good to go. He said "by making conservation too easy we made it trivial." One way we make it too easy is leaving the job to USDA and the local soil conservation districts, taking the onus off farmers and landowners, and never making their obligations to the land clear. If USDA has cost sharing funds you might choose to apply, or if there is a paying conservation program, you might volunteer to sign up. We let conservation become one more voluntary choice, great if you want to be Gene Swartz, but if you don't believe conservation is a priority, there is nothing we can do or say.

Most farmers I know believe NRCS programs are too rigid and rule bound. Popular conservation programs for land retirement and working lands incentivize or "bribe" farmers by paying them to do conservation. The 1985 Conservation Title was unique because it included more stringent rules like the provisions on sodbuster, swampbuster, and requiring conservation planning on Highly Erodible Land (HEL). These rules have been in place for thirty-five years and most land that can be farmed has already been converted to crops, so the rules have little residual effect.

If there is little bite in the federal rules then what about state and local efforts? Here there is more potential, unless the state has amended the model soil conservation law to reduce or eliminate the authority for local districts to establish soil conservation and water protection rules. Iowa still has enforceable soil loss limits and the high-water mark for conservation came in 1979 when the Iowa Supreme Court upheld the constitutionality of the law requiring landowners to spend money to limit soil erosion. In the forty years since the Court's ruling, local authorities have been reluctant to use the law. The agriculture community is happy with the approach and resists any efforts by local officials or citizens to increase attention to soil erosion.

To answer my question if we gave up on soil conservation, when did it happen, the best answer is it began in the late 1950s. USDA offered cost sharing for conservation but most American landowners never bought into Leopold's idea of land ethic. Perhaps it was just a little too preachy and out of touch with the dominator attitude of Empire driving agriculture for much of its existence, as Korten describes in *The Great Turning*. In the 1940s three new national organizations devoted to soil conservation were formed: Friends of the Land, the Soil and Water Conservation Society, and the National Association of Conservation Districts. By the end of the 1950s FOL was gone and no group took its place to speak intellectually about man's relation to land and soil. The SWCS and the NACD were more pragmatic, concerned with program design, implementation, and the jobs conservation might provide. In the late 1950s, a combination of Cold War politics, production-oriented farm programs, expanding export markets for commodities, and continuing improvements in seeds, fertilizers, pest controls, and farm equipment – combined to make conservation seem rather old fashioned and passé. The "abused" lands that drove creation of the conservation programs of the 1930s were back in production. The land was needed to fight the war and once the war ended, new farming technologies and conservation practices like terraces made soil losses appear "tolerable."

One reason we stopped caring about soil conservation, assuming we once did, is the lack of a moral ethic to the land, the answer Leopold told us was needed seventy years ago. Short of more assertive legal and regulatory efforts to establish and enforce a landowner's duty of stewardship there is little reason to expect much improvement. Our resort to laws and regulations are one of the stones we call bread, but the current social and political climate make them even less bread-like than before. Laws will work only if the will to enforce them is present, standing alone they don't nourish an ideal of stewardship, as would the bread of a land ethic. The effect of moving away from traditional ideas to address soil conservation means other forces will need to be considered in the years ahead if we are to re-energize our efforts. To help understand the motivations and ideas underpinning the larger conservation movement it is valuable to consider what shapes our attitudes and relation with the land, the subject we turn to next.

Lowell, my dad as a baby.

Grandmother Anna in 1881.

The Hamiltons circa 1956.

Mom and Dad with prize ear of corn.

Mom and Dad in California in early 1940s.

Dad in the muddy feedlot.

Mom waiting my arrival.

Zella Mae —my mom—getting water from the well—1942.

Me with Grandmother Anna and my mom, 1955.

Mom and a prize melon.

Dad with his Shorthorn steers.

Dad, my grandfather Ace Blakesly, and Uncle Tom Cheers.

Hamiltons at the Iowa State Fair — 1971.

Aunt Florence and Uncle Leo "Shorty" Wray - Mankin's grandson.

The Back Forty.

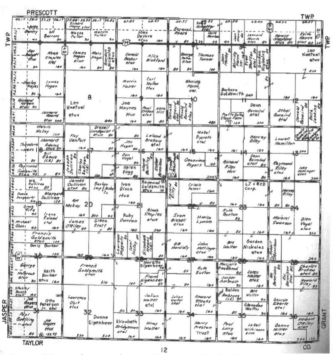

Mercer Township, Adams County, Back Forty at #13.

John F. Lacey.

Aldo Leopold.

Ding Darling understood the land's relation to humans.

Ding Darling Wildlife Refuge — Sanibel-Captiva, Florida.

Ding Darling at his
drawing board.

Some of the topsoil we love so much left by flooding of the
Raccoon River on the bike trail in the Waterworks park.

David Montgomery speaking at the Iowa Water
Conference in Ames.

A stream bank collapse on an Iowa river.

A tile outlet west of the Back Forty.

Cows in stream.

Corn in stream.

With first term Iowa congressman Tom Harkin, June 1975. Below: With Tom and Ruth Harkin at unveiling of official Senate portrait, Fall 2012. I chaired the committee raising funds for the portrait.

Historic marker for Icarians — off Highway 34.

With Iowa Attorney General
Tom Miller in front of Henry A.
Wallace portrait in Wallace State
Office Building, summer 1980.

Chapter Four – The Stones We Call Bread – What Shapes Our Attitudes to the Land?

Our attitudes about how we treat the land and the responsibilities that come with owning land are among the most critical issues shaping the Nation's ability to develop a more sustainable future. My path to a career teaching agricultural law began with studying forestry, where I was introduced to the writings of Aldo Leopold. He articulated the foundation for ecology, what today we refer to as environmentalism. A fellow Iowan and forester, his writings deeply influence my thinking about our relation to the land. In his famous *A Sand County Almanac*, Leopold described a land ethic this way, "An ethic, ecologically, is a limitation on freedom of action in the struggle for existence. An ethic, philosophically, is a differentiation of social from anti-social conduct. These are two definitions of the same thing."

In perhaps his most powerful metaphor, Leopold wrote, "[w]hen the logic of history hungers for bread and we hand out a stone, we are at pains to explain how much the stone resembles bread." He then described some of the stones we serve up in lieu of a land ethic: an economic system valuing little other than production, an educational system teaching no ethical obligation to the land, and a political system promoting conservation based primarily on economic self-interest. From a legal perspective, how society answers Leopold's call to land stewardship centers on the relations between humans, society, and the land. Land ownership reflects our belief in democratic institutions, balancing private actions with responsibilities to the public and the social welfare of the community.

I have spent my career working with the law, one of the stones society offers in place of the bread of a land ethic. Leopold was not a lawyer and he questioned the wisdom of relying on government regulations to achieve conservation goals. He believed our attempts to make conservation too easy made it trivial. By the late 1940s he grew concerned government programs, like the soil and water conservation districts he helped craft were proving ineffective, too slow in pushing community changes in attitudes to the soil. Just before his untimely death in 1949, he wrote, "To sum up we asked the farmer to do what he conveniently could to save his soil and he has done just that and only that… We have been too timid, and too anxious for quick success, to tell the farmer the true magnitude of his obligations. Obligations have no meaning without conscience, and the problem we face is the extension of the social conscience from people to the land." Leopold may have questioned our reliance on laws and regulations, yet he appears to have acknowledged the potential role law might play in moving us toward a land ethic. Speaking about the economic limitations on government conservation efforts, he asked, "What is the ultimate magnitude of the enterprise? Will the tax base carry its eventual ramifications? At what point will government conservation, like the mastodon, become handicapped by its own dimensions? The answer, if there is any, seems to be a land ethic, *or some other force* which assigns more obligation to the private landowner." (italics added).

Discussions of Leopold's ideas focus principally on his idea of a "land ethic," but much less consideration has been given to the "some other force" he mentioned. Famous Iowa agrarian, Henry A. Wallace, Secretary of Agriculture and later Vice President under FDR, captured the challenge Leopold later identified, writing in the foreword to *Soils and Men, the 1938 Yearbook of Agriculture*: "The social lesson of soil waste is no man has the right to destroy soil even if he does own it in fee simple. The soil requires a duty of man we have been slow to recognize."

Wallace is a key figure in American agriculture and politics of the last century, and the breadth of his accomplishments are monumental from his building the architecture of land conservation and farm programs to his development of what became the world's largest and most successful hybrid seed company. The rich content of his life, including the depth of his concerns about soil loss, are captured in John C. Culver and John Hyde, *American Dreamer: A Life of Henry A. Wallace*, (Norton 2000).

Wallace's quote is an early signpost in the long history of the challenge of promoting soil stewardship. Answers to his challenge can be found in the seventy-five years of history for how Iowa's legislature and courts have tried to embrace the landowner's duty of stewardship in law. Three legal precedents illustrate this effort. First, the General Assembly no doubt had Wallace's comment in mind in 1939 when it enacted the Iowa version of the model soil conservation law. Section 161A.43 of the Iowa Code provides the key legal precedent for the landowner's duty to the soil, stating:

> *To conserve the fertility, general usefulness, and value of the soil and soil resources of this state, and to prevent the injurious effects of soil erosion, it is hereby made the duty of owners of real property in this state to establish and maintain soil*

and water conservation practices or erosion control practices,
as required by the regulations of the commissioners of the re-
spective soil conservation districts.

By describing the landowner's obligation as a duty, the Iowa Legislature made clear the matter is mandatory not voluntary. All one hundred of Iowa's soil and water conservation districts have established soil loss limits and the law gives them the power and responsibility to enforce the rules when excessive soil losses are found.

Second, in a 1943 case, *Benschoter v. Hakes*, the Iowa Supreme Court considered whether the legislature could require owners of farmland to give four months advance notice before terminating a farm tenant's lease. The law was a result of recommendations made by the President's 1937 commission studying farm tenancy. Landowners said it was illegal for the state to require them to continue with a tenant another year just for failing to provide timely notice, especially when the lease agreement said no advance notice was required. Ruling the law constitutional, the Iowa Court held:

It is quite apparent that during recent years the old concept of
duties and responsibilities ... has undergone a change. Such
persons, by controlling the food source of the nation, bear a
certain responsibility to the general public. They possess a vital
part of the national wealth, and legislation designed to stop
waste and exploitation in the interest of the general public is
within the sphere of the state's police power.

Today this ruling and Iowa Code §562.6, the law requiring advance notice for termination, now set at six months, are the only statutory protections available for farm tenants, who farm over half of Iowa's land. The Court's recognition of the landowner's responsibility to the public is a powerful statement applicable not just for issues of soil erosion but also water quality and other resource protection matters.

The third and perhaps most critical legal precedent is the 1979 Iowa Supreme Court ruling in *Woodbury County Soil Conservation District v. Ortner* concerning the constitutionality of the Iowa soil conservation district law. The case involved a challenge to the finding by the soil and water conservation district a landowner had violated the soil loss limits and was required to change how he farmed some land to reduce the erosion. The soil conservation district have given him the option of taking a hilly eroding field out of crop production and putting it to hay or to install field terraces, 75% of the cost being paid by the district. The district court ruled it was unconstitutional for the state to require the landowner to expend money to control erosion on his land. The Iowa Supreme Court rejected the landowner's claim the soil loss limits were unconstitutional and ruled requiring landowners to either change how they farm or to spend money on soil conservation is within the power of the state. In reversing the district court decision for the landowner, the Iowa Supreme Court ruled:

> *It should take no extended discussion to demonstrate that agriculture is important to the welfare and prosperity of this state. It has been judicially recognized as our leading industry. The state has a vital interest in protecting its soil as the greatest of its natural resources, and it has the right to do so.*

The Court's statement essentially adopted Wallace's premise, at least for the public. The challenge is transferring the duty to individual landowners.

These three legal pillars establish a duty on owners of Iowa farmland to protect the soil and to act in the public interest. They provide the legal basis for public actions to promote soil conservation. Trying to understand and explain the role law plays in helping articulate the duty we owe to the land has been the focus for much of my legal career.

Reflecting on what shaped my interest in land, a major influence was definitely great writers and their books. In some ways, the nation's conscience and awareness of land and farming can be seen evolving through the sweep of literature shaping our societal understanding and policies to the land. The best starting place and my personal lodestone for insights of how the land shaped our people is John Steinbeck's *Grapes of Wrath*. This towering masterpiece, for me our Nation's greatest novel, follows the Joads and countless others as they were tractored off their land in the southern plains at the close of the Dust Bowl. These migrants in our own land found their way to the fields and orchards of California only to be greeted with hostility and brutal conditions. The hatred and deprivations they faced fuel the novel but their resilience and faith in the New Deal and in a caring government to aid them, are themes still echoing in our fields. Steinbeck's legacy lives in the land and his life is considered in a new biography by William Souder, *Mad at the World: A Life of John Steinbeck* (2020). *The Grapes of Wrath* and the USDA funded documentary film by Pare Lorentz *The Plow that Broke the Plains* helped mark the end of the Depression era focus on land and people, as the coming war with its demand for food and farmers signaled new and better days.

It is worth noting how there was a period in time in our past when people appeared to think more deeply and feel differently about our connection with the land. This more hopeful period began in the early 1940s when a group of like-minded, political and conservation leaders, like Wallace, Leopold, Louis Bromfield, Russell Lord, and others created a new organization, Friends of the Land (FOL). The most significant product from the effort was the quarterly journal *The Land*, published from 1941 until the early 1950s. *The Land* became a forum for creative thinking about land, conservation, culture, and agriculture. In some ways FOL was the forerunner of today's environmental organizations like the Environmental Defense Fund. It was also a progenitor of the modern land trust, the subject of Chapter Eight. The lands farmed and cared for by FOL's members, individuals who shared heightened concerns for soil conservation and land protection, were the demonstration grounds for what we know today as "sustainable agriculture." *The Land* was an intellectual outlet for new thinking about man's relation to the land, and it published essays on topics like soil conservation by Leopold, Wallace, and many more. It provided a home for Bromfield's vision of sustainably managed farms as the wellspring of rural economic vitality and for early writings of Rachel Carson. *The Land* is where readers learned about Edward Faulkner's 1943 best-seller, *plowman's folly*, and his radical idea of abandoning the plow for "trash farming," leaving crop residue on the surface rather than plowing it under. His idea was considered outlandish then, but today this style of farming, known as minimum or no-till agriculture, is used on tens of millions of acres. Many articles in *The Land* were written by people who today might be characterized as wealthy urban elites. At the time, some critics argued they were celebrity farmers like Bromfield, not the "real farmers" featured in the farm press.

After years of work by USDA in the 1930s to address the abuses of the Dust Bowl, the goals of conservation were becoming more widely shared in the US. *The Land* with its strong leaders and writings served a growing audience of readers, and FOL sponsored popular regional field days attracting hundreds to tour farms impacted by soil erosion and to see the benefits of new conservation practices. The 1950 book *Forever The Land: A Country Chronicle and Anthology*, edited and illustrated by Russell and Kate Lord, the dynamic couple helping drive FOL captures the energy of this history. But the war years were a challenge and in the post-war period FOL struggled to find a stable foothold amid the swirl of increasingly conservative farm politics and emerging cold war doctrines. The dominant voices of agriculture, like the ultra-conservative American Farm Bureau Federation (AFBF), found it easy to paint ideas promoted by FOL, like the value of co-operative action in the public interest and for collaborative watershed planning, as socialistic limits on private property and free enterprise, all sounding suspiciously like the Communism the nation was gearing up to fight. In the Eisenhower years, USDA and Congress were dominated by the votes and voices of southern agriculture, and by the politics of the AFBF. As a result, the progressive vision set out in *The Land* waned, and agricultural policy regarding the land was increasingly left to the USDA Soil Conservation Service, and the generally more conservative and private property oriented, farmer controlled Soil and Water Conservation Districts.

Louis Bromfield was one of the most interesting personalities to emerge from this period. He was a writer who vaulted to national prominence in the late 1920s and 1930s with award winning novels and a second career writing the Hollywood screenplays bringing his books to the screen. In the late 1930s as war clouds loomed, Bromfield brought his family home from France to a farm in Ohio near his place of birth. He used his wealth to assemble 600 acres of land in Pleasant Valley and create the farm he named Malabar. Over the next decade Bromfield wrote a series of bestselling books about farming at Malabar, notably the trio *Pleasant Valley* (1943), *Malabar Farm* (1947), and *Out of the Earth* (1948). Malabar soon became the most famous farm in America, and still remains, preserved today as a unit of the Ohio State Parks. It was at Malabar his friend Humphrey Bogart married a nineteen-year old Lauren Bacall and where field days drew thousands to learn about new conservation methods.

Bromfield's colorful life is captured in Stephen Heyman's 2020 biography *The Planter of Modern Life*, a timely elevation of awareness of Bromfield and the role he played in mid-century America. It is especially interesting to see how central agriculture and farming were then to the national conversation, when over five million families were still farming. His success as an author, all but forgotten now, his influence in Hollywood as a celebrity farmer, and his farming books, all struck a chord at a unique point in the nation's post war life. Thousands of returning service men were searching for relief and many turned to the land and farming to find peace. The economic difficulty of Bromfield's style of diversified, multi-crop farming was challenging. Soon the growing interest in new agricultural technologies, crop specialization, and the consolidating farm structure emerging in the 50s would help render it nearly obsolete in the minds of many. The official message from the USDA as articulated by Secretary Ezra Taft Benson was farmers either needed to get big or get out. Over the next decade many took the cue to exit a life on the land, helping fuel the post-war population boom in American cities and the emerging suburban culture.

Heyman makes clear how forward-looking Bromfield was, not just in his leadership to put soil conservation into a larger community context, but also in his attention to soil health and natural systems, and to viewing farms as grass factories for raising livestock. He was among the first national leaders to express a concern too much importance was being placed on corn and soybeans, and we were creating a monoculture destructive to the land. He was an early voice warning how DDT and other chemicals were poisoning wildlife, land, insects, and probably us. The concerns helped him recognize the link between better food and human health. It is one reason why most of the foods grown on Malabar were marketed directly from a farm stand. It is also why he supported organic agriculture, which he saw as a middle ground using the best science and modern agriculture practices. He may have been too much of a visionary for his time. His understanding of agriculture, especially the need for better land stewardship with more focus on the health of food and the land, mark him as a pioneer in the better food, better farming, better land movement discussed in Chapter Seven. In many ways Bromfield's writing about land and what it can do if we show it the care and respect it deserves, were largely forgotten for a generation. Not until Kentucky farmer, poet, and philosopher Wendell Berry wrote his 1977 classic *Culture and Agriculture: The Unsettling of America* would the land and farming enjoy such an impassioned and eloquent advocate. Berry's book so moved me, in a formal photo I had taken my last year of law school to send my parents on the farm, the book rests open on my lap.

From the perspective of the land by the end of the 1950s the vision and leadership to carry on the soil conservation work identified with FDR's era was largely abandoned, replaced by the economic determinism still haunting farm country today. Another book signaled the growing divide in America between a vision for the land based on stewardship and conservation as reflected in *The Land*, and the more utilitarian vision of agriculture as a factory for progress, harnessing the land with new technologies to meet the needs of people. The USDA 1958 Yearbook of Agriculture, was simply titled *Land*. The preface was written by then Secretary of Agriculture Ezra Taft Benson, a pious conservative who later served as President of his Mormon church. Benson captured the coming challenges, previewing how we arrived here today:

> Science has ushered in the Atomic and Space Age. Man has launched satellites and is now planning with a degree of confidence on reaching the moon. These thoughts and plans stir us. They are an index of the strength of human aspirations, imagination, and genius.
>
> But with all our Space Age planning, we still live close to the land. Many of us make our living from it. Many others derive pleasure from the recreation that the forests, fields, and streams afford. For each of us the land provides living space and is the source of our food, clothing, and housing.
>
> Land, indeed, is part and parcel of our growth as a Nation – of our history and our national attitudes toward freedom and democracy. Ours is a choice land, blessed of Heaven.
>
> As citizens, then, we should know more about land. We should get a panoramic view of the makeup of our country – cropland, grazing and forest lands, city land, lakes, deserts, and mountains, all of which form the natural resources base of our Nation …
>
> Such an inventory and projection can tell us what we

must do to husband our God-given resources and how we must deal with problems of land use and conservation. It will remind us of the ways in which we have been careless, unaware, and indifferent to our heritage. It will also indicate some accomplishments in the wiser use of our land. Finally, it demonstrates again how much we have for which we must be thankful to the Creator of all.

Several points are clear from this preface, beside the piety of his mind, notably his recognition of problems, a reference to the decades of land abuse fueling the Dust Bowl, and his optimism about our ability to harness the land for future needs. This view of the relation of people to land, was made clear in the Editor's preface on the next page, about our history on the land:

We consider the profound changes these later days have brought, and we try to see what they mean in relation to our land resources: The growth of population and cities; the growth of the size of farms and the decline of the farm population (for land, used by people for people, has meaning only in terms of people) ...

His parenthetical comment is vivid confirmation of Leopold's observation: a key problem in our approach to land stewardship is when we talk about the land we are really only talking about the people on it, not the land itself.

One effect of the demise of FOL and *The Land*, was the early sprouts of today's land conservation movement had to wait a generation to re-emerge until the environmental movement found its voice and footing with Earth Day 1970 and a series of legislative victories. It took Rachel Carson's *Silent Spring* (1962) and other events to help focus the public's attention on the environment. The story of Carson's life and the impact of *Silent Spring* on the national debate, is well told in William Souder's, *On a Farther Shore: The Life and Legacy of Rachel Carson* (2012 Crown). By the late 1960s the increasingly reactionary stance of much of agriculture was visible in the strident efforts to dispel concerns about the dangers of pesticides raised by *Silent Spring*. Its author and her followers were painted as enemies of modern agriculture and of the technologies needed to feed a hungry world, a criticism still echoing in today's debates. The more progressive parts of the conservation movement had evolved to become environmentalists, and their views of mainstream farming or what is called conventional agriculture (those involved like to call it "production agriculture"), shifted along an ideological divide. The effect was for some parts of society to see the movement to a chemical intensive, industrialized agriculture as more of a threat than a blessing.

Environmentalists became more vocal and alarmed about the impacts of industrialized agriculture, making it easier for those in the farm sector to portray them as anti-business and anti-farmer. The traditionally conservative voices of agriculture, dominated by Southern interests, opposed most progressive social movements for civil rights, women rights, worker's rights, and the "wisdom" of youth. Gone were the respected and moderating voices of "conservation agriculture" like Henry Wallace, Aldo Leopold, and Louis Bromfield and no one emerged in the agricultural community to take their place. One unfortunate outcome of the division, still present today, is many people in the environmental community see agriculture mainly as "unfinished business" in need of further legislative restraint. The exemptions agriculture reserved for itself in many key environmental laws of the era, notably the unscientific concept of "nonpoint source" pollution in the Clean Water Act, are now being re-examined. Fast-forward and you can see how the cleavage begun in the 1960s helps explain where we are today and how we got here.

The efforts of the "agricultural community" in the *Silent Spring* era illuminated two increasing trends of large agricultural suppliers, notably the fertilizer and chemical sector. First, their willingness to "speak for" farmers and second, the willingness of farm groups, inherently conservative and free-market oriented, to let them do so. The lesson many in agriculture took from this period was to fear anyone willing to question how and why farmers do what they do, or worse challenge the businesses selling farmers inputs and practices. One fundamental effect is how environmental concerns such as support for laws like the Endangered Species Act, are opposed by farmers and landowners who see the laws primarily as threats to private property and the autonomy of farmers, rather than as needed protections for the land and nature. Ironically, the void created by the demise of a group like Friends of the Land, at heart a farm organization, was filled instead by the more strident views of "property rights" defenders who want no public oversight on farming. The pattern that emerged in the late 1960s of resistance and opposition to anyone who questions modern agriculture has come to dominate political discourse over the last fifty years. That explains why today, progressive groups like the Environmental Working Group, known for its fact-based reports on issues such as water pollution and soil loss, are portrayed by the farming sector as anti-agriculture, with an agenda to starve the world's hungry, rather than welcomed as defenders of the land.

In the early 1960s, as to the land, the effect was USDA and the conservation districts were left as the lonely voices on land issues, but their focus narrowed to practical issues of farm program implementation and funding. More fundamental issues about landowner responsibilities or how the public and the land were negatively impacted by some farming practices went largely ignored. The "all is well" attitude came to dominate the communications from agriculture about conservation. The message is any efforts to protect nature will restrain individual rights, that is, owners' rights to use and abuse the land as they choose, and may increase the power of the government leading to regulation of land activities. The Cold War may be gone today but the forces it unleashed: an unbalanced and unrealistic view of property rights, resistance to "public values" in land protection, and privileging individual landowner freedom over the government's ability to restrain anti-social behavior, are all with us today. They are seen playing out in the Iowa debate over water quality and agriculture, addressed in Chapter Six, as they are in opposition to public land acquisition. The dominant view of many people involved in "production agriculture" is the public should expect landowners to engage in conservation only if the public will pay them to do it. Unfortunately, these same claims for unfettered "individual freedom" have played out in the widespread resistance to mask wearing and other public health measures designed to control the COVID pandemic, resistance often more acute in rural areas and farm country. The damage to public health and the loss of life caused by these attitudes are similar to the abuses these attitudes can bring to the land.

The Back Forty on Land, Law and Imagination

As a piece of land there are only a limited number of things I can claim credit for: crops grown, homes provided to wildlife, natural beauty offered, and satisfaction provided to people who own or use me. I also like to believe the land deserves credit for shaping the lives of the people who spend time walking and working on us. This is true for the boy who grew up on me in the 1960s, who spent his lifetime working with the law and on the land, eventually creating this book and letting me share these thoughts.

I remember him as a toe-headed kid walking my rows with his parents wielding a bean hook to cut the cockleburs so common in the days before the chemical companies invented the weed killers, economic poisons was their name then, to do this job. I remember him sneaking stealthily along my fencerows on cold fall days with his .410 hoping to flush a cock pheasant or a covey of quail. Sometimes in the spring he would even appear on the tractor pulling the disc turning under the bean stubble from last year's harvest, helping his father get me ready for another spin on the economic roulette wheel of 1960s crop farming. He didn't do a lot of fieldwork and I could tell his parents didn't dream he or his brother would stay on the farm. The farm was too small and too much of a struggle especially when college could open doors to a better and bigger life. The boy headed to the university, but in many ways, he really never left me. I take credit for that!

He got his degree from Iowa State in forestry of all things, I still puzzle over where that notion came from as there is not a tree growing on me or on many of my adjacent friends. As time would tell forestry was not as much the attraction as was the opportunity to study emerging environmental issues. In a way it was really all about me because if the land is anything we are the environment. He really never did get loose from his connection to the land. His career is like a roadmap moving from one land issue to the next. Arriving at law school he discovered the Eastern powers on the faculty had already killed the nationally known agricultural law program started there a decade before. To remedy this foolish action, his legal studies focused on issues most important to farm families like those he grew up knowing. His law school exit was a law review article "The Importance of Agricultural Law in the Law School Curriculum." The University of Arkansas and Drake would later both follow this plan when developing their programs dedicated to the subject. I don't think he could have imagined how one article written as a student would shape his career.

Becoming a professor specializing in agricultural law, was a focus few had heard of or could really understand forty years ago, even in a farm state like Iowa. Boil agricultural law down though and it is really all about me. Look at what he wrote about in the 1980s: "the right to farm", farm leasing, farm foreclosure, homestead protections, and debt relief so families could stay on the land. It was really always about people and the land – about me. When the 1980s farm financial crisis waned the next big issue on the legal horizon was the environment: water quality, nuisance suits over hog odors, soil conservation programs, and related matters. The Big Four Iowa commodity groups: corn, soybeans, cattle, and hogs, hired him to write *What Farmers Need to Know About Environmental Law*, the first guide of its kind in the country. The goal was simple, explain environmental laws in terms farmers could appreciate, what he likes to call "putting the corn down where folks can eat it."

About this same time the Iowa legislature passed the 1987 Groundwater Protection Act. The law did many things, such as closing the over 1,000 "drainage wells" scattered across northeast Iowa serving to direct surface pollution into the state's aquifers. The law created the Leopold Center for Sustainable Agriculture at Iowa State, with a 13-member Advisory Board to guide its research. Two representatives were designated for private colleges and universities and he quickly lobbied his university president to be named to the board. It was a position he held for over twenty-one years, providing a front row seat to watch the concept of sustainable agriculture evolve in Iowa and across the nation. He stepped down from the board so the Drake Center could apply for research grants on land policy, an expertise lacking at Iowa State. Leopold Center funds were used to develop the SALT project on Sustainable Agriculture Land Tenure, and to publish the practical *Landowners Guide for Sustainable Farm Leases*, written by Ed Cox, who joined the Center as a staff attorney after graduating from the law school.

Farm leasing led to his first international consulting trip, a three-week lecture tour of the Soviet Union in the fall of 1989. It seems a lifetime ago, but in 1989 the Soviet Union still existed. Premier Gorbachev was championing his economic reform ideas of perestroika, including reforming state-owned agriculture to allow long-term leases of farmland to individuals. The belief was granting farm leases would give private farmers incentives to mirror the productivity of American agriculture. History proves access to land is an important ingredient in any successful farming system but it is not that simple. In his lectures, when asked if fifty-year farm leases would make Soviet agriculture bloom, he would explain leases were a first step but more was needed. Stable land rights are only one part of agriculture. As the Soviets soon learned, other ingredients like low-cost credit, markets for production, access to appropriate scale machinery and inputs, and political stability are equally important if you expect former state workers to take the plunge and become the next generation of kulaks.

Access to land is the foundation and starting point for new

farmers, a subject he worked on for years. The 2010 Drake Forum on New Farmers, attracted hundreds of advocates to a conference in Washington, DC, to discuss new farmer policies and land access issue. He served on a USDA advisory board for creating a new generation of farmers on the land. What I appreciate is how he didn't just talk about the issue, he actually put his money where his mouth was, so to speak. When they decided to sell the last piece of farmland inherited from his parents, he and his wife sold it to a new young farmer. That is why the son of the couple who own me is now the proud owner of the tract in the quarter section to my northwest. The boy summed up his decision saying Adams County needed a new farmer getting a start owning land more than it needed a former farm kid holding on as an absentee landowner pretending he was still farming. They had the same thing in mind when donating what is now Hamilton Prairie to the Adams County Conservation board. His actions may seem peculiar to folks around here who can't understand why anyone would give away land or even sell it, but I am proud of what they did. I like to think they were honoring me in some way, as well as Anna and Mankin Wray, and Lowell and Zella Mae.

New farmers and land reforms explain his Cuba period too. Between 2012 and 2018, he made eight trips to Cuba, four times taking classes of Drake law students. The idea was simple, meet the Cuban people, learn from agricultural law colleagues, and study Cuba's new land reforms. When the Soviet Union blew up in 1991 the Cuban economy suffered a serious blow and was left with millions of acres of idle sugar cane fields. The Cuban food system, fed largely by imported food purchased with earnings from sugar sales to the Soviets, nearly collapsed. During what is known as the difficult years the average Cuban adult lost over twenty pounds. To the chagrin of many American politicians, the Cold War era policy of crushing the Cuban

Revolution with economic boycotts and international pressure still failed to do the trick. The Cubans cinched up their belts and carried on. It took another twenty years before economic reality and the need for food finally overcame Fidel Castro's ideological blinders to private enterprise. His brother Raoul, not as blinkered, recognized how the idle lands could answer several pressing needs. Why not find a way to put land into the hands of young families raising food for the emerging private economy and as a bonus get these former state workers off the national payroll?

The answer was a land reform initiative offering ten-year "usufruct" agreements, essentially leases, to people who could work the land, selling part of their production to the government but marketing the rest to the private restaurants and parradores springing up to serve the US tourist boom. In the first two years over 100,000 land agreements were signed and several million acres made available to a new generation of Cuban farmers. The reforms gradually increased the food supply but title to the land stayed with the state affirming the ideals of the Revolution. Drake students went to Cuba to study these reforms and meet with officials and farmers involved. Students saw we have nothing to fear from Cuba and as people we aren't that different. Both nations face a common challenge, finding ways to put young families on the land, so a new generation of farmers can take root.

Emiliano Lerda, his former student originally from Argentina, took leave from his legal work to accompany the professor on six trips. Lerda wrote the thesis for his agricultural law graduate degree from Arkansas on the Cuban land reforms. Insights gained from Cuban counterparts and access to documents, made him America's leading expert on Cuba's agricultural land reforms. Not that anyone in the US government really cared. Our official policy then, and now is to crush the Cuban state.

The reforms President Obama implemented allowing more Americans to travel to Cuba, like the Drake students, have been revoked, replaced by a new era of state sanctioned hostility. In any case, Cuba's land reforms remain and lessons are being learned.

The boy spent his life working with the law and the land, at the intersection where my future is impacted by how people treat me. A common feature of both the law and the land is imagination. What did Mankin Wray imagine when he took ownership, as you like to call it, over me? Did he imagine bumper crops of hay and oats, or of whatever he wanted to grow? He no doubt thought one day he would pass me on to his children to continue his legacy, as he did with Anna decades later. This is one of the land's great gifts to you, letting your imaginations run wild to dream how you will use us. The same is true for the law.

Imagination was what inspired Phillip Glick one of the team of young Ivy League lawyers Henry A. Wallace assembled at USDA, who wrote the 1937 model Soil Conservation District Act, changing the course of soil and water conservation for the next century. Fifty years later imagination led Paul Johnson and his legislative friends to draft Iowa's 1987 Groundwater Protection Act and create the Leopold Center for Sustainable Agriculture. The same creative imagination led Leopold to write his classic essay "The Land Ethic." Think of how imagination drove Raleigh Buckmaster, Gerry Schnepf, and Governor Bob Ray to create the Iowa Natural Heritage Foundation in 1979 to bridge the gap between the state's desire to purchase unique natural lands for public use and the state's inability to act quickly if private owners need to sell. This same spark of imagination and dreams for a better Iowa land future led Liz Garst and her family to create Whiterock Conservancy and turn 5,500 acres on the Raccoon River south of Coon Rapids into the largest family land protection project in Iowa. Today the land made famous by her grandfather Roswell, he of Kruschev's visit in 1959, is open to the public, preserved for people to hike the oak savannas and paddle the miles of bluff-lined river flowing through. The story of the empire he built on hybrid corn is told by his son-in-law, historian Harold Lee, in *Roswell Garst: A Biography*, (Iowa State Press 1984).

Yes, it takes imagination to give life to the land and to the law. It was clearly at work on Christopher Stone, writing his famous article "Should Trees Have Standing? Toward Legal Rights for Natural Objects," in the 1972 *Southern California Law Review*. Stone's article gave hope to Back Forties like me and to all the other parts of nature you have been slow to protect. Stone's question was clearly on the mind of Chief Justice Reynoldson of the Iowa Supreme Court in *Moser v. Thorp Credit*, the 1981 case about a farmer who abused a farm causing a lifetime of erosion in just two years. The case's unusual legal posture made it difficult for the Court to penalize the land skinner for his actions, but his actions lead Justice Reynoldson to write:

> *Perhaps before the current and exacerbating disaster in Iowa's hill country becomes irreversible the genius of the common law will devise procedures by which an abused farm through a next friend will be accorded standing to enjoin practices like those in the record before us, and to enforce remedial measures.*

In Purdy's *After Nature: A Politics for the Anthropocene* (2015), he writes about the role of imagination in the law. In reflecting on how Americans view the natural world, he notes it can be a function of whether we imagine it as a "wilderness designed by God to become a garden" or "as a storehouse of essential resources for national wealth." "Law is a circuit between imagination and the material world," he writes, acknowledging its variety of sources including "economic self-interest and political partisanship." He observes how, "imagination, too, is part of what makes law. Laws play out the logic of competing versions of environmental imagination." We definitely see the role of imagination playing out in asking "should trees have standing" or "can a next friend come into court on behalf of an abused Iowa hillside?" This same spark of imagination led John Lacey to see how interstate commerce could be the basis for federal laws to protect wildlife.

In February 2019, imagining better legal protections for nature led 61% of Toledo's citizens to approve The Lake Erie Bill of Rights Charter Amendment. The first of its kind in the nation, the law is the most significant step in the embryonic rights of nature campaign underway in the US. In 2014 algae blooms rendered Toledo's water supply unsafe to drink. The blooms were primarily caused by excess nutrients washing from farm fields and livestock facilities in the area. When agriculture and the state legislature failed to act, the voters responded. The ordinance was designed to protect the rights of the lake and watershed and to empower citizens to take legal action to protect the resources if the rights are violated. It is no surprise the ordinance, and the very idea of "rights for nature" were assailed by the farming and business communities as unconstitutional threats to the economy. The law was challenged and in early 2020 a federal court ruled it an unconstitutional violation of the 14th amendment and due process. The court reached this conclusion in part because the ordinance was too vague in identifying how the "irrevocable rights for the Lake Erie Ecosystem to exist, flourish, and naturally evolve" imposed specific obligations on the farmer, and lacked guidance on what guaranteeing Toledo residents' the right to a "clean and healthy" environment means.

You get the point, the court ruled Lake Erie is essentially just another Back Forty with no rights of its own, left only to whatever protections farmers in the watershed or the state government might offer, assuming they choose to do anything. The attempt to win legal rights for Lake Erie may have failed for now, but I believe Justice Reynoldson's hopeful prediction will eventually win the day, it is only a matter of time. Professor Purdy writing in *This Land is Your Land*, has it right, "the natural world, the land, is the thing you can always tell lies about, because it doesn't answer – until the time you can't lie about it anymore, because it is too late." The question for you is will you know when is it too late?

WHAT DID WE CHOOSE?

When *The Land* stopped publishing in the 1950s in some ways it marked the start of a new era of farmland consolidation, increased reliance on agro-chemicals, and the movement to our modern, "conventional" agricultural system. I was born on a small family farm in southwest Iowa at the time this transformation had begun. It seems such a distant era now. My first year of school took place in a one-room schoolhouse with eight grades of students and one teacher, and our farmhouse didn't have running water until I was six years old. One of my first chores was to carry buckets of water from the pump behind the house to the kitchen for use.

The economic and social changes experienced on Midwestern farms in the 1960s and 70s rewrote the structure of agriculture as traditional diversified family farms like ours, with a range of animals from dairy cows to chickens, gave way to specialized grain production and confined livestock feeding. As Leopold predicted, the change placed greater pressure on the pump we call farming. Concern for the land, or the well, in many ways went unspoken. For farmers dedicated to conservation like our neighbor Gene Swartz, caring for the land was a given. On most farms little thought was given to caring for the land, especially if it meant putting the brakes on increasing crop production. For most farmers who remained, the goal was seizing the golden era of farming proclaimed by Secretary Butz who urged "fencerow to fence-row" production. The role of the land was to produce, and new tools like improved seeds, powerful pesticides, better fertilizers, and more drainage were all it took to make the land respond. The good news for most farmers and the nation is the land did respond as the storehouse of soil fertility built over centuries and a supportive climate spurred America to new heights of production. Increasing grain yields helped mask troubling developments on the land, of growing soil losses and deteriorating water quality, issues to emerge in the next decades. The boom years of the 1970s also masked a rending in the social fabric of farming and farm life. The competition for more land pitted neighbors against each other and the vast divide in wealth inequality present to-day in farm country began to take root.

These forces and their effects were what Wendell Berry wrote about in his 1977 classic, *Culture and Agriculture: The Unsettling of America*. The book marked him as a prophet to many for his willingness to ask isn't there a better way for us to steward the land and rural communities? Berry wasn't alone in his concerns about what was happening on farms and to the land. The late 1970s saw a burst of attention to the structure of agriculture, asking what type of farming did the nation want: our traditional system of diversified family farms or one built on mono-cultures and large "corporate" farms? USDA examined this question in a major study commissioned at the end of the Carter years. Secretary of Agriculture Bob Bergland, former Minnesota Congressman and stout defender of family farming, spearheaded the

USDA Report on the Structure of Agriculture: A Time to Choose. The report was issued in December 1980 and the timing couldn't have been worse because the new Reagan Administration was coming to power. The report framed the stark policy choices facing Congress and the nation concerning which vision of farming and rural culture to support. The report drew no interest from Secretary of Agriculture John Block of Illinois and the new regime at USDA. They had little patience or political appetite for worrying about farm structure, especially if it might restrain the farm consolidation and crop expansion underway in farm country. As a result, *A Time to Choose* was consigned to the dusty shelves of libraries, waiting for the historians who may find it someday. On the land, the restructuring of farms continued at a rapid pace.

Another book written at this time poised a different question about our ability to choose, in starker and more land-focused ways. Researching the question "did we give up on soil conservation," I came across my copy of Neil Sampson's, *Farmland or Wasteland: A Time to Choose.* Published in 1981, the book is an excellent history of the development of American soil and water conservation policy and programs. The book is especially useful as a marker in time forty years ago when the need for more effective and focused soil conservation policies was becoming widely recognized. When he wrote the book, Sampson was Executive Vice President of the National Association of Conservation Districts and an influential policy advocate on USDA conservation efforts. The US was just entering the early stages of promoting "gasohol," which today has become the behemoth corn-based ethanol industry, consuming 60% of Iowa's corn crop. USDA would soon rename the Soil Conservation Service the Natural Resources

Conservation Service, acknowledging the larger suite of environmental issues it needed to address. The underlying tensions in US farm programs between promoting conservation and caring for the land or developing production-oriented programs, were growing. The export boom of the late 1970s encouraged more intensive commodity production and heightened the tensions. Not until the inevitable farm crisis struck in the mid-1980s did our belief in the unlimited marketing potential for US crops come into question.

Reading Sampson's book today makes it seem like we have been in a time warp for forty years. Issues he addressed in 1981 are subjects in today's headlines about soil erosion and water quality. In one section, he discussed our need to develop a new land ethic and to base conservation policies on concern for the land. He understood how challenging it would be to make the shift given the current agricultural policy environment. Consider this passage:

> Many farmers today are seriously abusing their land, not because they want to, but because they are either unaware of the damage they are causing or feel it is insignificant compared to the losses they might suffer if they changed their farming system. Often, they are assured by scientists from agricultural industries, agencies, and colleges that what they are doing is real progress. The criteria, too often is that if it is profitable it must be right.

Sound familiar?

In thinking about the subtitle, *A Time to Choose?* the question is what did we choose? Did we get it right? The simple answer is in large part we chose to punt and ignore the larger issues Sampson raised. We chose to green light essentially unlimited growth in commodity production, especially corn, promoting ethanol to absorb the surpluses we produced. We chose to significantly increase and revamp federal farm programs moving away from sixty years of production controls and supply management. The 1996 farm bill, dubbed "freedom to farm" was built on the assumption of unlimited export markets, and abolished the use of production controls and acreage limitations for most crops. We chose to promote expanded commodity production and provided farmers a financial safety net in the form of crop insurance. This new support morphed from disaster-based protections to a system of farm subsidies and guaranteed income, underwriting more production regardless of market signals or demand. The one bright spot in this history was the Conservation Title of the 1985 farm bill and the many new initiatives it brought. Developing a process to identify "highly erodible land" (HEL) and requiring some conservation protections for fragile lands like grasslands and wetlands were major improvements. Land retirement under the CRP helped lower average soil losses, but it is important to recognize the genius of the CRP wasn't simply as a conservation program. The CRP also served as a financial life ring for farmers struggling in the late 1980s by allowing them to put their whole farms in the program. By offering ten-year rental contracts at generous rates, the CRP placed a floor under sliding land values in regions like southern Iowa. Taking thirty million acres out of production, allowed the CRP to function like a long-term set-aside, but shifted the costs of this farm support to the conservation budget.

On farmland protection, a major focus in Sampson's book, we chose to do little at the federal level. Farmland protection is still left primarily to state and local governments, essentially cast as a land use issue rather than a national concern about food security or having the capacity to meet domestic needs as well as international markets and humanitarian food assistance. In the 1990s, Congress eventually provided USDA limited funding to acquire farmland protection easements, if states or local governments could generate the needed matching funds. The costs of protecting farmland are daunting, especially for land under development pressure with rising land values. Was anything we chose a positive development? The main improvement in conservation programs in recent years has been in creating "working lands" programs, like the Conservation Stewardship Program. The CSP pays farmers for how they care for land being farmed rather than paying only if the land is retired. New conservation practices being developed, like narrow strip intercropping with prairie grasses, are proving effective. The NRCS has shown new interest in promoting concepts like soil health and carbon sequestration through using cover crops. Yet in the grand scheme of land conservation, we are no closer to a "land ethic." We have yet to invest in developing the next generation of conservation policy advocates.

The land cannot speak for itself and since no farm organizations or commodity groups appear to view land conservation as a priority, they aren't going to pretend to speak for the land either. This makes sense and perhaps is just as well. As the editor of the *1958 USDA Yearbook on Land*, reminded us, when Americans speak of the land, we aren't really talking about it in a physical sense. Instead as Leopold noted, we mean the people who are on the land and what is good for them. By shifting our focus away from soil conservation, we were able to go on a farming bender, planting fence row to fence, bringing new fragile land into production, and plowing under millions of acres of pasture and set aside ground. The Soil Bank of the late 1950s, with its long-term land retirement contracts, was put on the shelve and wouldn't reappear for another thirty years. Only when the farm crisis of the 1980s required innovative ways to pour money into agriculture and prop up land prices was the Conservation Reserve Program born.

Jerry Hatfield notes his belief we need a revolution in agriculture if we really care about the soil that sustains our future. He isn't the only person who believes it. David Montgomery titled his 2017 book, *Growing a Revolution: Bringing Our Soil Back to Life*. He believes the revolution is already underway, noting "the foundation of the next agricultural revolution will be rooted in how we think about soil." Montgomery's premise is his concern, "the degradation of soils and loss of organic matter are the most under-appreciated environmental crisis humanity now faces." History shows "societies that do not take care of their soil do not last," but Montgomery believes "the stage is set for ground-up transformation and change, as the short-term interests of farmers increasingly align with preserving long-term soil fertility." His ideas about soil health, what he calls conservation farming, may be the foundation for a new era of resilient agriculture. We will return to this topic of the soil and its future in Chapter Nine, in looking to how the land can be our source of hope and renewal.

Looking back now over forty years of teaching and writing, the range of topics, travels, and activities covered surprises me. One explanation is I tried to stay busy, a trait inherited from my Mom who seemed to be in constant motion, "like a fart on a skillet" Dad would say. Driving home to visit, she was always busy, in the yard pushing the mower or deadheading her hundreds of daylilies. We were both over-achievers in our own way.

One of my favorite stories from growing up is one she might still find upsetting - the Second grade Christmas tree incident in 1961 with Ms. Harvey. As usual my folks were slow getting a Christmas tree that year. A tree was often an extravagance on the farm and some years a prickly red cedar cut from the ditch and sprayed with a can of flocking would suffice. This year was no different as December spilled away and still no tree. That is when this seven-year old decided to take matters into my own hands. On the last day of class when the teacher asked if anyone wanted to take the classroom tree home my anxious hand shot up, perhaps not a surprise to Ms. Harvey, and I was awarded possession.

When the day ended I hauled the somewhat dried-out tree down the stairway to the bus. Riding home it sat proudly up front propped beside me. The bus driver pulled up to the farm and I wrestled the tree down the steps, across the road, and through the yard to the back door. Mom greeted me but rather than welcome me as the hero my gesture clearly deserved, she was aghast. "Why did you bring home the tree" she said, "now everyone will think we are too poor to buy one!" I can't be sure, but my most likely reaction was to burst into tears as she had hurt my tender feelings, always near the surface. I was too young and impatient to understand my teacher's offer was intended for a classmate whose family couldn't afford a tree. Viewed in this light, my act of bravery providing a tree for my family was really a selfish act denying the opportunity to another classmate more in need. From mom's perspective, my childish action was laden with social stigma in our community. Who would think so many social and class issues could be contained in a dried-out Christmas tree! The lessons were too big for a seven-year old to comprehend, I just wanted us to have a tree! Today, issues of poverty, class, and social stigma surround us and are often tied to the land, just as freighted with emotion and stigma as that December day in 1961. That is why before we can consider the future, we need to take a closer look at how landowner' attitudes to the land are today often highlighted by a history of fear, conflict, and inequality.

Grant Wood's *Approaching Storm.*

Chapter Five – Iowa Land and Landowners: Fear or Opportunity

Our relation to the land changed as modern agriculture changed. Today many issues involving the land seem to focus on fear and conflict, revealing a fragility of agriculture surprising for how it confounds the expected image of strength and stability. In many ways, our fragile relation to the land contrasts to the optimism of the relation in the past, in the years of settlement and expansion. Part of the change reflects the adverse impacts of modern agriculture catching up with us, and part stems from a society more willing to focus on issues of equity, inclusion, and inequality. The good news is the current state of tensions on the land can't obscure the land's resiliency and its ability to offer hope. The discussion about hope from the land will wait for our last chapter. Before considering our reasons for hope we first need to examine what brought us to a pattern of fear and conflict on the land.

Iowa Through the Lens of Appalachia

In *Ramp Hollow: The Ordeal of Appalachia*, Fordham University historian Steven Stoll explains the region's history through the lens of displacement as subsistence agrarians lost their access to the land to the extractive industries of coal and timber. The process reduced the people to wage employees and destroyed the common lands supporting their lifestyles and culture. Stoll doesn't venerate subsistence farming as an honored goal but explains how it provided the people of

Appalachia with autonomy in a shared economy, one more sustaining than the economic and social degradation brought once the coal and timber industries took charge.

Reading *Ramp Hollow*, the parallels to our experience of the last half-century of change in Iowa agriculture are striking. Similar forces have reshaped the rural economy, culture and for many, our relation to the land. The same forces decimating much of Appalachia help explain deteriorating attitudes toward soil conservation and land stewardship. The Iowa agriculture of my youth in the 1960s, though not purely subsistent in nature, had more in common with the model than we might realize. Farms were smaller, around 200 acres and more plentiful, with over 150,000 farms, meaning neighbors were closer and more numerous. Farms were more diverse as to the mix of crops and livestock, perhaps not as productive if measured simply in yields but more economically resilient, often more profitable, and importantly, more enjoyable for the families living on them. Land was usually owned by the people who farmed it, and tenancy was not seen as an enviable goal. The widespread production of livestock, hogs, chickens, cattle and dairy cows, meant much more land was in pasture and hay. Animals grazed the marginal land and stalk fields after harvest, and the animals did the work of spreading manure across the landscape.

Farming in the US has been in constant evolution since our founding but agriculture began to change more rapidly in the late 1950s and the changes have continued unabated since. At that time, a series of forces, either unleashed the potential of agriculture as an industrial force or led to the destruction of the diversified family farm, take your pick. The shift to exporting grain, moving to commodity specialization rather than mixed grain and livestock farms, consolidation and growth in farm size, increasing scale of equipment, and growing reliance on expensive inputs of seeds, fertilizers, and chemicals all contributed to the "modernization" of agriculture. Moving swine production into confinement buildings, concentrating the pigs geographically, and using production contracts between farmers and vertically integrated companies resulted in a radical, though little noticed, change in pork production. Over the last thirty years the number of pigs in Iowa increased by half to 25 million, while the number of farms raising pigs shrunk by over 90%, from 70,000 to around 6,000 in 2020. These changes transformed the politics of pork, and as many consumers know, changed the nature and taste of pork itself.

From the perspective of land tenure, the period saw a doubling in average farm size to over 450 acres, rapid increases and periodic fluctuations in land values, a sharp rise in farm tenancy especially of cash rental rather than crop sharing, and more land owned by non-farming heirs and other investors. These changes were gradual over forty-years and like the proverbial frog in the pot, many of the people living in Iowa and rural America didn't notice the cumulative effects until recently. There have been periods of disruption, like the 1980s farm crisis when land values collapsed by 60% only to regain the losses within a decade. There have been shifts in exports and market prices, as trade relations with major partners like China and the EU have gone through periods of strife. Even with these fluctuations, the shift to a more industrialized agriculture was steady and is still underway.

One key effect is the dramatic increase in production of corn and soybeans. We added close to 9 million acres of row crop production in Iowa alone over the last 50 years. All these acres were converted from hay, pasture, forests, and marginal bottomlands. Today we have around twenty-four million acres of cropland planted to corn or soybeans every year. The increase in corn acres and yields led to frequent surpluses, impacting market prices. In turn, the surpluses drove the search for new outlets, new export markets, and new uses, like high fructose corn syrup. In recent decades, the main answer to abundant corn supplies is producing corn-based ethanol for fuel, a use now consuming an almost unbelievable 60% of the corn produced in Iowa.

When you ask how these structural shifts in agriculture are reflected in attitudes toward land stewardship, soil conservation, and water quality, the parallels to the Appalachian experience become more apparent. The extractive industries in Appalachia are coal and timber, in Iowa they are corn and pigs. The economic and political parallels of these industrial shifts become clear once you look for them.

In our current debate about water quality, the subject of the next chapter, most attention focuses on reducing the nutrients leaking from the intensively farmed millions of acres of corn and soybeans. Most ideas to address water quality focus on edge of field practices and improved fertilization and drainage systems. These ideas are all premised on accepting the need to continue maximum production of corn and beans. Few people dare question if we have over played this hand and whether some land is better left in grass and habitat. We are essentially mining our soil and water resources, extracting fertility and future productivity to raise crops used for industrial purposes or export. In many ways, we have re-colonized our state without recognizing it. Granted there are economic benefits of increased crop production, and anyone who owns Iowa farmland as I have, enjoys the steady increases in land values. The actual benefits to the state are less clear, when an increasing share of any profits from farming are captured by a declining number of ever-larger farms. Because over half the state's land is farmed under tenancy, much of any apparent gain in farm income is transferred as rent to absentee owners, 20% of whom live outside the state.

Consider the role of pork production, a sector Iowa has longed prided itself on for being first in the nation, supplying 25% of America's pigs. Here the parallels to Appalachia are even clearer. We are proud of Iowa's rank as the nation's leading pork producer but this claim glosses over questions of who actually owns the pigs and who benefits from any profits they might produce. The shift of over 90% of swine production to contracting in a vertically integrated system, and away from independent family farms owning the pigs, means a few dozen corporations, many from out of state, own most of the pigs and enjoy most of the profits. One of the largest pork integrators, Smithfield Foods is Chinese owned meaning the profits don't even stay in the US.

An excellent example of the shift in the structure of Iowa hog production is the story of Iowa Select Farms. The company was started in 1992 by Jeff Hansen an Iowa farm kid from Iowa Falls and his wife Deb. What started with three sows has now grown into a behemoth. The company is estimated to own over 242,000 sows, employ over 7200 people, and produce around 15% of Iowa's hogs, with facilities on hundreds of farms spread around the state. Hog farmers, now called growers, are legally considered to be independent contractors, meaning they have little legal status to seek judicial recourse if anything goes wrong. Their returns are the contract payments, usually just enough to cover the costs of financing the buildings and caring for the pigs. Many industrial scale contract swine farms are so large, the actual labor is done by low wage employees, often immigrants from south of the border. The same is true for the slaughterhouses, where the COVID pandemic illuminated the lack of concern for worker safety. Growers may benefit if they raise crops to sell to integrators for hog feed and they do get to keep the manure to use for fertilizer. Other environmental issues: smells, water pollution, and manure spills are left for the neighbors and local communities to experience. Mountain top removal is the environmentally destructive coal mining practice now plaguing Appalachia. The proliferation of Concentrated Animal Feeding Operations or CAFOs, and converting marginal land to crop production are Iowa's versions.

The collective political impacts of shifts in swine production can be seen in attitudes and challenges for natural resource protection. Local residents are increasingly vocal about concerns over locating new CAFOs nearby but decades ago Iowa's politicians yielded to the powerful lure of industrialized farming. The answer was to remove any local control over livestock production in favor of weak and often unenforced state standards written largely by the industry. On the issue of water quality, farmers naturally focus on increasing grain yields to stay ahead of rising input costs and shrinking margins. The need to keep our proverbial foot on the accelerator of all-out production leads directly to farmers claiming the permanent conservation practices or cropping changes needed to reduce nutrient run-off and soil loss are unaffordable. This is a reason few are willing to adopt the conservation farming practices promoted by soil health experts like David Montgomery. The nutrients leaking from increased tile drainage and over application of fertilizers and manure simply become problems for others living somewhere downstream to address, be it in Des Moines or the Gulf.

The increasing role of non-operator landowners and investors who control over half of Iowa's cropland mean many "landowners" are disconnected from the land. The success of their "farms" is measured largely by the cash rent tenants can afford to pay rather than the soils conserved or water quality improved. The tenants decide the crops to raise, how to raise them and how much attention, if any, is given to conservation. The short one-year term typical of Iowa farm leases mean most tenants have little incentive to invest in long-term conservation practices. Attention to soil stewardship is left to those who can afford it or who are motivated to use public conservation programs to support the efforts. Society and our legal system asks and expects little from landowners.

The shifts in the economic and social structure of farming and land ownership in Iowa are the manifestation of our industrialized agriculture. They help explain the apparent coarsening of our attitudes to the land. Today we appear willing to tolerate levels of soil loss and water pollution that would have shocked our forbearers, like Ding Darling, Aldo Leopold, and Henry A. Wallace. The structural shifts help explain our political impotency and unwillingness to address these ills or confront their causes. Instead we place faith in voluntary actions and public funding to carry out what should largely be private responsibilities. Seventy years ago, Leopold warned us how believing economic self-motivation will lead farmers and landowners to protect our common heritage of natural resources was destined to fail. We still lack the land ethic he wrote of, or an adequate substitute for it. The history of Appalachia bears this out and the tragedy unfolding on Iowa's fields does as well, that is, unless we begin to take more seriously our responsibilities to the land. It is not too late to change, to follow the paths being made by farmers and landowners showing how land can be conserved, grass-based farming promoted, and water quality improved. Making the needed changes will take leadership, and recognizing the costs our current system imposes. Only a greater appreciation for working with nature can help sustain our future.

Fear as Seen by the Back Forty

I like to think one of my key roles is providing my owners with joy and opportunity. I don't ask much, you can leave me alone for years and I will be here when you come back. The weeds may have grown and a few trees sprouted up but I will be here waiting for you to do something, it is your choice. That is why I am struck by how much time owners spend worrying about things going wrong, the fear of what might happen. This goes way beyond worrying if bankers may come to take me way. Our last real dose of that was in the mid-1980s during the farm financial crisis when most of us lost half our value – at least on paper. It didn't affect me because the old fellow who farmed me then had no debt and no mortgage to worry about. I don't think he liked the news my value had gone down, but he didn't plan to sell me, so it didn't make any difference. He couldn't borrow as much against me as collateral but he didn't need to borrow any money.

Borrowing money against the land is how most of the neighbors got into trouble, some eventually losing the land. They used high-priced land, valued at inflated prices, as collateral to borrow at high interest rates to buy more high-priced land. It didn't matter if the price didn't pencil out, meaning the value of the corn it could produce wouldn't pay for it. The banks were willing to lend money confident land values would continue to go up. If they didn't the banks could always foreclose on the land. The banks weren't the ones risking their futures, at least not as directly as their farm clients. When the music stopped in the early 1980s, the financial house of cards came down. Many who leveraged their land found themselves caught with nowhere to turn. Some younger farmers looked to the bank of Mom and Dad, asking them to mortgage the home place to refinance the loans. Some who did paid the ultimate price, losing Junior's new land and the family home place as well. The toll was real. In the 1980s Iowa lost over 30,000 farms falling from around 125,000 to just 95,000 but 1990. It was a sad and trying process to watch. Farm activists like Prairiefire filled the Statehouse lawn in Des Moines with white crosses representing the thousands of Iowa farm families who lost everything.

You know I will never understand why headlines reading "Farm Land Values up 10%" are seen as good news in farm country? They are only good news if you plan on getting out or plan on borrowing to buy more land. It seems news of higher land prices just fuels higher prices for everything else. Landlords reading the headlines expect higher rents, thinking "I should get more rent for my land if it is worth that much!" Where is the good news for tenants in that? Makes you wonder whose head the farmer is using and whose head is using the farmer? Come to think of it, Wendell Berry from Kentucky asked just this question in one of his farming books.

News stories appeared in the 1980s saying I lost half my value, but I knew better. I hadn't changed a bit and was just as valuable as ever, if you knew what to look for. The fear farmers and owners have today is different than their fear in the 1980s. Today the fear is more political, the fear someone is going to disagree with how they farm or expect them to do something for the benefit of the public and community. This is a whole different issue than worrying about the bankers. With bankers, you just borrow money and sign documents, all the terms and risks are right there on paper. Today the worry is more of being out of control, at the mercy of others, people who don't share the same values, don't appreciate how hard you work or the risks you take, and who maybe aren't even interested in trying to understand what you do or why. The fear is these people want to put you out of business or tell you how to farm. This is different than bankers, they just want to get paid and really don't care how you come up with the money!

PURDY AND HIS LAND INSIGHTS

Thinking about how the changes in agriculture impact our relation to the land raises several troubling issues challenging our future. One is the environmental vulnerability we face in using land for farming, as discussed for soil conservation and detailed in the next chapter on water quality. A second issue is the inequality we have embedded in the land, not just the history of how land was acquired and distributed but new inequalities being magnified by expanding farm tenancy and land being consolidated into larger and larger farms. One of the most thoughtful observers examining the impact these changes have on the land is Jeremiah Purdy, a law professor at Columbia Law School. His 2019 book, *This Land is Our Land,* is a tightly written and brilliant essay about land in the larger context of our national tensions. He offers several insights helping explain our current situation, in particular on environmental issues and inequality.

As a starting point Purdy makes the astute observation in "the natural world, the land, is the thing you can always tell lies about, because it doesn't answer – until the time you can't lie about it anymore because it is too late." Consider how well this explains our willingness to believe the myths we create, such as those concerning soil conservation. Our willingness to lie about what we are doing to the land is reflected in how we accepted the rapid changes in Iowa's pork sector with its negative impacts on the land, water, and neighbors. Farmers face a much different future disenfranchised from the historic promises of farming's independence. The question now is if it is too late for us to continue lying about the land?

The idea it may be too late is intimately tied to environmental vulnerability created by changes on the land. In speaking about recent water quality disasters in West Virginia and Flint, Michigan, Purdy notes how "environmental vulnerability is intimately involved in American inequality." Perhaps the most poignant example of this increasing inequality on America's land is the rapid increase in farm tenancy. We don't like to think about farm tenancy in terms of inequality but isn't that what it is? The inequality is present not just in the relation of the tenant to the landlord but also for the land itself. There are differences in how land is treated by a farmer owner and how the land may fare if farmed by a tenant faced with paying high cash rent. Of course, there are examples of tenants who take care to steward land they rent, but I always reminded my students, few people wash their rental car before returning it.

Another of Purdy's powerful comments is his idea "the land remembers." How we farm is always visible on the land, and eventually it catches up with us, unless or until we treat the land right. Leopold said, "truth is what wins out in the end." This is worth contemplating when it comes to farm tenancy. Tenancy has been a concern since the history of agriculture, whether for the serfs under feudal ownership in Europe, or America's farm tenants during the Great Depression. The President's Farm Security Commission report from 1937 was the high-water mark for these concerns in the US. At that time, farm tenancy was recognized as an "evil," and government efforts were taken to reduce the incidence of tenancy, to address its inherent inequalities, and to increase the ability of farmers to purchase and own their land. But in the post-war era of modern agriculture, this view dimmed and we came to tolerate increasing farm tenancy. The shortcomings of farm tenancy were well known: the short-term planning horizon, farming the land harder, lack of wealth building, and reluctance to invest in soil conservation. The concerns are still present and haven't changed; instead we changed. What changed was the desire of more people to own farmland but not be the farmer and for farmers to want to farm more land but not own it. These trends are encouraged by many farm economists who say renting land is the way for farmers to spread risk and have access to more land.

Our inability and unwillingness to confront increasing farm tenancy reflects the sanctity given to private property and the inability (or unwillingness) to question how people choose to farm or own land. This is why efforts to restrain non-operator landowners, i.e., absentee owners, have never been popular or successful. Ideas like higher property taxes or giving existing farm tenants a right of first refusal if the land is sold are considered un-American. On the other hand, assisting new farmers to buy land, a topic considered in Chapter Seven, by offering lower interest rates and easier credit, is more popular and politically acceptable. The fact the efforts are often ineffective due to the difficulties new buyers face in a competitive land market against more capitalized landowners, doesn't mean we didn't try.

The real concern about tenancy we avoid talking about is inequality and how tenancy increases the vulnerability of those involved. Vulnerability is present for tenants who can be turned off the land next year, and for the land if an absentee landowner is unwilling or unable to invest in soil conservation. We have difficulty even talking about the inequality associated with farm tenancy because it goes against our belief all people are equal and should be free to make their choices. To acknowledge increasing farm tenancy presents threats recognizes the inherent imbalances present in a capitalist free market system, i.e. some people have a lot more power and not all people are equal. We gloss over or ignore reality and treat tenancy as a matter of "choice." Choice is easier to talk about because it rests on individual autonomy even when the choice may not be real or effective.

That tenancy is not a problem is a lie we tell ourselves about the land, a lie we justify by noting some landlords do care for the soil as do some tenants. This partial truth allows us to gloss over the fact tenancy is inherently unequal. Some slave owners may have been more benign than others and some slaves may have been better treated than others, but that doesn't change the inherent and abhorrent nature of their slavery.

Another factor corroding our relation to the land Purdy notes, is the growing mistrust of the federal government on issues of environmental protection. This anti-government, anti-public view is popular in many quarters of modern agriculture, especially with conservative farm groups like the Farm Bureau. Concerns about government over reach may be historic, for example many found fault with programs of FDR's New Deal, but the idea the government is the enemy found its most vocal advocate in Ronald Reagan. His anti-government rhetoric fueled the growth of the Sagebrush Rebellion in the West, challenging the federal management of public lands. This philosophy lives today in the Bundy acolytes and other anti-government radicals who demand the federal public lands be given to the states so they can be privatized and exploited. Purdy adds a dimension to this reality, observing one feature of American politics is "the willingness to suffer at the hands of the institutions your people identify with, and to forgive them nearly anything out of loyalty." This idea applies to agriculture in so many ways. Farm groups support only voluntary, non-regulatory "solutions" to environmental issues, absentee owners are trusted to place a priority on conservation over production, livestock integrators are trusted to make contracting relations fair, and fertilizers dealers are expected to recommend only the amounts needed to not threaten public waters. None of these assumptions are true or reasonable. We aren't willing to believe these institutions could fail us because we are invested in supporting them.

When you combine economic and political inequality with the lack of power found in relations like being a farm tenant or a contract hog grower, the attendant environmental vulnerability is no surprise. Purdy notes power rearranges people on the land and our willingness to lie about the land is essentially a political bid to remake reality. The good news is we didn't get to this point by accident, we built the institutions being relied on, free markets and government programs. Some believe these institutions are not equipped to deal with the problems and instead we must hope for a hack to radically alter our systems. Purdy rejects this, saying "Putting hope in the hack gives up on specifically political, let alone democratic, responses to environmental questions." Aristotle said man is "a political animal" with the ability to invent powerful constructs, like life, rights, citizen, votes, democracy, legitimacy, and law. Fifty years ago, our nation made a choice to use a set of national laws to address environmental questions. Purdy notes, "The great power of a political species is to change the architecture of its common world." This gives us the "uniquely constructive power of political sovereignty." Today we have to confront the fact many forces are using political sovereignty to secure a fragmentation of the planet, into safe spaces and sacrifice zones. This is why considering the issues of the land are central to the future of society, as the land will be the base for our solutions. To understand our changing relation to the land it is valuable to consider how often land has been the subject of conflict, and how its ownership reflects threads of the racial discrimination woven into our society's history.

LAND AND DISCRIMINATION

America's history is steeped in a broth of racism so strong if you tried swallowing it in one gulp you might gag on the stench. A great deal of our racism is tied to the land, whose land was stolen so settlers could claim it, whose labor was stolen to work the land, and who was denied the opportunity to own land. In some cases, we went so far as to take land away from lawful owners, forfeiting the land to the government through extra-judicial means, arcane legal rules on racial identity, and wartime attitudes about who could be trusted to be good Americans. If you doubt the accuracy of this indictment, consider these examples:

Millions of slaves imported and raised to work the cotton plantations and other agricultural lands across the South;

Tens of millions of acres of land "acquired" from indigenous Native American tribes, some "purchased" through one-sided "treaties" usually broken as soon as signed, but more often land taken by war, armed conflict, theft, exter-

171

mination, and forced expulsion to the west.

Thousands of people residing legally in the US denied the right to own land, such as Asians barred by Chinese Exclusion Acts and other anti-Asian laws enacted in the 19th and 20th century;

In many states after the War, both North and South, the same exclusions applied to freed slaves denied the right to purchase land;

Hopeful examples of land redistribution, like General Sherman's January 1865 Field Order No. 15 setting aside a large block of land on the coast in South Carolina and Georgia for ownership by freed black families, were quickly reversed and the distributed land restored to white ownership by power of the law and violence;

Abandoning Reconstruction and the promised 'forty acres and a mule' denying freed blacks the opportunity to own land, to gain economic independence, and to build wealth. National policy ignored the resurgence of white supremacy and resigned the new citizens to generations of slave-like conditions working as share croppers on the former plantations, under the brutal yoke of Jim Crow.

These examples illustrate the linkage of racial discrimination to ownership of land. Another is the "re-appropriation" or forfeiture of lands held by South Asians, considered "white" under state property laws, until a 1923 US Supreme Court decision revoked their right to own land by ruling they were not "white." A final example is the tragic internment of over 120,000 Japanese Americans, mostly US citizens, beginning in February 1942 and lasting four years. Many lands owned by these citizens were lost, through forced sales made prior to internment or by other nefarious means.

Restraining who can own land in the US, especially farmland, is still a topic of state legislation and restrictions, although today the focus is on foreigners rather than our citizens. My thinking on the topic is bookended by events more than forty years apart. In May 2020 PBS aired a documentary series on the history of Asian Americans, detailing several restraints on land ownership, even some I had never encountered after spending a career working on land issues. The second event was my first major assignment as a newly minted Assistant Attorney General for Iowa.

Much of my July 1979 was spent writing an Attorney General's opinion on the constitutionality of Iowa's recently amended law restricting non-resident ownership of farmland. The lengthy opinion held the law constitutional for several key reasons. It did not violate the supremacy clause or interfere with federal enforcement of immigration laws because it incorporated the federal definition of "non-resident aliens." Regulating who can own farmland has historically been considered an issue of state law and not one for federal courts. Under the equal protection clause Iowa had a rational basis for restricting non-alien ownership based on their lack of connection to the communities where the land is located. The more restrictive strict scrutiny test, a constitutional standard few discriminatory laws can meet, was not applicable because the category of non-resident aliens includes billions of people not US citizens, meaning they are not a discrete, insular minority. The Iowa law bore no evidence of racial animus or discriminatory purpose, it was just protecting opportunities for Iowans. The 1857 Iowa Constitution protects the rights of anyone who is a resident of the state to own land, a provision written when most of Iowa's farmers were immigrants, like my mother's Danish ancestors.

The legacy of racism and land discrimination woven into our Nation's history has many explanations, though none are very palatable today. With native American's it was a question of perceived necessity. We had to move them out of the way because they didn't "use" the land or understand our ideas of ownership. Seen through one lens this is a classic exercise of political power to promote greed and exploitation. Seen through another, perhaps more patriotic lens, it was Jeffersonian nation building by yeoman farmers. The truth is the Indians were in the way so they were dealt with in ways, and with tragic consequences, they and the Nation still grapple with.

As to slaves, the first justification was they weren't people, certainly not on a par with whites, when it came to things like owning land. Once the Civil War ended and the former slaves were freed, justifications evolved to include fear of how independence, success, and wealth building by a black society would challenge dominant white society. If blacks could own farmland, it would erode a ready supply of low cost, malleable workers to toil as sharecroppers. White owned plantations faced an existential threat if no one worked their fields. Sharecropping was the legal device invented in the South and designed to perpetuate near slave-like conditions and control over families. Sharecroppers are not tenants and have no legal property rights in the land or in the wealth and independence it offers. Instead they are essentially bonded workers but with no rights to wages or other protections employees might have. White society feared if blacks owned land they could access income, self-employment, and wealth to pass on, and would seek and expect political power. Each step threatened white culture and the political and economic systems. Echoes of the unequal treatment of black landowners by the legal system still reverberate today. The reluctance of black families to use legal tools to formalize passing land between generations, creates what is known as "heirs" property, fractionated and unrecorded land divisions passed to generations of heirs. Failing to record the transfers leaves the current fractional "owners" vulnerable to losing their claims if another heir records a deed transfer. The uncertain nature of these land titles makes it difficult to obtain loans and mortgages using land as collateral. The uncertainty and legal risks associated with this history contributes to declining black land ownership, an issue many legal scholars, members of Congress, and USDA officials are struggling to address today.

Restraints on Asians were classic examples of racism and "anti-other" hatred, more easily enforced due to physical appearance. The success of Asian farm families fueled jealousy on the part of white neighbors and others who craved the opportunity to take their lands. For some, the WWII internment provided the perfect opportunity and excuse to act. This part of America's land history doesn't get taught in schoolbooks. This failure is the type documented in James Loewen's 1995 book, *Lies My Teacher Told Me*. Perhaps the collective lacuna in our story of the land is understandable. Who wants to be reminded of the crimes and ill deeds of our ancestors? Especially when it clouds the view of heroic struggle and survival we embrace. Worse yet, what if considering this history might threaten the legitimacy of our own claims to the land! Therein lies our problem. James Baldwin put it best when he noted: "People who imagine that history flatters them, are impaled on their history like a butterfly on a pin and become incapable of seeing or changing themselves, or the world."

The Back Forty on the First Big Lie
[Not the New One]

I can't help thinking about this history of racial discrimination and what it means for me. The concern I have is how you constructed a social and political worldview making it too easy to avoid confronting the reality of your actions. You did it in regards to how you obtained "ownership" of me from the Potawatomie, a part of my history no one remembers or teaches. It isn't that my legal title is somehow in doubt or that you will go back and right the wrongs of history by giving me back. That ship has sailed. You did the same for racial injustice and I fear the pattern is playing out in how you are coming to treat the land. In his fabulous book *Begin Again*, Eddie Glaude Jr., examines the life of James Baldwin and his role in the civil rights struggles of the 20th century, to see what lessons we can find for today. Glaude shapes his analysis around Baldwin's efforts to confront the big lie – white America's unwillingness to abandon the belief white people matter more than blacks and then constructing a society to ignore and minimize this failing. Glaude's motivation is asking whether the Nation's current experience, as exemplified by the televised murder of George Floyd in 2020, and confronting the reality of racial injustice will reach a different end, a time when the lie will finally be put to rest.

If you read his book, and examine it through my lens, that of the land, the parallels between white America's attitude toward racism and how it treats the land are clear. My intention in making this connection isn't to minimize the nature of racial injustice, instead it is to ask if the history and pattern of land abuse is not similar? If it is, you must ask what lessons you draw from his analysis of Baldwin are applicable to me – the land?

Glaude's premise is using the lens of truth telling, not unlike my premise. Is there a better story, if we examine the lies you tell about the land and tell the truth about where we are? This theme of truth telling and examining lies told about the land are themes in Terry Tempest William's *Erosion*, and Purdy's *This Land is Our Land*. What is the lie you tell when it comes to the land? Is it what Leopold identified as the key log we need to move – your treating land only as an economic issue? Is it what Wallace warned about – your unwillingness to recognize the duty owed to the land even if you do own it in fee simple? Is it your view the land is all about private property and landowner rights without recognizing any responsibility to the public, who created the context for your rights to exist? It is all these things and more – the lie is you love the land, when the evidence shows many of you don't.

Don't get me wrong, some people do love the land, you will read their examples showing what loving the land can mean. But the evidence of how you abuse the land is present as well. Your history with soil conservation is largely a story of avoiding responsibility for your actions. Glaude might say, in your debasement of the land you debase yourselves by willingly accepting the damage and explaining it away, the ephemeral gullies are your truths. The power of the lies you tell about the land help you avoid confronting the truth. You rationalize your treatment of me and spin your myths about the progress you make, all the while my soil erodes, my health declines, and you pollute the waters with my soul. Because I am not human and have no rights, at least legal rights you respect, the land is just land and it is no crime to mistreat me. When those who love the land, environmentalists and conservationists, challenge your right to act this way you respond with vigor and vitriol. Who are they to dare challenge the primacy of your gloried property rights! Glaude notes to call your reactions a backlash is inaccurate, doing so accepts the legitimacy of your claims of right and gives you power to set expectations for what is acceptable. The opportunity and challenge we face today is the need to re-examine what you believe is acceptable in how you treat the land. As Purdy notes, land is something you can always lie about – until the time comes when you can no longer hide the truth. Today is a time for truth telling and confronting your lies, giving witness to their effects, and setting alternatives.

It is only natural you to want to avoid such a confrontation, preferring to wash away your sins without admitting any crimes. One reason you fear critics is because they remind you of your misdeeds and ask you to confess. This is why you hated the now deceased and sorely missed Bill Stowe, who dared to sue you for polluting the river he used to water 500,000 customers. Living with and defending your lies is not without costs. It is a large part of what makes you worried and fearful. Knowing you are mistreating the land takes the joy and fun out of farming. It makes me sad, not only do you not respect me, you are blind to the satisfactions and joy I can offer.

In the summer of 2020 the Nation faced growing public dissent and protests over the racial injustice many people experience at the hands of the police. Thinking about the moment, led me to reflect on how the wealth inequality feeding our social strife finds its history in the land. The following essay was my attempt to address the issue. A mutual friend shared it with his friend, noted journalist Bill Moyers, who posted the essay for his readers. It generated a great deal of reaction as friends and strangers reached out to comment. A law school classmate I had not seen in forty years even contacted me after reading the essay, such is the reach of new media. I include it here to help illuminate the sentiments shared by the Back Forty.

IOWA'S WHITE PRIVILEGE HAS A
BILLION DOLLAR PRICE TAG

I remember the first time someone called me out for my white privilege. The charge came decades ago from a black food activist in Detroit. Naturally I was offended - the label stung coming from someone who had no idea of my nature other than the color of my skin. To me, my so-called white privilege was growing up in an ill-heated farmhouse without running water watching my parents eke out a living on our small farm. Where was the privilege there?

Time can soften many memories and events of recent weeks have forced our nation to address the legacies of racial injustice and wealth inequality plaguing us today. Recent events made me think more deeply about the term white privilege and what it may mean in our Iowa context. The term has been used frequently in recent weeks along with the idea of systemic racism. On hearing the terms, it may be natural to strike a defensive pose and say not me – how can you accuse me of exercising a privilege I neither claim nor recognize! But it is important to understand being the beneficiary of white privilege does not make you a racist – that is a function of your thinking. White privilege is a function of how society treats us.

That is why this moment is so important because it is a time to stop and think. As Iowan's we pride ourselves on our state's history of commitment to civil rights and racial equality. There is truth to these claims but the idea we are free of racism is more a myth of our own making than reality. If we are honest with ourselves white privilege is all around us – in fact it is almost foundational to our state. How is this true? The most significant evidence is in our pattern of land ownership and system of farming. You need look no further than agricultural policy and the generous public financial support we provide farmers and landowners to see white privilege at work. Yes, it is alive and well in Iowa and has a price tag measured in billions.

In the last two years alone, Iowa farmers and landowners will have received several billion dollars in public subsidies – not just the crop insurance protecting farm incomes, but farm program payments and a new crop of benefits in the form of market facilitation payments to compensate for markets lost to trade wars and new COVID-19 payments to compensate for losses due to falling prices. The people who receive these payments – several hundred thousand Iowa farmers, family members, and landowners are almost exclusively white. We have so few minority land owners in Iowa you could gather them in a bank basement. So where is the white privilege in that you ask? Well you can answer that question yourself by explaining why society has chosen this group of citizens as being worthy of a bounty of public welfare?

The answers we provide are predictable – it's so we will have a stable food supply and plenty to eat, it is to keep the rural economy afloat, it is to make sure land prices don't collapse and trigger a farm crisis, and so farmers don't go out of business. There is some truth to all these answers and the good news is the public broadly supports helping farmers in times of economic stress like we are in now. But do we really fear our nation going hungry or believe farmland will go unplanted? The reason we chose to send them the checks is because we choose to privilege those who farm and own land.

Don't get me wrong I am not blaming the farmers and landowners being showered with support for cashing the checks. Any of us would do the same if we were among the chosen. If we have learned any political lesson in Iowa it is "when the getting is good – get all you can." The truth is most of the funds going to the farm sector won't stay there long anyway. It will go to pay for the high-priced seeds and chemicals the Bayer's and Syngenta's sell – and to pay for the big green machinery you see in the fields.

A good deal of it will pass through farmers into the hands of the landowners – the landlords who control over one-half of the farmland in the state. If you want to know why cash rents don't decline even in the face of declining crop prices or farm incomes, it is because we prop up the land market with farm supports. The truth is we launder money through farmers to support a whole array of related agricultural businesses. It works well for them because they benefit but do not have to do the political heavy lifting to get the funds – farmers do that for them.

What is the point, why pick a fight and label this as white privilege? The reason is because we as a nation will never to be able to understand or address issues at the heart of racial injustice and wealth inequality if we don't appreciate how the deck is stacked. Issues like claims of reparations for slavery or the roots of black wealth inequality are found in our reversal of Reconstruction. By abandoning the promise of "40 acres and a mule" we resigned millions of former slaves to generations of slave-like conditions as sharecroppers on Southern plantations. How different would life be today is they had been allowed to take their place as land owning and independent farmers – like so many of our ancestors. As Iowan's we are privileged in many ways, with our land, people, and history, but we must be willing to show humility in recognizing how the privileges came to be.

LAND, LEGACY AND LOSS

As the economic toll of the COVID-19 pandemic became more apparent, for some in agriculture, especially hog producers, the potential of "losing" the farm was real. In Levon Helms' song the *Growing Trade* the farmer sings, "This land is my legacy, it's all I've ever known." The song reminds me of the incredibly powerful connection people can have with their land, especially farmers whose homes and livelihoods merge in one place. Being the one to "lose" the farm is the most shameful sin possible in the liturgy of agriculture. Doing anything necessary to "hold on" to the farm is its flip side, even if it means joining "the growing trade" as Helms sings. This link is among the powerful ingredients fueling many farmer suicides. The strong connection farmers have to their land is reflected by the fierce resistance they have to its potential interference by others.

"Involuntarily" losing the farm can come about in many ways:

> If land is taken by the government through eminent domain, it always leaves a bitter scar even if just compensation is paid and the public need or benefit is clear. The compensation is never enough and any "replacement" land never has the same emotional connections.

> If land is lost through economic forces such as the 1980s farm crisis, then others bear responsibility: the bankers who should have known better than push the loans, the market manipulators, the government, or someone else. There are always others to point to rather than accept responsibility for our own decisions. It is easier when many people are in the same situation, as this makes it a collective problem, not a question of individual culpability.

If the farm is lost due to COVID, this will be the cause: an unprecedented, unforeseen, and unavoidable event, bigger than any of us. It may not make the loss less painful but it will provide an excuse and something to blame. Focus then can shift to why politicians didn't do more to help you hold on?

If you lose the land through the actions of family members, to siblings in a partition fight or will dispute, or heir's property to a cousin who recorded a deed transfer, there is another to blame in a legal system stacked against you.

In all these cases, the loss of land is still real, leaving a permanent mark and memory. They contrast to deciding to sell, "losing" the farm voluntarily. Putting a conservation easement on the land through a USDA program, like restoring a wetland under the Wetland Reserve Program (WRP), is voluntary. These actions are often done with alternatives in mind, such as a section 1031 "like kind exchange," a tax provision allowing owners to trade land for other land better suited to their needs, but avoid paying taxes on gains in the transactions. In many cases, deciding to sell may mean cashing in on some high valued land to actually retire, to stop being land rich and cash poor for once, and to see how the other version works.

My decision to sell our farm on an installment land contract entered with neighbor Chris was an intentional and planned action. In these cases, the emotional cost of "losing" the farm is absolved by the loss being a voluntary decision made of free will, not due to legal or economic coercion. This is why a "sale" to pay the nursing home bills, such as we were forced to do with the Back Forty as Dad lay dying, was less satisfying, somewhere between voluntary and involuntary. The solace was we "at least had some land to sell." Weighed against it was the fear "how much longer can this go on" and what will happen when there is no more land left to sell? Given the backdrop of emotion and connection to the land, it is easy to understand why landowners resist government regulations or actions they believe will restrain their ability to use and enjoy the land, or dispose of it when necessary.

The Back Forty on "Losing" the Farm

To a tract of land, who owns me is somewhat irrelevant. Different owners may treat me with different levels of care and respect, some may expect more or give back less. In many ways, the story and the expectations are always the same, "produce for me" is the mantra and so we do. Another facet of the owners' attitudes is how set they are on maintaining control. To them the idea of "losing" the farm is a cardinal sin, perhaps the most ignominious fate to befall a landowner. To us it really isn't such a big deal. The main thing that happens is the name on a piece of paper in the County Recorder's office is changed and the County Auditor will send the property tax bill to a different address. The boots that walk on us, assuming we ever feel the step of a human rather than the tread of a tractor tire, might change too. But we don't, we are still here and will be next year, next decade, next generation and even next century. You could say forever or what you like to refer to as perpetuity. The boy who grew up to become a law professor responded to student questions about the "rule against perpetuities" – an arcane legal rule designed to prevent legal entanglements of land longer than the life of the owners' last child – with a handy answer about what is perpetuity. In his view "perpetuity is the day after I am dead" because then he wouldn't be around to care or know what happens to the land.

Wow that is a lesson lost on most landowners! It seems in addition to using us, one of their favorite activities is thinking up ways to extend control into the future, long after they are dead, to guide the actions of their heirs. Remember how Mankin tried to control the Salem Church land. Lawyers refer to this as "dead hand control." The favorite theme in a lifetime of dinner table admonitions by parents to farm kids is "you must never sell the farm." That explains why many parents try to include legal devices to the effect "you must never sell this land." You know the boy had it right, at least in my view. Once you are dead what is the big deal about needing to control my fate and who owns me? Life is for the living and the land should be too.

When I hear people talk about "losing the farm" I want to shout "not to worry, I am not lost, I always know exactly where I am." Perhaps what they really mean in worrying about "losing the farm" is more about missing out on the opportunity to use, control and enjoy me, certainly the right to farm (or exploit) me to make a living. In this vein, I am really just one more capital tool or asset similar to their pigs and tractors. They never seem to get upset about "losing" them! If they were really worried about "losing" me I wonder why many of them don't show any concern for how I am actually being lost? The top soil washing off my hillsides, the soil fertility I feel being sapped away each year, the soil health, my tilth and my ability to hold and absorb a good rain when it comes rather than feel it quickly pour over and off me, these are the real assets contributing to my value and making me healthy. Someday people may wise up and realize these are what is being "lost" while they are busy farming me hard to hold on!

AGRICULTURE'S FRAGILITY

Driving to Storm Lake was like passing through an endless sea of green. Fields of corn and soybeans, webbed with a network of fence lines, county roads, and every now and then a stream or river. The bounty and potential of the land were almost overwhelming, enhanced by the ridge top vistas of more green stretching miles in every direction. As a lifelong Iowan and son of the soil I couldn't help feel a swell of pride and history in the view. It seemed to represent the perfect ground to grow a spirit of optimism and draw a life of fulfillment, laden with hope for a big crop and better times ahead. To the knowing observer however, the green fields masked a range of tensions and worries, sharpened by a growing drought threatening the apparent bounty. Other fears though go deeper, to the very psyche and psychology of farming in modern times.

All the apparent prosperity and strength passing by my window, hid an equal mixture of fear and anger, a fragility in farming, a product of our times and a source of growing tensions clouding our future. My August 2020 trip to Storm Lake was ostensibly to see an example of the tensions and conflict play out in real time. My plan was to attend the quarterly meeting of the North Raccoon River Watershed Coalition, made up of representatives from the dozens of towns, counties, and soil and water conservation districts in the nine-county watershed. Years before they had entered a 28E agreement creating an intergovernmental body to develop plans for improving the water quality in the watershed, and to get some of the millions in a HUD flood grant the state received. The meeting agenda featured a new controversy, after four years of planning, county supervisors in the seven northern "farm" counties had recently passed resolutions to rewrite the watershed map to exclude Polk and Dallas counties, the two more urban counties at the south end of the watershed. Triggering this unexpected twist was the scheduled vote to finalize the watershed improvement plan and establish goals for the nutrient reductions to be achieved. The fight was allegedly over whether the goal should be set at 41%, as provided for in the Iowa Nutrient Reduction Strategy, or the higher goal of 48%, established by EPA under the total maximum daily load (TMDL) plan created by the state to move the Raccoon River off the Clean Water Act "impaired waters list." In reality, the fight was more fundamental. No one in attendance, whether state or local officials or city environmentalists had any faith either goal will ever be reached, a fact several speakers acknowledged. The real fight was over the counties' fear someone, at some future time, might actually expect improved water quality and use the established reduction goal to implement regulations to make it happen. As highly unlikely as that is to happen, the political fears of the supervisors were real. However, by the day of the meeting, the boards of supervisors in three of the concerned counties had rescinded the resolutions to alter the watershed, due to public criticism. The effect was the watershed will stay intact and the final vote to adopt the resiliency plan with the 48% goal passed 14-11. Even with the vote, the issue of who should control the watershed will no doubt surface again.

Making the 140-mile drive to attend was well worth it because it opened the window on a larger issue surging through Midwest agriculture. The fear expressed by the farming county officials representing farming constituents wasn't just about water quality and possible regulations. Behind their fear is a larger reality, farmers are trapped in a system leaving them essentially powerless to market forces and low prices, locked in unequal relations with the businesses who thrive on their trade. The other side of the vise pressing in is a consuming public increasingly willing to question the safety of what farmers produce and even the morality of their farming practices. The feeling they have lost the trust of society, feeds a "victim" mentality letting farmers assume no one appreciates them. Farm groups and commodity organizations help fuel this "us against the world" view, as reflected in how the "critics" of agriculture, like Bill Stowe, are portrayed. The "no one loves us" mentality is supported explicitly with constant reminders of how important farmers are to society, such as the ANF "American Needs Farmers" stickers worn on University of Iowa football helmets and seen on pickup bumpers across the state.

The resulting stew of grievance and self-pity often finds expression in anger and resentment, not unlike that played out in Storm Lake. Anger at the environmentalists and city folk who expect clean water, and at those who expect an odor free countryside but who do not want to foot the bill for these "benefits." Resentment is leveled against the experts and officials who think they know the answers and appear happy to impose new costs and restrictions on farmers. The cumulative effect creates a brittle wariness and fragility in the farming community, in sharp contrast to the self-image of resilience and strength most farmers believe they embody. This is the image marketers for the seed and chemical companies promote in slick TV ads extolling the strength of farmers. Fear and fragility drive the reactionary, anti-regulatory mind set so common with farm groups, expressed in actions like trying to redraw the map of a watershed as if doing so will make water quality issues go away. The defensive crouch agriculture quickly takes against any criticism is easily and often seen by others as anti-public and a threat to important social goals. The stance is all the more ironic given how the farm sector expects and receives billions of dollars in annual public subsidies with few questions asked about how the money is used or what the public receives in return.

The anger, fear, and fragility found in much of conventional agriculture have other more corrosive effects. These emotions take a good deal of the fun and joy out of farming. This is a shame because farming at its essence is all about joy. Being able to harness sun, rain, and seeds to create new wealth; to work with livestock to bring forth new generations of animals; to work the land to feed the nation and support the family; and working to sustain our future can be and has made farming one of the most fulfilling careers possible. These rewards are what draw thousands to dream of becoming farmers and what fuels the hope of farm families to pass their land on to the next generation. As fear and anger grow in farm country it threatens to erode not just the experience of those who farm but the reality of these hopes and dreams. The fears are reflected in the language and terms commonly used in agriculture, the euphemisms employed to cover the darker aspects of farming – such as referring to slaughter houses as meat harvesting facilities or calling pesticides "crop protection products." A good rule of thumb is when you feel the need to invent new words to hide your reality from the public, and yourself, you have a problem. When I was a boy we were all farmers. The label of choice today is "production agriculture," a dog whistle used to distinguish those not worthy of being called farmers - the small farmers, market gardeners and organic growers – from the larger farmers who really matter.

Underpinning the helplessness flowing under the surface in much of agriculture is the inherent vulnerability to economics and weather.

If you are constantly subject to the vagaries of the weather, which without warning can change a clear blue sky to a tornado, it makes you hyper-vigilant about the attacks you can control. Few of these forces are in a farmer's control, making criticisms or threatened regulations even more galling, but at least those can be confronted. This vulnerability feeds the feeling "no one appreciates the risks we take." This explains why the farm community does not perceive the billions in public dollars spent to subsidize "crop insurance" as a form of welfare. Instead farmers see the programs as an entitlement and a small public compensation for the risks and abuse they take. There is a certain truth in this feeling, farming is different than most other jobs for the risks and vulnerability to weather and nature it involves. The irony is how most people in farming or at least those who claim to speak for them, don't want to believe human activity contributes to a changing climate and the increasing variability of the storms and weather they experience.

In many ways, this situation is a tragic tale feeding its own mythology. It makes the question of how to break the cycle an important one for the mental health of farmers, for the fertility and sustainability of the countryside, and for the long-term health of society. The great news is the answers for how to break the cycle and the vehicle for doing so is right below our feet. It is in the land and the delicious food it can produce. That is a story we will turn to, but first we need to consider how protecting water quality influences how we treat the land and the quality of the food we grow.

Chapter Six – Who's Water, Our Water

A blog post by a University water engineer in a somewhat obscure research program doesn't often generate front-page headlines and ignite a statewide debate, but in May 2020 Chris Jones from the University of Iowa hydro-science lab managed to do so. The title of the post seemed innocent "Iowa's Real Population" but the content was explosive. Jones, one of Iowa's most widely respected water scientists has had what you might call an interesting and varied career path. He worked for years at the Iowa Soybean Association and then at the Des Moines Waterworks before joining the University of Iowa and Dr. Larry Weber's highly regarded program examining flooding and water quality. Jones is known for applying a rigorous scientific approach, driven by historical data, to Iowa's water issues – and for his willingness to speak truth to power. The blog in question was classic Jones, examining how rapid growth in Iowa's livestock population and the vast quantities of feces and urine produced, are impacting water quality in Iowa's streams and rivers. Manure is disposed of by spreading it on the land untreated, unlike the sewage treatment plants required for handling human wastes. Jones looked at the number of cattle, hogs, and chickens raised in Iowa, about 110 million head, and calculated the quantity of manure they produce annually.

The crowning step in his analysis was converting the quantities of livestock manure to the human populations required to yield the same amounts. His conclusion? Iowa with a population of 3.2 million people plus the 110 million farm animals has a manure population equivalence of 168 million people, about the same population density as Bangladesh. The front-page headline in the *Des Moines Register* captured the point, "UI research shows state ranks No. 1 in 'No. 2.'" That type of headline will get readers' attention! To help people visualize what all the manure means, Jones took his calculations one step farther and produced a map of the state's major watersheds, labeling them by the countries or cities containing similar human populations. The North Raccoon River Watershed, where Sunstead is located and the subject of the Storm Lake meeting, has a population equivalence of Tokyo. Jones' follow-on post titled "50 Shades of Brown," compares Iowa's human and livestock waste production to the quantities produced in other states. You can imagine the results, Iowa ranked No. 1 with an effective population density of 2,979 people per square mile. Adding 52 million chickens to Delaware's human population ranked it second with 2,391 people per square mile. Wisconsin, a farm state known more for dairy cows than people ranked third at 1,554 people per square mile. Illinois only came in at 18th at 930 people per square mile, edged out by California at 15th with 1,090.

You can imagine the mixed reactions to Jones' blogs, cheers from those who have fought for years protecting Iowa's water, and outcries from the agricultural groups who found the news discomforting and the comparisons unfair. One can assume the phone lines of university leaders in Iowa City and at Iowa State in Ames lit up. Predictably, shrill efforts to discredit Jones were led by the shills from the Iowa Farm Bureau who rushed to assure Iowans there is nothing to fear from all the poop. They pointed to one Iowa State researcher's conclusion the state can use twice as much livestock poop to feed our corn crop, without risks to water quality or health. Of course, this fallacious "conclusion" assumes the manure is evenly spread around the state's twenty-four million acres of farmland to fertilize crops with the required amount of nutrients applied at appropriate times. If only these assumptions were true! The truth is Iowa livestock facilities are heavily concentrated and produce more manure than can be readily used on nearby lands. Iowa even allows spreading manure on frozen ground, increasing the likelihood of spring run-off. Some farmers use manure as a crop nutrient and account for it by buying less fertilizer. For most operations though, livestock manure is treated as a waste to get rid of, rather than a valuable asset. How do we know this, from research done by none other than Chris Jones! He studied Iowa counties with the greatest livestock populations, meaning the most manure, and examined records for commercial fertilizers purchased in the counties. If farmers use manure as fertilizer and take credit for the nutrients the assumption is they reduce the amount of purchased fertilizer accordingly. What Jones found was commercial fertilizers purchases in high livestock counties were similar to those counties with low livestock populations, meaning nutrients in manure being spread on land also being fertilized are a prime source of the excess nutrients polluting the state's rivers and streams.

There you have it in a nutshell, a state dominated by agriculture with a worsening water quality crisis but a farm sector and political establishment happy to wish the problems away. The response to anyone raising concerns, are platitudes and claims agriculture is doing all it can to protect the water, it just needs more time. Bill Stowe, the now deceased head of the Des Moines Waterworks got fed up hearing the excuses and concluded agriculture would never get serious about dealing with water quality unless someone and something brought the issue to a head. That was why he encouraged his board to bring a lawsuit against drainage districts in three counties upstream on the Raccoon River, as discussed below.

It didn't have to turn out this way. In the late 1980s the state had a window in time, a political moment, to develop a more responsive and effective policy to limit water pollution and put agriculture and farmland use on a more solid, sustainable path. The opportunity came in large part from the election of several modern-day environmentalists to the Iowa House of Representatives. Most notable was Paul Johnson, a soft-spoken dairy farmer and tree grower from near Decorah on the Upper Iowa River, in the drift-less region of Northeast Iowa, and an acolyte of Aldo Leopold. His key partner was David Osterberg, a quirky college professor at Cornell College in Mt. Vernon, best known for living in a converted chicken coop. It is fair to say they were non-traditional lawmakers but the duo came to play a central role in leading the Democrat controlled legislature to enact laws to protect the state's soil and water. Most significant was the 1987 Groundwater Protection Act, which among other things mandated closing the over 1,100 surface drainage wells used in the flatlands of northern Iowa to "drain" surface water directly into underground aquifers as if they were bathtubs. The law created the Leopold Center for Sustainable Agriculture at Iowa State, discussed in Chapter Three, funding the research with a small tax on nitrogen fertilizer. The tax was a bitter pill resented for decades by agribusinesses, until finally in 2018 a compliant legislature and University went along with industry efforts to kill the Leopold Center, but that is getting ahead of the story.

The loss of power felt by the agriculture community was made more bitter when Prof. Osterberg became chair of the powerful House Agriculture Committee. From this position he got House passage of progressive laws like a 1989 act requiring the Attorney General to develop model livestock contracts for producers to use in comparing terms offered by the swine integrators just beginning their take-over of production in Iowa. Only a last-minute intervention by the Iowa Pork Producers Association prevented the Iowa Senate from enacting the law. Defeat of the legislation meant Iowa lost its chance to protect independent hog producers, as well as neighbors, land, and water. The transformation of Iowa's swine industry into today's vertically integrated, contract system as detailed in the previous chapter, was free to proceed unhindered.

This wasn't the only legislative protection for the land the state managed to avoid. Another innovation the pair helped pass in 1989 was a law to create an independent "environmental advocate" given broad powers to initiate legal proceedings involving Iowa's environment. In many ways, the law answered Chief Justice Reynoldson's question, "who will speak for the land?" Unfortunately, but not surprising, Iowa's Republican Governor Terry Branstad vetoed the law, claiming existing environmental agencies could perform the functions. Assuming lawsuits and litigation, what he called a cops-and-robbers approach, would protect the environment was unnecessary. As the intervening thirty years proved, neither assumption was true. Iowa's environmental agencies and boards show a disturbing unwillingness to control water pollution, especially involving agriculture, the source of over 90% of nutrients and silt polluting the water. Budget cuts, staff reductions, and making the employees who work in natural resource protection "at-will" employees subject to firing for any reason, combine to render the state's environmental protectors largely impotent and unwilling or afraid to act. Those who believe regulations and law should play no role in protecting the environment or restraining farming practices welcome this outcome.

Iowa's Water Quality Battles
Capture the National Debate

Water quality is intimately connected to how we care for the land. Efforts to protect water have been underway for generations, and the issue plays a critical political role in national and local debates. At the national level water quality is front and center in discussions about the health of the Chesapeake Bay, about addressing the Hypoxia zone of depleted oxygen in the Gulf, and about the future of Lake Erie. Water pollution can come from many sources, yet in these examples the major contributor is agriculture, especially the manure and nutrients running off fields when it rains. In no state has the fight over efforts to protect water quality from the effects of farming been more protracted and bitterly fought than in my home of Iowa. The debate here captures the larger political and legal issues at work in other regions and nationally. That is why this chapter examines the Iowa water quality story to see what lessons can be learned about how water issues relate to the land. More selfishly, my involvement in the debate over the last twenty years can hopefully yield insights and experiences illustrating how the issues may evolve.

Two major actions help frame understanding Iowa's water quality issues. First is the 2013 adoption of the Iowa Nutrient Reduction Strategy or NRS for short. The second is the 2015 headline-grabbing lawsuit the Des Moines Waterworks filed against trustees of several drainage districts in three upstream counties in the Raccoon River watershed. The goal of the NRS is to develop a science-based strategy for how Iowa can eventually reduce the huge quantities of nutrients carried into the Mississippi River and on to the Gulf. Iowa is estimated to contribute as much as 40% to the Hypoxia Zone. The goal of the waterworks suit was to find a legal mechanism to hold upstream users accountable for polluting the river it uses to provide drinking water for 500,000 residents in the Des Moines area. At first, the two goals might appear to coincide making collaborative solutions possible. As politics and time revealed, a cooperative solution was the last thing most groups representing agricultural interests had in mind. Time also shows both efforts have failed, the waterworks litigation by judicial edict, and the NRS, failing for now from a lack of leadership, funding, and perhaps even good faith, by Iowa's agricultural and political leaders.

Understanding the Des Moines Waterworks litigation

In March 2015 Des Moines Waterworks filed a federal Clean Water Act lawsuit against several agricultural drainage districts in three upstream counties on the Raccoon River. The citizen suit alleged the districts built and maintain systems of drainage ditches to artificially collect, convey, and discharge polluted groundwater into Iowa's rivers and streams. The argument was this made the districts point sources under the CWA in need of EPA permits to operate, no different than a municipal sewage treatment plant or factory. Then and now, EPA and the state do not treat drainage districts as point sources, instead they are considered exempt nonpoint sources carrying stormwater from farm fields. The lawsuit alleged the contaminated water flowing in the ditches is primarily ground water coming in from tile outlets in farm fields not surface runoff. The distinction is important because the exemption for nonpoint sources includes "stormwater discharges," meaning the case potentially hinged on whether the court would treat the water flowing from tile outlets as groundwater or stormwater. When Congress wrote the CWA it surprisingly did not define stormwater discharge and over fifty years the federal courts have never addressed the issue the case raised. The importance of the groundwater-surface runoff distinction made the evidence of how the water was contaminated and when the water quality was measured, critical issues.

The lawsuit was not directed at farmers or landowners, instead it argued the drainage district trustees were responsible under Iowa law for the ditches. The suit illuminated the unusual relation between Iowa's drainage districts and county governments. Under Iowa law, districts can choose to be managed by a private board of trustees or by the county supervisors serving as trustees, as had the districts being sued. The choice of drainage districts the waterworks sued was strategic. They were predominantly agricultural and the waterworks had obtained verified measurements of significant nitrate water pollution in the ditches, utilizing US Geological Survey test sites. Evidence showed after big rains pollution in the ditches actually decreased as surface run-off diluted the water, but several days later after heavy rains the water flow coming in from tiles lines increased and nitrate levels spiked making water in the ditches more polluted.

As you can imagine the lawsuit was a thunderclap, unleashing a deluge of criticism from politicians and farm groups who argued Des

Moines was declaring war on rural Iowa. At some point a book will be written about the litigation but here are the key points. The agricultural community, led by the Farm Bureau, commodity groups, and major agribusinesses, funded a multi-million legal defense for the districts. The central goal of the defense was to admit no liability or responsibility for the districts or for farmers, the "don't pee a drop" defense. The earliest funding attempts raised significant legal and ethical issues, shenanigans Art Cullen detailed in editorials in his Storm Lake newspaper. They resulted in changing how the defense was funded and in Cullen winning a Pulitzer prize for his writing. You can read about all this in his book, *Storm Lake: A Chronicle of Change, Resilience, and Hope from a Heartland Newspaper*, (Viking 2018).

In court the case took several unexpected turns. Judge Mark Bennett, a respected and brilliant jurist, determined before he could consider the case, state law issues on liability for drainage districts needed to be answered, so he certified several questions to the Iowa Supreme Court. The key issue was even if the drainage districts were determined to be point sources, could they legally act to address water quality? The districts argued Iowa law restricts their authority to only creating drainage systems. In January 2018 the Iowa Supreme Court agreed, ruling drainage districts are powerless to address water quality, only legislative action could grant this power. On receiving this answer, the new federal judge hearing the case dismissed the suit, ruling there was no remedy the court could grant against the districts. By then the waterworks board had spent over $1 million waging the lawsuit, and taken a torrent of political criticism including legislation introduced to eliminate it. The board decided against further appeal. The result is under Iowa law drainage districts are free of any responsibility for water quality, and the Clean Water Act issues raised in the suit remain unanswered. The agriculture community harbors bitter resentment over the episode, as seen in the Storm Lake effort to rewrite the watershed map. On the brighter side, if one exists, the litigation changed the trajectory of the water quality debate in Iowa, generating political and public pressure to fund improved water quality, a fight still underway.

UNDERSTANDING THE IOWA NUTRIENT REDUCTION STRATEGY

The NRS is a science-based report for how the state can meet the goal of a 45% reduction in nutrients, as required under an agreement with the EPA. The goal relates to EPA's efforts to address nutrient losses into the Mississippi River impacting the Gulf hypoxia zone. The involvement of scientists, many from Iowa State University, gave the NRS a solid footing in understanding water movement and how potential changes in farming practices can reduce nutrient losses. The actual drafting of the NRS report though happened behind closed doors, accompanied by political intrigue. The water quality staff of the DNR was not consulted and the Iowa Farm Bureau wielded undue influence on the final report. Developing the Nutrient Reduction Strategy was part of the farming community's efforts to deflect responsibility and delay any reckoning for as long as possible. One reason the agriculture community responded so viciously to Bill Stowe and the Des Moines Water litigation was because the lawsuit threatened agriculture's hope to use the NRS for decades as a shield from public or official scrutiny.

The NRS has several problems, most telling is the absence of any description of how Iowans will benefit if the water quality improvement objectives are met. It is not clear meeting the 45% reduction goal for the Mississippi will have any identifiable impact on the water quality Iowans experience if they try to use local streams and rivers. EPA's goal is not a clean water plan for Iowa. Rather than focus on "nutrient reduction," a goal with little meaning for most Iowans, state efforts should focus on identifying how improved water quality will benefit Iowans and communities through access to cleaner and safer waters.

One surprising gap in Iowa law on water quality is the lack of any provision establishing a responsibility on the part of citizens, farmers, or landowners to not pollute or degrade the surface waters of the state. This contrasts to the duty in Iowa Code §455E.5(4) on groundwater protection: "all persons in the state have the duty to conduct their activities so as to prevent the release of contaminants into groundwater." The lack of a parallel duty for surface water, reaffirms how the goals and practices identified in the NRS are optional for farmers and landowners.

One consistent theme in the NRS and in statements by public officials is the view there is no role for regulations in protecting water quality. The state's efforts rely entirely on voluntary adoption, an approach actually codified in the law. The "no role for regulation" mantra is essentially an anti-government ideological stance that ignores the reality of how law works in society. This approach may be understandable politically, but it is illogical from a public policy perspective and will inevitably prove unworkable. Regulations are how we implement legislative and societal goals. Whether the issue is speed limits in school zones, caps on alcohol consumption and driving, or promoting child safety such as requiring kid seats in cars, key social objectives are promoted through uniform regulatory requirements. We do not make these programs voluntary and hope citizens will comply. The importance of a social goal is reflected in the types of regulations used to achieve it. While voluntary action is hoped for and desired, failing to establish expected conduct on the part of citizens through publicly developed regulations mean the objectives will not be reached. A lack of regulations essentially signals the issue is a low priority, and places those who chose to act at an economic disadvantage to those who do not. Current political realities may mean implementing regulations to protect Iowa's water quality is not possible now, but growing frustration with lack of progress on water quality and the limited voluntary actions make adoption of regulations inevitable. Excellent examples from neighboring states, Minnesota's buffer law and Ohio's requirement farmers adopt nutrient management plans, show how effective and relatively unobtrusive, wisely chosen regulatory approaches can be.

A key portion of the NRS was development of a series of scenarios detailing the changes in farming practices required to reach the water quality improvement goals. The scenarios included projected "costs" of the practices to identify the potential price tag for implementing the plans. As might be expected the potential "costs" in annual expenditures and long-term costs for most scenarios were in the billions of dollars. The key value of the scenarios was to validate or "sanctify" the NRS as meeting the required goals of the EPA. A logical expectation for the next step would have been to turn the scenarios into plans for action, with budgets developed for how the practices will be funded. This has never happened, in large part because the magnitude of proposed changes on the land are so unrealistic. For example, the requirements from Scenario #1 include:

> - Maximum Return to Nitrogen Rate (of fertilizer application) applied to all corn and soybean crop acres, [using fertilizer at rates recommended by University agronomists, rates 30 lbs. lower than commonly used],
>
> - 60% of crop acres planted in cover crops, estimated at 12.5 million acres,
>
> - 27% of all crop land treated with wetlands, estimated at 7.7 million acres,
>
> - 60% of all drained land treated with bioreactors, estimated to require over 140,000 bioreactors, while the state currently has around 60.

Given the magnitude of what was being proposed it is no surprise the scenarios used to validate the NRS have largely disappeared from discussions. However, they are important in identifying the changes in farming practices and the number of acres where actions, such as installing wetlands, will be required. These projected actions will require significant changes in actual cropping and land management practices across vast amounts of Iowa's farmland. This is why the scenarios are essentially an exercise in magical thinking. Believing we can change how 60% of all the land cropped in Iowa will experience major changes in management, voluntarily, defies reality. It is no surprise in recent years any discussion of such large-scale changes in farming disappeared from the discussions. In effect, the scenarios vanished once they served the purpose of getting the NRS "approved" as the basis for Iowa's water quality policy. This step became official in 2018 when the Iowa General Assembly codified the NRS as Iowa's water quality policy, found at Iowa Code §455B.171. Other political failings of the NRS include the failure to identify timelines to achieve the goals, the lack of support for water quality monitoring, and no strategy for how it will actually be implemented. The actual "strategic" decisions for who will act, who will pay, and how it will be administered are left for future action. Iowa is now eight years into implementing the NRS and has little to show other than a modest increase in the use of cover crops. In fact, recent studies show the amounts of nitrates being exported in Iowa's rivers has actually continued to increase, fuel for critics who believe what began in good faith as a scientific exercise has devolved into a political effort to delay action.

WHO'S WATER? OUR WATER

The Iowa agricultural community has spent the last two decades downplaying and rejecting any role it may play in Iowa's deteriorating water quality. From the "deny, deflect, delay, and deceive" approach of the Iowa Farm Bureau Federation, to the agricultural groups and businesses funding the legal costs for the drainage districts in Des Moines Waterworks case, the themes are consistent: we aren't to blame, others are responsible, its goose poop and golf courses, we are doing all we can, and it really isn't a serious issue anyway. These tunes are all in the songbook to play as circumstances or threats of being forced to accept responsibility require.

One central goal is to control the debate and shape what the public knows and thinks about water quality. In Terry Tempest Williams book *Erosion*, one of her many astute observations concerns the power of telling the story. She explains how those threatened strive to control the story and keep it fragmented so threats are easier to confront. You clearly see this in the "story" agriculture tells about water quality and soil conservation, centered on the claim farmers are doing all they can and progress is being made. The effort in Iowa is to make sure the public never sees the whole interconnected nature of the story, only pieces more easily rationalized or explained away. The slick propaganda videos produced by Farm Bureau for its "Iowa Minute" TV commercials are perfect examples. Each appears to address a legitimate issue but the treatment always comes wrapped in a web of half-truths and misdirection, with the same ending - don't blame farmers.

What really is our Iowa story when it comes to water quality and soil conservation? As I see it, our attitudes toward the land and water are a blend of tensions and contradictions. Tensions include people who say they love the land and water and "are doing all they can" to protect them, contrasted to the reality of soil losses and declining water quality. The voting public says it wants more public land and cleaner water, but allows a vocal minority in the agricultural community and General Assembly to resist raising the sales tax to fund cleaner water or expand public land access. We understand the concept of watersheds and believe ourselves to be people who will do anything to help our neighbors. Perhaps, but most landowners can't draw a map of the watershed their land is in or tell you where the water goes after leaving their farm. We believe ourselves to have high moral standards but have no problem embracing the moral hazard of sending silt, manure, and extra nutrients flowing off the land and out of tile drains, downstream to damage our neighbors.

One way the agricultural community tries to control or spin the issue of water quality is providing new names or labels to describe it. A few years ago, a concerted effort was made to organize public responses around the theme "One Water." This innocent sounding idea, highlighting the hydrological connection of all water, was to help everyone see how we all have a role and responsibility for water quality. No doubt some who promoted the idea did so in good faith. But if you retain a healthy vein of skepticism mixed with a dash of cynicism as I do, it is easy see the label as a deceptive attempt to mask the truth and shift attention from those responsible for the vast majority of water pollution, farmers and agricultural businesses. We all have an interest in the water flowing in the rivers but we certainly don't share equally in being responsible for how it gets polluted. Agriculture is the main driver of degraded water and this fact shouldn't be glossed over to make us feel good about our limited progress or to make the public feel it is letting the home team down by expecting more be done.

Serving on the environmental committee for the Central Iowa Water Trails, I encountered a new variant on using labels to confuse the public about what they should expect from our water. The water trails project is a grand proposal for a $115 million public-private initiative to create a recreational system for the rivers and streams flowing through greater Des Moines. Building it will take innovation and imagination, and if it is successful it will mark a new era in Iowans being able to connect with the rivers. One issue lurks in the background of the efforts, a bit of a chicken and egg question. Water quality in portions of the watershed at times of the year is so degraded the wisdom of increasing human contact with river water can raise public health concerns. A key question is what to do first, work to clean up the rivers or spend millions creating opportunities for people to use them? One political calculus is if more people use the rivers and experience degraded water quality they will support more aggressive and effective actions to clean them up. However, a key challenge to this is the investments to "use" the rivers are happening at the lower end of the watershed in the more heavily populated metro area around Des Moines. Political and economic tensions will result because most of the pollution comes from the millions of acres of farmland upstream, including the drainage districts sued by the waterworks. So, the fight will be similar to the one played out in Storm Lake but on a bigger scale.

In preparing for increased public use of the rivers, the water trail committee reviewed drafts of proposed Frequently Asked Questions or FAQ's to use for public education and advocacy. One question in a preliminary draft illustrated the agriculture community's success in shaping public thinking about what to expect from Iowa's rivers. The question was "why are Iowa's rivers brown?" and the proposed answer explained this is the normal historic condition of the rivers and does not pose a public health threat. Not surprisingly, the phrasing drew push back from scientists and environmentalists on the committee. The Missouri River is historically brown due to erosion from the hills in the northern great plains, but Iowa's rivers and streams were never "historically" brown and do not flow that way all year. The "brown" we see is soil eroding from farm fields and stream banks. There is nothing natural about it unless you accept the extensive soil erosion encouraged in recent decades, by plowing fragile lands and farming up to the riverbanks. Adding to the brown water are the drainage tile being installed, speeding more water into streams, increasing their velocity to tear soil from stream banks and scour sediment from streambeds. The brown comes from modern farming, it is not a natural feature of Iowa's waters. Subsequent versions of the FAQ amended the answers for why Iowa's rivers are brown some times.

The examples demonstrate the need to ask a more fundamental

question about Iowa's rivers and streams, whose water is it? Legally the water belongs to the public, as declared by the Iowa legislature in the 1965 law making all the water in the state "public waters" regardless of the source. This is why the thirty-part educational video series my Center produced in 2018, was titled "Our Water Our Land." The truth is, it is our water. It is not brown water or one water, or someone else's water to pollute, it is our water. Iowa citizens have the right to expect more from those who treat the water as their own and from those responsible for protecting it, our political leaders and agency personnel. This legal reality creates a responsibility on the part of all citizens, and a public trust duty for public officials.

Iowa courts recently had an opportunity to identify exactly what the public trust doctrine requires of state officials. In 2019 two citizen groups sued several state officials arguing the state is violating the public trust doctrine by not acting to prevent pollution in the Raccoon River from farm sources. The suit alleged the 2018 legislative act adopting the "all voluntary" approach of the NRS is unconstitutional because it allows private actors to pollute the river. By supporting this approach state officials have abandoned their duty to protect the river for other users. The public trust doctrine is not well understood or often utilized, but it is a powerful idea and predates creation of the state. It is the historic underpinning of the public right to use rivers, for example by preventing private dams and navigation obstructions. The district court hearing the case rejected the state's motion to dismiss and ordered the case to proceed. The state appealed to the Iowa Supreme Court arguing the case involves a "legislative question" making it inappropriate for the courts to decide what the state needs to do to protect the river. I joined with several other law school colleagues to submit an amicus brief arguing it was important the courts retain jurisdiction over the matter because of the significance of the public trust claims. Ironically, signing the brief to submit to the court was the first time in almost forty years I had actually used my license to practice law. The Iowa Supreme Court heard arguments on the motion to dismiss in December 2020. Unfortunately in June 2021, the court issued a 4-3 decision, ruling the public trust did not apply. In a somewhat shocking conclusion the majority stated it was not the role of the court to hold the state accountable to the public. While three Justices filed dissenting opinions, for now the public trust doctrine remains unrealized.

Will Iowa's Water Ever Get Better – or Are We Fooling Ourselves?

A recent conversation with a person responsible for providing safe drinking water to a large number of Iowans was sobering. He noted matter-of-factly, there is no reason to believe water quality in Iowa's rivers and lakes will improve appreciably in the near future. As a result, public water systems relying on surface water sources like his, face the reality of finding other supplies. The comment made me wonder *are* there any reasons to believe water quality in Iowa or the nation will improve given current economics and politics? The simple answer is no. There is no reason to assume fewer acres of corn and beans will be planted or less fertilizer and pesticides will be used. There is no reason to believe fewer head of livestock or poultry will be raised, or less manure applied, in fact, livestock numbers are more likely to increase. There is no reason landowners will stop installing more drainage tile or any drainage districts will close. There is little reason to believe farmers will stop planting next to stream banks or install enough conservation practices, like buffer strips, to make a difference. There is every reason to believe more anhydrous ammonia will be applied each fall and manure will be spread whenever necessary, even on frozen ground. It is foolish to assume the weather will get less volatile or heavy rainfalls less common, instead the potential is for more flooding and larger rain events. Given this reality why would we expect water quality to improve? Is the answer simply because water quality needs to improve if we want to have a safer, healthier future on the land? The good news is we have the policy tools available to change the current reality and protect the water, by changing the policies now in place.

WHAT IS IOWA'S AGRICULTURAL WATER QUALITY POLICY?

Reports show Iowa is making little "progress" in addressing water quality, leading to the question, what exactly is Iowa's water quality policy for agriculture? The answer is we really don't have one – if by policy we mean:

- a set of articulated standards of expected conduct,

- an identifiable goal to strive toward, with objective and measurable indicators of progress or compliance, and

- a widespread social recognition and acceptance of the need to act, and an appreciation of the expected benefits.

Given the lawsuits and legislation on water quality it is easy to assume Iowa has a robust water quality policy. The truth is little in Iowa law protects water quality from agricultural activities. When it comes to Iowa water quality and agriculture our policy can best be summarized as high hopes and best wishes, or less charitably, faith in magical thinking, like the Nutrient Reduction Strategy. Here are actions Iowa law allows farmers and landowners to take:

- installing as much tile drainage as desired with no need to evaluate the impact additional water will have on streams;
- farming next to the stream banks with no set back or buffers;
- applying as much fertilizer as affordable and applying unlimited amounts of manure to any acre;
- converting pasture and grasslands to crops and removing any timber, fence line trees, or other habitat without restraint;
- allowing livestock to have unlimited access to streams and rivers;
- letting water leave the land without monitoring the quality, this is left for someone downstream to address.

In effect, there are no performance standards or limitations on farming activities that can result in water pollution, other than some limits on the timing and location of manure disposal, and rules requiring permits for larger animal feeding operations, depending on the number and type of animals. Enforcing these rules most often happens after the fact in conjunction with investigations of reported fish kills, such as when a waste lagoon overflows or excess manure enters a stream. Is it any wonder Iowa water quality continues to deteriorate given these policies? Instead of promoting water quality or soil conservation, Iowa policy is designed to maximize crop production from every acre. Iowa is driving with our foot on the accelerator of all out production of corn and soybeans and only periodically do we tap the brakes when nature, floods, or the changing climate tap them for us.

The tragedy is Iowa's farmers, conservationists, and public officials have the tools and know the approaches to improve quality in meaningful ways. One bright spot is the potential to use watersheds to organize and prioritize our work. Harnessing the structure of Iowa's 1,600 small watersheds offers a way to organize and localize efforts. Doing so can promote practices like cover crops, stream edge buffers, constructed wetlands, and targeted retirement of unproductive acres to reduce nutrients entering the water. Iowa has one hundred county soil and water conservation districts and can re-energize them to multiply and magnify the watershed efforts. Enacting reasonable regulatory standards for farming practices with the potential to degrade water quality such as tiling, manure disposal, and fertilizer management will help protect water. Doing so will also support the efforts of the farmers committed to stewardship and level the playing field so they aren't placed at a competitive disadvantage with farmers who don't take the steps. Water quality can improve with better leadership, more honesty, more public support, and additional funding. Many forces are pushing for action, not just to improve water quality but to address other challenges, like the public health issues from water polluted by blue green algae and microcystins. Addressing flooding risks and increasing the resiliency of towns and farms are shared goals. Helping mitigate the impacts of climate change and integrating efforts to improve soil health and manage carbon into how we farm loom as huge opportunities for the future. Laws and policies can be designed to address all these issues, helping to improve water quality and the economic performance and social sustainability of Iowa agriculture.

The Back Forty on Watersheds and Morality

When the rain comes I enjoy feeling the water seep down into my soul. I know it will feed the roots of the plants and crops growing on me. Decades ago my owners "tiled me" as they like to say – burying lines of clay pipes about three feet down to help drain the excess water from my surface. By keeping the water table several feet down, tile lines encourage roots to grow down to gather nutrients and support the plants. My tile lines are all connected and the water drains slowly to the southwest where an outlet pipe just east of the county road empties into a ditch. This is essentially the headwater of Willow Creek as it begins its journey west for several miles joining up with other creeks to flow into the One Hundred and Two River. Quite a name, historians believe it originated as the distance from the confluence with the Missouri River to the point where the river crossed the Sullivan line, marking what became the Missouri-Iowa border. The beauty of this system is the natural watershed, the topography helping gather water from all the land like me resting in the natural drainage of the river. All land is in a watershed, the water has to flow somewhere.

Watersheds are nested in each other like the Russian Matryoshka dolls the boy brought home from his lecture tour in the Soviet Union in 1989. Scientists at the US Geologic Service have a naming system for watersheds, called a Hydrologic Unit Code or HUC. I doubt they had Twain in mind when they came up with the name but HUC is sure evocative of rivers. The larger the watershed the lower the HUC number, so something like the North Raccoon is a HUC-8. The smallest watersheds and the most valuable when you think about an individual field like me, is the HUC-12. I am in HUC-12 #10240013, one of more than a half dozen similar HUC 12's that flow into the 102 River. A large watershed like the Mississippi River can cover a quarter of the continent. As you go upstream, each river emptying in has its own smaller watershed, and each stream emptying in the river has any even smaller watershed. You have the Missouri River, then the Platte, then the 102, and then on to Willow Creek, you get the idea. Since each large HUC 8 watershed like the North Raccoon River is assembled from smaller watersheds, that means it can be disassembled into smaller pieces, to identify where the pollution may be coming from impacting its quality.

Iowa has over 1600 HUC 12s in its borders, meaning each of the 99 counties has at least a dozen, averaging about 20,000 acres in size. Of course, they come in all shapes and sizes because their borders are determined by the topography of the land. At 20,000 acres the typical size is about 30 square miles and while no HUC 12 is box shaped, an area 5 miles by 6 miles is easy to visualize. You see that is what makes a HUC 12 the perfect size for working on water quality. It has a defined boundary and a defined point where the watercourse connects to a larger river or lake. This makes a convenient location where water quality can be monitored and measured to determine if efforts to clean the water have any effect. It can also make the perfect place to install something like a constructed wetland to improve the water quality. The size makes it easy to identify all the farmers and landowners farming in the watershed, you could probably bring them all together in a church basement. This makes it possible to see who is doing what on the land and to identify how water quality may be impacted. This is why HUC 12s are the right size for taking actions: you can see the land, you know the players, and you can evaluate how any changes impact the water quality. If you want to know if the water flowing out of my tile lines, and from all the other fields I see stretching for miles to the southwest, is clean, the answer is to use my watershed as the vehicle to do so. This is just common sense. If you are serious about addressing water quality you need to use the natural tools the land provides!

As long as I am talking about water quality, there is another issue bothering me and it is a question of morality. Looking east I see where the Salem Church used to stand and see the cemetery full of gravestones. I know the pious folks buried there considered themselves moral people. Morality can take many forms and has a variety of strands, enough to fuel the conflicts and divisions generating much of human history. Regardless of the creed or faith a commonly held moral ideal is to treat others like you want to be treated. You call this the Golden Rule. If belief in the Golden Rule is so common why isn't it afforded to how you treat me, or the water, or your neighbors downstream? When it comes to water, people seem happy to do as they please, use it to carry away soil washing down hills, to carry off nutrients and extra nitrates applied to insure a big crop flowing out of tile lines, and to carry off manure applied to the surface before a rain. The fact these things get carried off in water is only part of the problem. What happens once the water leaves the land? It flows downstream so the pollution becomes someone else's problem. How fair is that? You pollute the water knowing it will go downstream for others to deal with – everything flows downstream – and avoid responsibility for protecting the water. This is what the people who study these things, philosophers, call a moral hazard. The hazard is by not taking responsibility for what you do to the water, you avoid any costs and pass the problem to others who did not cause it. This is inherently immoral. Your immorality inflicts costs and risks from your behavior on neighbors, communities downstream, and society.

A second dimension makes your conduct not just immoral but arguably illegal. Iowa law makes all the waters in the state, like the water flowing off me toward the 102 River, public water owned by the people of Iowa. If water leaves the land polluted by your actions, it is the public's water being impacted. You are essentially taking property belonging to others, something you have no right to do. The fact your neighbors may be doing the same thing might offer you solace, but it doesn't make your conduct any less immoral or anti-social. Most people agree it is immoral for one person to damage the property of another. A legal system that sanctions such behavior is itself immoral, at least for that issue. It is reasonable to assume people who pollute the water, like farmers who insist on planting to the edge of the stream, do not see themselves as immoral, but isn't that what their actions reflect? One can argue, and I know the land agrees, a goal for society should be making the arguably legal conduct, morally intolerable if it damages others or the public. If you want to be a moral person, like the good Brethren buried across the road, you need to meet your duty to protect the waters of state.

WATERS OF THE UNITED STATES (WOTUS) RULES: A HOAX WITH LEGS

At the national level the most significant water quality issue of the past decade concerned efforts of the EPA to clarify the reach of the Clean Water Act (CWA). In 2015 the EPA issued what it called the Waters of The United States Rules, or WOTUS. The rules were developed in a multi-year process and designed to address jurisdictional uncertainties created by several US Supreme Court cases. The rules attempt to draw the line where EPA's jurisdiction stops and state jurisdiction starts, but either way, all waters in rivers, streams, and lakes are subject to someone's authority to protect it. An aggressive and deceitful public relations campaign orchestrated by national groups has resulted in most of the agriculture community believing the rule's represent an existential threat to the future of the nation. This happened even

216

though the CWA exemptions for normal farming practices and agricultural storm water runoff, called nonpoint source pollution, mean the EPA rules have little if any impact for farmers involved in crop production. Unless you plan to fill a wetland or build a CAFO near a river or lake the EPA rules are not applicable, but you will have trouble finding anyone in farm country who believes this is so. You will also have trouble finding an Iowa farmer who has ever met someone from EPA or who can identify how the WOTUS rules might actually apply to them!

The WOTUS opponents engaged in a disinformation campaign unlimited in the specious claims being made, including that farmers would need federal permits to walk cows across pastures or plant crops. The controversy made legal challenges to block the EPA rules a cottage industry and led to Congressional efforts to stop implementation. Opposition to WOTUS became a rallying cry in rural America to generate votes for President Trump, and his administration quickly rewarded supporters by reversing the Obama era rules. Not surprisingly, this action was challenged in court, making the current array of WOTUS related litigation a crazy quilt of competing claims. The situation has become even more complicated, as the new Biden administration has proposed scrapping the Trump EPA actions. The real beneficiaries of the Trump rule change, estimated to remove federal protection from as much as half the nation's wetlands and thousands of miles of streams, were developers and mining interests. They moved quickly to advance plans to "improve" formally protected lands, while the opportunity existed. In an example from late 2020, the Army Corps of Engineers determined it couldn't stop a proposed titanium mine planned for a few yards from the edge of the fragile Okefenokee

Swamp in Georgia, because it no longer had "jurisdiction" over the area. The agriculture community was happy to be the handmaiden for developers, and others who benefit most from removing federal protections from streams and wetlands. No doubt the farm community will portray any changes proposed by the Biden Administration as an attack on farming. The episode is a sad example of how some in agriculture will resist any efforts to protect soil and water, ironic given the billions of dollars in public subsidies the sector enjoys.

WATERSHED CITIZENSHIP

I believe Iowa and the nation can find the willpower and wisdom to protect water quality, to conserve soil, and to address the challenges of climate change. My optimism is tempered by a healthy vein of skepticism making me a realist willing to question our claims, and ask if we can do better. The Chinese artist and social activist Ai Wei Wei notes "Liberty is about our right to question everything." The ideal of Liberty is part of Iowa's state motto, "Our liberties we prize and our rights we will maintain." When we stop asking questions or looking for better answers then society is in danger. In March 2019, I spoke at the annual Iowa Water Conference in Ames, having last appeared four years before to explain the Des Moines Waterworks lawsuit then in the news. This time the hosts asked me to talk about watersheds and citizenship, familiar concepts but ones not typically joined. After spending time thinking about "Watershed Citizenship," I believe it may be one answer pointing us toward better care for land and water. Key elements missing in our water quality efforts are personal responsibility, and any sense of obligation to the land, a consciousness needed to underpin stewardship and citizenship. We will never have cleaner water or healthier soil if we think someone else is responsible for doing the work, the truth is the job is ours.

We all know the concept of citizenship, it is embedded in our culture and education. It is embodied in ideals we learn from childhood: the pledge of allegiance, the 4-H pledge, the Boy Scout code, and the Golden Rule. We are all good citizens, could we admit to being anything else? What does it mean to be a good citizen? Is it only obeying the law, paying taxes, voting when you feel like it, and saluting the flag? These are ways we experience citizenship but isn't it really about more, about being an active and responsible member of whatever communities you belong to?

As I see it, citizenship is grounded on basic concepts: being accountable *and* taking responsibility for your own conduct; being informed *and* making choices; and engaging in issues shaping your community. Citizenship is not something we subcontract out to others, it requires our participating in the process. It is based on understanding how law and society works *and* supporting the institutions underpinning the community and our way of life. Citizenship is premised on being part of something. We may be individuals but we are also citizens in a nation, state, county, and even watershed. There is an implicit aspect of mutuality and reciprocity to the other people who are your fellow citizens.

The idea of Watershed Citizenship takes the power of citizenship and applies it to the scale of a watershed to inform our actions. It is like Leopold's Land Ethic in focusing on the individual's role in stewardship, but it broadens the focus from the individual to a community. Water is the collective resource we steward as individuals and as members of the community. This helps us avoid the moral hazard of water quality being a "downstream" issue, and someone else's worry. In a watershed we are both upstream from some and downstream from others.

The reciprocity of citizenship is premised on the Golden Rule, the Back Forty referred to - treating others the way we want to be treated. We learn this ideal from childhood and reflect it in many ways, like "Don't eat the last cookie." If we pollute the stream aren't we taking our neighbor's last cookie? The Golden Rule is really about our obligations to others. When Leopold wrote about our relation to land, he noted the idea largely missing from discussions of conservation is obligation, observing how our education "makes no mention of obligations to land over and above those dictated by self-interest." Being a citizen means you have responsibilities to others, but citizenship is not just about obligations it is also about rights. As citizens, we are co-owners of all the public lands and waters, state parks, and the rivers and streams. As citizens, we are beneficiaries of laws designed to limit anti-social behavior and protect the environment. As watershed citizens, we have the right to expect others won't pollute the water, just as they expect us not to abuse the water and land.

My career teaching law involved seeking justice and using the technologies of justice to create more opportunities for individuals to build a better society. Watershed citizenship fits well in the context of our search for justice, as stewarding the land and water are forms of justice and citizenship. Is it too far reaching to view water quality and conserving soil as issues of justice? If we do an injustice to our water, don't we do an injustice to ourselves and our neighbors, and more importantly to our children and future generations? Citizenship carries an obligation through time, it is not just a reflection of current acts but is a way to honor those who made our way possible and an obligation to those who follow. Is it unfair to ask what legacy we are leaving our children if we are unwilling to address the reality of water degradation and soil loss today? Our decisions and actions, not just words, reveal our embrace of citizenship. What do our decisions reflect?

A favorite episode of "Our Water, Our Land" was Episode 20 about restoring Lake Darling in Washington County. The very existence of the lake was threatened by siltation and pollution but local residents organized to save the lake. After years of private fund raising, state support was secured and a lake restoration plan implemented. A key was the agreement by a majority of farmers and landowners in the watershed to install permanent conservation measures to protect the long-term health of the water. Their actions demonstrate what can be achieved through cooperative action in a watershed and lessons from the experience can apply across the state and nation. The question they faced is what is the farmer and landowner's responsibility to the community of a watershed? There is no magic answer, instead each landowner, farmer, and watershed citizen must provide their own. It begins by recognizing we are part of a larger community and have obligations to others residing there. How we meet the obligations is the measure of our citizenship.

In *American Georgics: Writings on Farming, Culture and the Land*, ed. by Hagenstein, Gregg, and Donahue (2011 Yale) the editors include a passage of the essay "The South Astir" (1935) by H.L. Mencken, one of my favorite writers. Mencken wrote:

> Unfortunately liquidating a dogma is always very tedious
> and hazardous business. All the fools holler for it loudly,
> for it saves them the trouble of thinking, and the minority

of prudent men find it difficult to think in the din. Such a hollering of fools, with no counter uproar by the prudent, gives the noisiest of the former the appearance of being leaders of opinion, and if they go on long enough that appearance is converted into reality. ....

Reading this passage about confronting dogma brings to mind today's debate about water quality and the role agriculture plays. It is exemplified by the outrageous claims made in the WOTUS hoax. Even though claims the rule will severely impact agriculture are easily debunked, the powerful false narrative lives on. The same is true for claims of "great progress" made under the Iowa Nutrient Reduction Strategy, and the dangers of litigation like the Des Moines Waterworks suit. The dogma underlying the claims is premised on several "truths": farmers do everything possible to address soil and water concerns; government regulations must play no role (unless providing public funding); and any regulation or court decision is an affront to private property, threatening agriculture and basic freedoms. The claims play out against a background of economic determinism restraining farmers' choices, and high costs and low profits make being able "to afford" conservation or water quality difficult. If our economic system and markets don't value water quality or soil health, or concerns like climate change, species loss, or land conversion – and in fact may weigh these goals as costs rather than benefits, then why should we believe economics alone will ever protect the resources? The truth is economics alone will not, more is needed.

Posing the issue raises many questions, one of the most important is the content of our "education" about conservation, assuming such education even exists. Is our common answer conservation means doing only the minimum the government requires? If more is expected then the public must pay. Undoubtedly the government will play a key role in conservation but in recent decades we have given government too large a role. The voluntary nature of our conservation programs leaves participation to the discretion of landowners and farmers. Little effort has been made to explain or expand on ideas of duties and responsibilities owed by private landowners. The result is great variation in conservation and environmental stewardship depending largely on the attitudes, awareness, and economic abilities of individual farmers and landowners. Thankfully some farmers accept and embrace duties to the land, even though doing so is constrained by economic realities of commodity prices, rental rates, and farm income. Unfortunately, many other farmers and landowners do not choose to embrace conservation for a variety of reasons, including adherence to the dogma of property rights and "no government regulations." The fear is any form of regulation will reduce farmers and landowner opportunities and freedom, even requiring them to forego some desired action. One reason the Des Moines Waterworks lawsuit was so threatening was it raised the idea private landowners have a responsibility to the public. It illuminated what appears to be for many their philosophy of land ownership: the land owes me everything because I own it, with no corollary of what the owner might owe to the land. Admitting some duty to the land would humanize it with a living quality, so better to treat it as an inanimate well from which to pump our economic desires and on which to paint our self-image.

Even if this is the attitude of many owners about their duty to the land, there is hope some attitudes may be changing. The transition of land to a new generation of owners, public support for efforts to improve water quality, and the voter approval of conservation funding initiatives all reflect changing attitudes. These voices may now be muffled, but there is reason to believe they are growing. More landowners are confronting and even surmounting the dogmas shaping their relation to the land. In his essay, Mencken wrote about how dogmas are finally reversed:

> How and why such pestilences end is always a bit mysterious. All one can say with any assurance is there seems to be a law of diminishing returns for imbecility, just as there is for taxes. Over a long stretch of years the general appetite for buncombe and banality looks to be quite without limit, and then of a sudden the byways begin to rustle with whispers of doubt. Such uprisings, of course, seldom if ever originate among the actual folks, they are the artifacts of minorities in the ... region.

What we hear happening in our state and nation are the rustling whispers of doubt. How the whispers, now in the minority, can grow into winds of change is the focus of the final three chapters. One of the first places to see the changes coming is the food we eat and what it means for the land.

Art Cullen.

Mark Ackelson, long time President of the
Iowa Natural Heritage Foundation.

J.W. "Jake" Looney next to Terry Centner and Linda
Grim —two of our first LLM students from the class
of 1982, at the 35th Anniversary in Fayetteville.

Louis Lorvellec arriving in
Des Moines for a visit.

With Khanh and Louis at
a European Agricultural
Law Congress 1991.

With Louis at a European Agricultural Law conference.

With Gus Schumacher and Amy Goldman at the
James Beard Awards in New York City.

With Hugh Joseph, Michel Nishan, and Gus at a W.K.
Kellogg Foundation, Food Policy meeting in Arizona.

At March for Science
in DC—April, 2018.

Outside the Global
seed vault at Svalbard.

View of the Upper Iowa River from Heritage Valley an Iowa Natural Heritage Foundation project east of Decorah.

Trail along the Loess Hills ridge line.

Time To Take An Inventory of Our Pantry

Ding knew how profligate we can be, will climate
change make us be more sensitive?

Ding knew the land and nature can heal—if we let them.

Law School photo with Berry's classic—1978.

At the COP15 Climate Summit in Copenhagen.

With Khanh, Cary, and Amy, with NordGen
staff in front of Seed Vault doors.

Inside the Seed Vault.

With Senator Obama in August, 2007,
at a rural summit in Tama.

With Paul Willis and Bill Niman.

With Secretary Vilsack at the Iowa State Fair.

Matt Russell with then US Senator Tom Harkin, demonstrating an EBT machine at the Des Moines Farmers Market.

Two favorite photos from eight trips to Cuba.

Spring flowers at Sunstead.

Khanh and Neil at Sunstead. (Photo by Martha Valencia)

Chapter Seven - Better Food, Better Farming, and Better Land

SWEET POTATOES AT SUNSTEAD FARM

Pushing a fork into the ground to dig sweet potatoes is like beginning a treasure hunt, you never know what you will find. The 2020 crop at Sunstead was a bumper as the Georgia Jets sized up nicely, even with our limited rainfall. Some lunkers came it at two or three pounds each, and one plant yielded so much I weighed them separately and the one plant produced twelve pounds! Sweet potatoes made a nice bounty for October, and several batches went to Chef Derek at Django, our favorite customer who managed to hold on as the pandemic decimated other restaurants in town.

There were plenty of sweets to use for Thanksgiving. Rather than have our usual large gathering of friends, we did "pick-up dinners" to lower the COVID risks. The decision was much needed as Iowa's new cases and deaths surged to records in November 2020. Such was the benefit of having a Trumpian governor with little regard for public health, her citizens, or common sense for that matter. Our total meal count came to over forty and I was pressed into directing traffic so no collisions happened as people converged at pick up time. Khanh roasted four turkeys plus ten more legs and thighs so there was plenty but by the time it was over most of the turkey and fixings were gone – as well as the sweet potatoes.

I feel sad for people who never have the opportunity to garden, to raise some of their food. There is no better connection to the land – and to what we eat – than raising some of your food. This year, Thanksgiving meant peeling and chopping about twenty-five pounds of sweet potatoes and coating them with a topping of butter, brown sugar, and bourbon. Roasted for three hours at 350°, they were delicious, somewhere between a vegetable and dessert. I even added some of this year's honey to the blend. When we purchased the farm in late 1996 one thing was certain, I wanted to keep bees. After taking an evening extension class offered by the state department of agriculture, and building a set of bee boxes from kits sold by Dadant in Hamilton, Illinois, things were ready to go. Spring came, my bees arrived and an adventure in bee keeping began. It is an exciting hobby and can be relaxing, sometimes. Sitting on a stool in the garden, watching bees on their flight path back to the hive is a form of farming meditation. There are times when bee-keeping is not for the faint of heart, like when pulling frames of honey comb, and trying not to be unnerved by riled-up bees swarming your face net. We went many years without bees, but one evening in spring of 2019, Khanh said "we should get bees again." So we did.

An October 2020 cold snap drove the bees deep into the hive, and provided a perfect opportunity to pull the extra super, the top box of frames added in summer for bees to store honey, with a minimum of bee disruption and stinging risk. What a rich reward it was. With a little time and effort, fifteen pounds of golden honey was the bounty. We savor it every morning in our coffee. Bees are back at Sunstead.

This is a good time to explain the origin of the farm's name Sunstead. In winter 1996 after purchasing the ten acres, and waiting for our springtime move, I happened to read a 1935 book by Gove Hambidge, *Enchanted Acre: Adventures in Backyard Farming*. It is the story of the life he and his wife created on their small garden farm on a northern Westchester hillside in New York, a farm they named Sunstead. I was acquainted with Hambidge from his work with Henry A. Wallace at USDA, where he edited the famous series of USDA Yearbooks of Agriculture, including the 1938 classic *Soils and Men*. Hambidge was one of many progressive thinkers FDR and Wallace attracted to redefine the role USDA could play in American life. To me, the name Sunstead or home of the sun, seemed perfect for our new farm, and so it is. For a number of years, I designed an annual Sunstead Farm t-shirt for friends and our garden crew. Each version featured a different regionalist lithograph from our collection, a work by Wood, Benton, or Curry. In the late 90s, I was wearing a Sunstead shirt one July day at the Seed Savers Exchange annual campout, when a young man exclaimed "Sunstead – that was the name of my grandfather's farm!" You can imagine my surprise to learn he was a grandson of Gove Hambidge, living in Minneapolis, carrying on his grandfather's love of gardening and working the land.

FOOD DEMOCRACY

I have been immersed in Iowa's rural and farming culture since growing up on my parent's Adams County farm. The Back Forty thinks I was even conceived there one late April morning under a warming sun, on a quilt nestled in the fencerow after Mom brought Dad his mid-morning snack. I can't be sure but it makes a nice story. Forty years of teaching agricultural law and food policy classes gave me a front-row seat and ticket for direct involvement in many progressive evolutions in America's food system. My writing and activities covered a range of issues: sustainable agriculture, small farm initiatives, food policy councils, access to healthy foods, land tenure, and supporting the next generation of farmers. Projects focused on the role law and policy can play in creating better opportunities for farmers, consumers, communities, and the land. As you know by reading this far, I am optimistic we are building a more just and sustainable farming and food system in the Nation, though we have much more work to do. My confidence stems from my belief these developments reflect the values of what I call food democracy. The tenets of food democracy are found in our desire for better food, our demand for information and better choices, and our preference for local action and personal involvement. The forces reflect strong democratic tendencies and illustrate how citizen actions can shape a more sustainable and healthy food future.

These trends have a common denominator, the democratic yearnings of the American people. Economists and marketers will tell you the price of food is the most important determinant in consumer demand. No doubt cost is an important factor and one to consider when food availability and hunger are real issues. But cost or price is not the only concern for consumers and eaters. I believe an increasing number of consumers do not want to eat cheaper or less expensive food, instead they want to eat better food, better in whatever way that means to them. It could be locally grown, it could be organic, it could be an heirloom variety, or it could be food grown on a farm they can visit by people they know. These factors may raise the cost but they do not necessarily have to – the real issue is access and availability. In recent years shelves of books have been written about our food and about the opportunities for people trying their hand at farming. One of the most eloquent books exploring a unique "better food" and the challenges of growing it and bringing it to market is David Mas Matsumoto's 1995 classic *Epitaph for a Peach*. America's farmers and food companies are experimenting with many ways to make our food better. The desire for better food powers other social forces, the need for information to have more choices, and for there to be alternatives in the marketplace and the food aisles. These forces are driving shifts in food production, processing, and marketing. These shifts are accompanied by political and legal debates over fundamental policy issues relating to food labels, support for local production, the emergence of third party certification of food traits, and examining the relation between nutrition and public health. The path forward is clear, better food can lead to better farming which in turn can support better land. This chapter examines how these forces can work together to improve our options and opportunities.

I always tell my classes and audiences you are only as far away from agriculture as your next meal – meaning you are only as far away from the land as the food you eat. For decades a challenge in teaching agricultural law classes was getting law students to enroll. Often the reaction was "I am really not interested in working with farmers" so why take your class? From my experience it was clear many exciting legal trends and developments were surging through the food and farming world. The challenge was how to engage students. For decades, mainstream or "conventional" agriculture has spent little time worrying about consumer interests or concerns for what is happening on the land. This was certainly not true though for the growing number of farmers in the burgeoning organic farm movement, or for chefs like those in the Chefs Collaborative working to promote the value of local foods, or for the food policy advocates, nutritionists, and others concerned about how we treat land and animals and how this impacts the safety and quality of the food we produce. It was at this time, around 1996, when these insights led me to take several actions. First, I wrote several law review articles about what I saw happening, with titles like, "Tending the Seeds: The Emergence of a New Agriculture in the US," and "Greening Our Garden: Public Policies to Support the New Agriculture." I developed a new law school course on Food Law and Policy, not focused on questions of who and where food is grown, but instead on issues from the consumer and public perspective, topics like food safety, food labeling, direct farm marketing, food security and hunger, and broader issues of health and nutrition. Taking a food perspective on the law was like walking through a window and turning to see a whole new set of issues unseen when only thinking about farming. By taking a food-based approach to legal topics, the subjects became bigger and broader, and my audience grew. Students might not care about farming but everyone cares about food and eating. My students understood we can certainly choose what to eat, but we can't choose not to eat, at least for very long. Examining the law from the perspective of food provides a new perspective to understand how law impacts farmers and the land.

Growing up on an Iowa farm, the interests of consumers were seldom considered, or ever mentioned. The small patch of strawberries Mom kept for selling fresh berries to town folk was our only real connection to people eating something we raised. Consumers came up in conversation only indirectly, usually in my father's constant refrain the main thing politicians were interested in was a "cheap food policy." Things haven't changed much in fifty years. Today, farm groups are happy to put up billboards claiming "every farmer feeds 140 people" or whatever the latest number is, but it certainly wasn't true on our farm or any others in Iowa, then or now. We didn't feed anyone, unless people had a powerful hunger for soybeans or corn. The truth is we didn't raise food, we raised raw ingredients other people used to produce something people ate. This is still the case for much of American agriculture.

Most Midwestern farmers, then and now, are disconnected from consumers' concerns and desires. Those are for the food marketers and manufacturers, the General Mills and Campbell Soups, people selling food people eat. Farmers paid a steep price for this disconnection, primarily in the hardening of their attitudes toward consumers. Farmers and farm groups came to resist and resent consumer concerns, an odd stance given these people are their customers. Another cost is losing the satisfaction and fulfillment associated with feeding grateful eaters.

For over two decades Khanh and I have operated Sunstead, our small market garden. For years we sold at farmers markets, and we have a small CSA operation. Our main customers are chefs, friends like Derek, who count on us for the fresh, delicious crops of leeks, basil, heirloom tomatoes, and herbs Sunstead is known for. In some ways I have difficulty even calling Sunstead a farm, certainly it is not comparable to the farm my parents spent fifty years on with their land and the crops they raised being the only source of income. But for USDA purposes and definitions, Sunstead is definitely a farm by the scale of "off-farm" sales the Census of Agriculture uses to classify farms. Here is a little-known fact about how USDA determines the number of farms in the country – a number currently at around 2.1 million. For USDA purposes if the operation sells more than $1,000 of production – or could have – it is considered a farm. It is only by using this low threshold the nation is able to claim two million farms still exist, but over 1.5 million of them are like Sunstead, relatively small in terms of annual sales. The issue of who is a farmer or what it should take to be classified as one is a sticky political issue with no correct answer, but the relatively inflated number of farmers makes it easier for USDA to obscure issues such as who are the beneficiaries of federal farm program payments and the importance of off-farm income. In my view, the status of being a farmer is as much a state of mind – are you raising food and caring for the land – as it is the number of acres you farm or bushels you might raise.

The differences between our farm and my parents' go much deeper than just the size of the sales or if it is a "full-time" venture. We regularly experience two important features in our farming life my parents never had the chance to enjoy. The first is the ability to set our own price for crops we sell. The Chicago Board of Trade doesn't list a price for ten pounds of fresh picked basil. The price is between you and the chef, a function of what we need to charge and what the chef will pay. In fifty years of farming my parents never set a price for any crop they sold. When we raised fat cattle the order buyer came to the farm and made an offer for the lot. In decades of trucking corn and beans to the elevator in town, the price that day was chalked on the blackboard behind the counter and if you didn't like it you could always turn the truck back home. The truck never went home full. The inability to set a price but instead being forced to take what someone else offers has fueled in generations of farmers a sense of unfairness. Farmers feel impotent in the face of powerful forces, the grain companies and packers who control their fortunes. Searching for ways to

245

be free from the market dominance of others has driven many farm families to look for alternatives, such as by marketing "food products" rather than producing and selling commodities. Unfortunately, in the worst cases, the option some farm families choose, such as many who raised dairy cows, is to leave farming all together.

The second way our experience at Sunstead differs from my parents is perhaps even more important although it doesn't come with a dollar sign. This is the thanks and feeling of gratitude we gain from satisfied customers. This powerful surge of connection can come in many ways. It can be when "Sunstead Farm" is listed on the menu as the source of ingredients in a special dish, or when customers report back "those baby beets you sold us were the most delicious we ever ate." These experiences and comments make the act of growing food come full circle. Putting our face on the food we grow, allows us to see the faces of our customers and to know the joy our food brings them. This invaluable physic connection with grateful eaters is something my parents never experienced. No one ever called to say those were the best soybeans they ever ate. Even when we raised fat cattle no one knew the prime steaks came from our farm, instead the butcher or the packer got the profits and the thanks. I can't help but think my parents' farming experience suffered from this lack of connection to people they were helping feed. Moving forward, one of society's most important opportunities, is helping make the connections between better food, better farming, and better land. This is the dynamic at the heart of the Niman Ranch Pork Company, making connections and using them so farming is more satisfying and farmers are more profitable and sustainable.

THE NIMAN RANCH STORY

The story of Niman Ranch Pork Company begins in the mid-1990s when Paul Willis, a farmer from Thornton in north central Iowa, visited a friend from the Peace Corps ranching in California. The friend introduced him to Bill Niman, who was raising cattle on his ocean-side land in Marin County, and having success selling pasture-raised meat to high-end Bay area restaurants like Alice Water's Chez Panisse in Berkeley. This led him to create the Niman Ranch meat company and add other meats like the lamb being grown by Jeannie McCormack, their mutual friend. Bill hadn't located a pork producer using the same care as the other meats he sold. When Jeannie introduced them, Bill learned Paul raised hogs on his farm in Iowa. When Bill asked Paul "what do you want for your hogs" it was the first time Paul had ever been asked the question, then he knew he was no longer in the commodity business. Several conversations led to a deal being struck and in February 1995 the first thirty carcasses from Paul's pigs, slaughtered in Iowa, were trucked to Bill's meat cutting facility under the Bay Bridge in San Francisco. The pork tasted great and was a hit with the customers and as a result a business relation and friendship grew. From those first shipments of a few head a week, the Niman Ranch Pork Company has evolved into a network of over 700 farm families, shipping over 20,000 head of hogs a month into the Niman Company meat distribution system. Most farmers are located in Iowa, but producers in neighboring states are part of the operation. All the farm families are committed to raising high-quality pork, treating the animals with respect, and to meet exacting standards for animal care. As Paul likes to say, raising hogs the old-fashioned way, outside and on the land. The Niman pigs may have one bad day, but their lives are unlike those of the millions of pigs who spend every day of their lives cramped in smelly, noisy confinement facilities.

I first met Paul in the late 1990s when we were speakers at a sustainable agriculture conference at Sinsinawa Mound in southwest Wisconsin. We found a common bond in our love for the land and great food. Our friendship made it possible for me to watch the evolution of the Niman Ranch Company from its early years and to see what it means for farmers, consumers, animals, and the land. The last twenty years has had its share of ups and downs for Niman Ranch. Growth of the Chipotle chain and a commitment by founder Steven Ells to use Niman Ranch pork made it possible to add another hog farmer with each new Chipotle, until this pace became impossible to sustain. During this period, the realities of seeking venture capital to support the company's growth resulted in his eventually losing control, and Bill Niman left the company and the dream he started.

His name remains and fortunately so does his commitment to caring for the animals and the farmers, keys to producing the high quality, delicious meats demanded by the chefs who are Niman's main customers. In 2016, Niman Ranch was acquired by the Perdue family from Maryland, famous for leadership in the chicken industry. Observers feared the acquisition meant the Niman Ranch commitment to meat quality and animal welfare risked being smothered by the new owners' desires for profits and market share. Time has shown the fears were wrong. If anything, the Niman Ranch philosophy of raising high quality meat by caring for the animals and the families who raise them, has had a stronger influence on Perdue and its poultry operations. Today Perdue is the largest producer of organic chicken in the country and is leading the industry in changing how poultry is produced and marketed, removing antibiotics from the feed, improving housing conditions, and giving growers more ability to shape relations with the company. Acquiring Niman Ranch has helped both companies grow, and provide consumers with the better foods they want and support the better farming practices the country needs.

The essence of Niman Ranch pork is found in the quality and taste of the meat it sells. This is what makes it not just a favored supplier to chefs across the country but a popular brand in meat cases of Whole Foods, Trader Joe's, and local grocers known for quality products like Marczyk Fine Foods in Denver. You can't produce high quality pork consistently without having farmers committed to their animals and the Niman Ranch network of farm families distinguishes it from every other meat company in the country.

Niman has always valued and honored the farmers who raise the hogs, paying them premium prices above the market, for raising pork to meet the company standards. The recognition and the relationships are about more than money, they are built on respect and a shared vision for a brighter, healthier farming future. One unique way this is shown is through the annual Hog Farmer Appreciation Dinner held each fall in Des Moines. The dinner has evolved on a brilliant plan: bring in a half-dozen of the nation's most innovative chefs who feature Niman meat on their menus, and have them prepare a pork-centric meal for several hundred Niman farmers and family members, company staff, meat distributors, and customers. Throw in a sprinkling of the nation's food writers, like Tracey Ryder and her network of *Edible* magazine editors, along with folks from the Iowa food scene and you have an event. The dinner is the culmination of several days of farm tours for chefs and meetings for Niman Ranch employees and farmers, to focus on better food and better farming.

One highlight of the dinner is the awards ceremony, recognizing the top ten farmers producing the best tasting meat. Each farm in the Niman system has a number, Paul of course is Farm #1. When animals are slaughtered the number is coded with the primal cuts and on a regular schedule, pork produced by all the farms is cooked and sampled to insure the taste and quality meet the standards the company knows customers expect. This process is used to judge and rank the farms based on the quality of their pork. We have had the honor of attending every Niman Ranch dinner over the last twenty years and there is nothing like it in the food and farming world. Having top-flight chefs prepare innovative pork focused dishes, served family style at long tables to families who raise the meat is a unique culinary experience, not just for the incredible food. Most of these farm families will never have the opportunity to dine at the chefs' famous restaurants or get to eat their pork prepared in these ways. You can only imagine the pride a Niman farm family experiences being recognized before their peers for producing the best tasting pork, a nice reward for the hard work and love that goes into raising hogs.

At the close of the evening, after the awards are given and the over-the-top meal consumed, the chefs appear and talk about what the meat and the farmers mean to them. It is a special moment to hear the chefs describe how the farmers' commitment to producing delicious meat fuels their success. You have to be a hard-hearted soul not to shed a few tears hearing this mutual love and respect for better food, better farming, and the animals involved, come full circle.

There is even more to the evening and it gets better! Starting twenty years ago Bill and Paul decided Niman Ranch needed to support the next generation of farmers, children of the families raising their hogs. What started the first year with a few thousand dollars in donations from suppliers and supporters has grown today so that in 2020 Niman Ranch Pork Company awarded over $170,000 in scholarships to forty-eight students, all children of Niman farmers. The scholarships support the education of kids who want to either return to the farm to carry on the tradition of raising animals for Niman or who want to stay in rural America in some capacity. Several years ago, Niman Ranch created the Next Generation Foundation to administer and raise the scholarship funds and I am honored to serve on the foundation board.

A network of farmers numbered in the hundreds may not sound significant if you worry about the future of farming in the US, but trust me, it is very significant. By giving these families a market for their hogs raised "the old-fashioned way", Niman has made it possible for them to stay in farming. Rather than having to choose between leaving hog farming or signing a contract with an integrated packer like Smithfield, to raise pigs in foul smelling confinements, Niman Ranch gives the families the chance to farm, care for the land, and raise animals in ways they feel are best. Niman farmers retain their independence and the freedom to farm in ways better for eaters, better for the animals, and better for the land. Tell me what is wrong with this story? Companies like Niman are giving consumers more opportunities to vote with their forks and pocket books.

THREE MENTORS WHO SHAPED MY WORK ON FOOD AND THE LAND

If you stop and think, your life is shaped by the people around you

– family, friends, neighbors, and co-workers. The role others play is especially significant if you are fortunate enough to have a select few you consider mentors – people who open doors, provide advice and support when needed, and who create opportunities because they believe in you. My work on food, law, and land issues was immeasurably influenced by many, but three individuals stand out as my mentors, friends who changed the direction of my life and work. Sadly, all three have now passed on as untimely illnesses stilled their vibrant lives when they still had so much to share. Although they are gone and deeply missed, their work, deeds, love, and advice still guide me every day. We all shared three traits – we grew up in farm families tied to the land, our careers focused on the intersection of farming, policy, and food, and we were all ambitious dreamers who loved thinking up new ways to improve the lives of people who farm and of those who eat.

First in my pantheon of heroes was J.W. "Jake" Looney, a law professor, economist, rancher, and judge. Jake spent his career teaching and as Dean at the University of Arkansas Law School, and after retiring to his ranch near Mena in southwest Arkansas, a second career on the bench as a judge. In 1981 Jake recruited me to interview for the position of law professor to help guide the new Masters of Law or LLM program in agricultural law the University was unfolding. As you know from this book, it seems trite to say that opportunity changed my life and set me on a career spanning these forty years. The beginning was less auspicious. Jake called me at the Farm Division of the Iowa Attorney General's office, saying he was going to be in Des Moines and wanted to visit about the new LLM program. After the call, my boss asked what Jake wanted. I told him of our meeting but explained I wasn't sure if he wanted me to enroll as a student or be a professor! Our meeting clarified it was to teach and that winter Arkansas hired a twenty-seven-year old farm boy to develop classes for their new agricultural law program.

Jake taught me many things in the years that followed: how to be an energetic classroom teacher and engage students; how to be a curious scholar focusing on issues relevant and impactful for the farming and legal communities; and how to distill the law so people can understand it, by taking a practical and human approach to how the law serves individuals and society. We shared many adventures over the years, from his trips to Des Moines to teach summer classes, my annual returns to Fayetteville to continue building the program, and on travels around the nation and the world speaking at agricultural law gatherings. Jake was happiest on his ranch in Mena, taking care of his momma cows and calves. There was always another pasture to buy and more cattle to raise. Jake was infected like many involved in farming with the itch to buy more land. This approach seemed to always leave him strapped for cash, worrying about how to keep his ranching operation afloat. My advice was to stop buying land and sell a few cows, advice he never took. Who knows maybe the struggle of his ranching operation kept him grounded and in touch with the economic realities most farm and ranch families face. I will always be thankful Jake called that day and changed both our lives.

The second man in this story also had a connection to Jake and Arkansas. In 1989 a French law professor, Louis Lorvellec, took a sabbatical from running his graduate program in food and agricultural law at the University of Nantes and moved his family to Fayetteville to study in the LLM program. I meet Louis shortly after he arrived and we began a friendship that evolved over the next decade into something like a brotherhood. It lasted until May 2000 when Louis lost his battle with leukemia, a passing felt deeply on both sides of the Atlantic. During those years we were together on many occasions. Louis arranged for me to spend a week in Nantes each year as a professor invitee', explaining the history and operation of American agriculture, large farms, and GMO's to all his students. Being unable to speak French was not a problem as Louis arranged for his students to receive a special "bilingual" designation on their diplomas for taking classes in English. Louis and his wife Souzic visited the US on many occasions when he would teach summer classes at Drake or speak at our American Agricultural Law Association meetings. These "exchanges" were one of the many life lessons Louis taught me, "the importance of sending the elevator back." When someone creates an opportunity for you, it is important to return the favor so they or someone else can share the same benefits. I have tried to send the elevator back throughout my career, in respect of his wisdom.

Louis was famous for his humor, his equanimity, and a calm, inquisitive approach to life. Shaped by his boyhood on a small farm, Louis was a Breton first and only then a Frenchman. In reality, he was a citizen of the world. Fluent in many languages, his warm engaging personality and his lack of pretense made him widely loved and respected by students, lawyers, and colleagues in the larger world of food and agricultural law. We traveled the globe in those years, often to attend Congresses organized by a group he helped start, UMAU – Union Mondiale des Agraristes Universitares or in English, the All World Union of Agricultural Law Professors. When Louis died it was as if a flame had been snuffed out and the extensive travels we shared in Europe ended. Not just had my translator and friend who opened so many doors gone silent, some of my fire had gone out as well. I think of Louis often and when giving public talks, an "L" in the mnemonic I write atop the first page, reminds me why we do this work. Writing this, I can see him now with his mischievous grin and hear him say "Neil – you know …" Louis was famous for his expressions and one often comes to mind when I find myself being too quick to judge another's action. We were talking about what appeared to be troubles in a friend's marriage. I don't remember how he said it in French, but translated it was "Neil, you know we do not light the candles in their house." The idea we can never know what goes on behind a couple's doors once closed reminds me Louis knew we are all human and need to be humble and kind.

The third star in my constellation of mentors was Gus Schumacher, a widely loved and respected figure in American food and agricultural policy. His roots were in his family's long history of truck farming near New York City but his political career began in Massachusetts. In the 1980s he served as state commissioner of agriculture under Governor Michael Dukakis and confirmed his passion for making sure everyone has access to healthy nutritious food. Combined with his political instincts and his unique people skills, this passion for food and people led Gus to a distinguished career at the top of US agriculture and food policy. In the Clinton years, as USDA Under Secretary responsible for international and domestic programs, Gus helped oversee the expansion of US farm exports and of domestic nutrition programs. He helped secure the USDA funding my Drake Center used to create state and regional food policy councils in fifteen states. The hallmark of his career was a program he began in Massachusetts providing coupons to seniors to redeem at farmers markets to purchase fresh produce. When Gus joined USDA under President Clinton he brought the seniors farmers market coupon program with him and eventually saw it expand to a national program offering millions to aid seniors buying fresh food from farmers. In the 2018 Farm Bill, Congress honored his memory by naming it the Gus Schumacher Nutrition Incentive Program or GusNIP, a fitting testimony of the respect so many had for him. His legacy is the millions of dollars for food assistance provided each year to address the scourge of hunger that still haunts our nation, such an anomaly in this land of bounty

I feel so fortunate to have been one of the many food activists who fell under Gus' spell and who looked to him as a role model. We were together on a summer morning at the Des Moines farmers market in the 1990s, when an older woman hugged him with tears in her eyes explaining she had just used her senior's coupon to purchase ripe raspberries, something she hadn't been able to afford for years. Gus had an uncanny way of connecting with people and he was always quick to pull out his Canon Sure Shot to take a photo, as he did that day. Being with Gus made you feel special and at the center of the action. It felt like we had a special bond, though I know there are dozens of others who feel they shared just as special a connection with Gus. When he died several years ago of a heart attack many feared his energy might be drained from the local food and healthy eating movement he championed after leaving USDA. Thankfully the work he began with friend Michel Nishan at Wholesome Wave, to expand access to nutritious food and expand the nation's nutrition programs continues, needed now more than ever. His example and inspiration live on in the multitudes he touched.

I can't count the number of nights spent in the guest room at Gus and Susan's home in Georgetown. It functioned as a halfway house for food activists and friends visiting from around the nation. A week after he died my cell phone rang and I was startled to see "Gus Schumacher" on the caller ID. It was Susan using Gus's phone to reach out to friends to share memories and talk. I didn't go to his funeral, packed with the legions of people he befriended over his long career. Rather than travel to DC, I used the money the trip would have cost to do something else in his memory. A Drake student group had constructed three mini-food pantries placed on the edges of campus. They look like the tiny libraries you see but bear a sign saying if you are hungry take what you need and if you have food to share please leave it. Each Sunday for the next year I would buy a trunk full of food – canned soup, vegetables, tuna, and mac and cheese and haul it around campus to make sure the shelves of each pantry were full. I never saw anyone taking food but invariably the shelves would be empty. Gus knew as well as anyone in the nation, how the evils of hunger often go unseen. My gesture was a small one but it was doing something. If there is a message in Gus' life and from Louis and Jake's as well, it is the importance of doing something. We each have an obligation to make society and our nation's food system better. May you be as fortunate to have in your life friends and mentors like these.

The Back Forty on the Better Food Movement

You might not think I have much to say when it comes to this idea that better food is a pathway to better farming and better land, but you should know better. It is true, like Iowa's 24 million other farmed acres, crops raised on me don't getting eaten by people, at least directly. The corn and beans I produce do get used. Some of my harvest is eaten by the hogs producing your bacon and by the laying hens producing your eggs. My beans might be crushed and sold as your jug of cooking oil or turned into margarine to spread on your toast. The fact I am used for what might be called conventional farming doesn't mean the Better Food movement is not empowering for the land. The land has a broad range of potential roles and benefits it can produce. I can grow crops but can also create and store carbon in my soil, helping clean the water. I can grow many more crops than just corn and beans, it all depends on what the farmer wants to plant, a decision determined by the availability of markets. I could grow grass to feed cattle or I could support a fleet of chicken tractors with hundreds of hens laying eggs and eating my bugs. Yes, I may now be part of a several thousand acre grain farming operation but I could also be the small farm giving a young family their place to start. Some of these opportunities will never be mine and I might spend my next decades raising corn for ethanol to burn in your car, but these other things could happen. If they don't happen to me, they might happen on another piece of land like me, just located closer to town or where eaters yearn to buy food raised by people they know on land they can visit. My potential and that of all other land is real. As the better food movement grows we will be here serving as the canvas where your better food future can be painted.

The key to understand is how the land actually makes the better food and better farming movement possible. Many features making foods more attractive to consumers relate directly to practices employed on the land. Consider the growing consumer interest in foods like grass-based dairy products. The Organic Valley dairy cooperative even has a line of milk with that name. Pasture raised poultry and grass-fed beef is seeing a surge in interest and appreciation. Seth Watkins, a friend and farmer from southwest Iowa, has converted most of his crop ground back to grass so he can expand his grass-based cattle operation and work with nature to improve his land. The hog farming practices used by Niman Ranch farmers involve raising the babies in pastures and then feeding the pigs in open-air, deep-bedded hoop houses. Niman Ranch, is a prime example of how producing better food through better farming translates into better land. Much of the Better Foods movement focuses on local foods, raised on nearby lands, kind of a food-shed approach. I like that because to have local food you have to have farmland available to use. Protecting the farmland nearest to cities, lands under the strongest development pressures, is the main concern of American Farmland Trust, one of the land trusts discussed in the next chapter.

Demand for local foods helps support two primary forms of marketing: farmers markets and community supported agriculture or CSA farms. A powerful draw for consumers who shop at farmers markets is knowing the food is grown locally, by people they can talk with and come to know. Farmers markets embody the Buy Fresh Buy Local ideal and help put a face on the food. People don't shop at the farmers market because the grocery stores shelves are empty. They go for the social experience to make a connection to farmers and food, and because it makes them feel good. When Secretary of Agriculture Vilsack first unveiled the Know Your Farmer Know Your Food campaign at USDA in 2009 some Senators criticized him claiming farmers markets are only important to wealthy urban foodies. They couldn't have been more wrong. If you follow the farmers' pickup trucks home from the markets to the Laconas and Lovillas and other small towns in rural America, you might see farm families counting the day's proceeds. Then you will understand how farmers markets are a form of rural economic development, bringing city food dollars back to the farm and to the rural countryside.

Some farmers use the CSA model, selling annual subscriptions paid for in advance. A CSA farm is inherently place-based and is useful in developing a network of loyal customers. CSA members may even come to think of the farm as their land. I like that idea of other people being invested in caring for the land and the success of a farm. In some cases this is literally true, as farmers are using cooperative financing to share landownership with members. These examples show local food is about more than just farmer-eater connections, it is another way to link customers and eaters to the land. This can build a core of informed citizens who care about local land use issues. Community support has been invaluable for several farm families who have found their direct marketing farms embroiled with local zoning officials over land use rules. Disputes over how many cars can park at the pumpkin patch on a Sunday, or whether all the food being sold is actually raised on the farm have led to conflicts and court cases. Being able to call on a network of social media followers to let local officials know how much the community values their farm, has helped save farms from oppressive rules or even closure. There may be a great deal of media interest in new and innovative food products like "cell grown meat" and I am excited about the potential farmers have to build new markets for eco-systems services and carbon credits. But it is important to remember first principles – land is the source of the food you eat and enjoy, and local land will be critical in producing the better foods more consumers want and need.

CHALLENGES IN MAKING THE BETTER FOOD, BETTER LAND LINKAGE

The better food movement has many challenges. One potential limitation is being able to communicate to consumers how better farming is linked to the better foods they buy. We don't lack for food labels, and in recent years many new food terms have flooded the market: organic, natural, free-range, humanely raised, pasture raised, and antibiotic free. The issue isn't a lack of food labeling, instead it is a lack of connection between what is said on food labels and the farming practices used to grow the food. This is especially true when it comes to issues like soil conservation, water quality, and soil health. Presently there is no effective way to communicate to consumers how the soil and land is treated for "conservation" purposes or to link these better farming practices to a food product. Organic may include better farming methods but the term only covers some of what is being done to improve farming. Better soil conservation and farming practices are being more widely employed in producing grains, but most grains are fed to animals or used in other products, like pancake mixes. Being able to attach the "conservation farming" label to these consumer foods is a difficult matter. Even when grains are consumed in more direct forms, such as in cereal and flour, determining what label or description adequately captures the "better farming" involved in growing the grain is a challenge. An alternative to labeling food products is certifying the farms where it is grown as having met a set of farming standards. This type of third-party certification is possible and is essentially what is done for products like Niman Ranch meat, now approved by Certified Humane, for meeting its standards. So far efforts to certify farms by the conservation practices used, such as their commitment to resilient agriculture, remains a willow wisp. But hope may be on the horizon. Burgeoning attention to climate change and recognizing how farming practices are keys to storing carbon in the soil may help spur creative efforts for food marketing and labels for farming practices. Using the "better farming" label to communicate to consumers, may create the potential branding linkage to food products, an important step now missing as David Montgomery points out in *Growing a Revolution.*

A second challenge faced in developing a more robust, better food, better farming connection in the US comes from a more unexpected place. The movement runs counter to the "official" view of the role of agriculture, at least the views expressed by recent USDA officials like former Secretary Perdue and his underlings in the former guy's administration. There is no better evidence than the vocal opposition from the United States to the European Union's announcement of the new "Farm to Fork" agricultural policy in 2020. The EU is charting a new course for its farmers and food system, based on resilient agriculture practices, reduced reliance on chemicals, increased organic food production, and consumer health as a way to reform farming practices. In a July 2020 video conference with his European counterparts, Secretary Perdue warned of the dangers in this new policy, claiming to deny farmers access to modern technology will place the EU at a competitive disadvantage with American agriculture and our reliance on agro-chemicals to increase production. The European ministers explained the purpose of Farm to Fork is to protect the health of the land and people, and to insure long-term stability and sustainability of European agriculture. This explanation fell on deaf ears with the Americans and senior USDA officials continued attacking the Farm to Fork idea, going so far as to claim it will increase hunger and famine in the world. There in a nutshell is the difference in our approaches. The EU is moving forward with policies to promote and safeguard the health of the land, while American policy has been based on assuming the land is just fine and new production technologies are worth any risk they might pose. In other words, the health of the land can be taken for granted, a view reflected in how slowly we have embraced the idea of soil health. Our approach to agriculture and food, reflected in our heavy reliance on agro-chemicals, confirms what Drs. Hatfield and Cruse observed: we essentially treat the soil as a growth medium rather than as a living part of the natural system of agriculture. One of the exciting opportunities that comes from having a new Administration in charge of American farm and environmental policy is the potential for major changes in how our attitudes to food, farming, and conserving the land may be reflected in national priorities.

SHAPING THE PUBLIC'S IMPRESSION OF FARMING'S FUTURE

Another challenge in making the Better Food, Better Farming linkage concerns how the public's view of agriculture is shaped, and whether the public has confidence farmers are working in their best interests. The images of farming and its future the public sees on television and in the media, help shape this issue. Contrasting images and the unfortunate impressions some popular treatments may leave were present in two television shows I happened to see. In a September 2020 episode of Andrew Zimmer's "What's Eating America" on CNN, he visited the world's largest vertical farm, and spoke with an "expert" on the future of food. Their conversation was disheartening. They described the large warehouse facility as not just the future of food but in fact necessary because millions of acres of farmland are now so degraded by erosion crops won't grow. Both propositions are preposterous. Vertical farming may be a passing fancy, attractive if you see it as an answer to urban food deserts, but the building costs and energy needed to grow mostly micro-greens and salad, raise serious doubts if vertical farming will ever be an answer to urban food needs, or a wise or necessary substitute for raising food on land. Clearly, we have challenges with soil erosion and land stewardship but these can be addressed and we do not have a shortage of farmland, either in America or near most urban areas. This does not mean there is not an important role to play by urban agriculture, whether in community gardens or mini-farms. Novella Carpenter captured the challenge and excitement of urban agriculture in her 2009 book, *Farm City: The Education of an Urban Farmer*. It is a great leap from people raising food in neighborhoods to believing vertical farms will answer food deserts.

The CNN episode got worse when Mr. Zimmer went on to expound enthusiastically about how once we begin feeding ourselves from vertical farms we can retire millions of acres of land now being farmed unsustainably and instead use it to grow native grasses to sequester carbon. He didn't address how we will go about convincing the thousands of farm families now owning and working this land to quit farming and make the shift, it was just assumed to make sense. This is definitely not the future of farming nor should it be. We are not going to address urban food needs with vertical farms and we are not going to retire tens of millions of acres now being farmed just to sequester carbon. Our solutions as discussed in Chapter Nine, will need to be more comprehensive and sensitive to the needs of farmers, eaters, and the land if we expect them to work.

The problem with shows like this is how the experts reveal so little understanding about how land is owned or how agriculture operates in the economy. For our purposes let's call this category of viewpoints the "beautiful dreamers." On the other side of the media equation, you find another equally problematic version of our future. We will call this category of viewpoints the "woe is me, no one loves farmers." A prime example of this thinking was an episode of Kamu Bell's "United Shades of America" also on CNN, in late July 2020. Much of the show concerned the serious issue of black land loss and how discrimination and violence, like the infamous Greenwood Massacre in Tulsa one hundred years ago, play major roles in the wealth inequality found in farming and landownership, a reality discussed in Chapter Five. The portion of the episode that caught my eye though was the last segment featuring a white farm family from Oklahoma. The interview was primarily with the father, a leader in the Oklahoma Farmers Union, America's most historically progressive farm group. Unfortunately, the conversation followed a predictable path with the farmer explaining all the ills and woes they face, from the loss of exports, to consolidation of meatpacking, to a lack of anti-trust enforcement leaving no profits from feeding cattle, and on to how little value the wheat they sell returns once it is turned into cereal. The interview left you with the collective impression the farm was a depressing enterprise, constantly losing money, barely able to survive. Woe is me indeed.

The challenges farmers face from natural causes like weather and an increasingly consolidated market place are real, but watching shows like this can't help but leave viewers asking if things are so bad in farming, why does anyone do it? The show is just one example of the "woe is me" variety of farm coverage but the pattern is familiar. First, farmers explain how they cannot make any money, leaving one to wonder how did the farm survive until now? Second, the subtext is essentially no one loves farmers and people will be sorry when they go hungry once farmers are gone. I have heard this refrain all my life in farm country – you will miss us when we are gone. But our food supply has never lagged and the average percent of income Americans spend on food continues to drop, even as farm numbers continue to decline. So what should we do? That is one ingredient usually missing in these shows - any suggestion for what needs to be done to improve the situation for farmers or agriculture. Instead the shows typically next shift to a segment showing a recent college graduate on a small farm selling vegetables at a farmer's market, explaining how to make a living on ten acres.

Don't get me wrong, farmers markets are an important outlet for many small farms and an exciting way for consumers to buy food, but they are not the future of American agriculture and few people, even the best direct marketers, make a living on ten acres. The problem faced by most conventional crop farmers, like the family from Oklahoma, is how the United States has developed a farm policy built on government subsidies, crop insurance, and ever-expanding production. The system locks grain farmers into raising commodities for sale, often at barely break-even prices, yet it always benefits the agro-chemical companies selling farmers the high-priced seeds, pesticides, and fertilizers they need to stay on the merry-go-round. Farmers make enough to hang on for another year, and if the market doesn't provide the income, the public steps in as it did in 2020, providing over 40% of farm income through $46 billion in taxpayer subsidies. The question is how, when, or even if, US agriculture can break out of this vicious cycle and get off the ride of trying to produce our way to nirvana. This is a central challenge facing many farmers, and one reason why an increasing number are finding hope in the idea of producing better foods and using conservation farming and resilient agriculture to build soil health and address climate change. Many of these farmers see emerging opportunities to "market" environmental services – such as water quality and capturing carbon – from their land as keys to the future.

Given the contrasting visions of farming you can see how the public's perception of agriculture and the future can be influenced. On one hand, we have the view "agriculture is over," farmers can't be trusted, and climate change means food will need to be raised in whole new ways like vertical farms. On the other hand, we have the "no one loves farmers but you need us," just don't ask us how we treat the land perspective. What is missing is the reality many farmers do care for the land and are seeking a future raising the foods consumers want and need. If there is a middle version to the story, one where farming is profitable and rewarding and a more hopeful occupation, isn't this the goal we should be seeking? A future where consumers can be confident the foods they eat are safe, wholesome, and raised on well cared for lands? These farmers and foods exist and there is a better food and better farming option if we will support it. We are fools to believe we can either give up on farming as a lost cause or believe alternatives like vertical farms and lab grown meat are the answers. They may provide a sliver of the food supply, as did food fad "innovations" like the "Flav'r Sav'r tomato" and Better Life Grains from decades ago. Instead of chasing impracticable alternatives we need to work with the farm families who own the land to help them care for the land and to have a stronger voice in policy making. We can support policies and systems letting farmers obtain a fairer return in the market and develop more equal relations with the companies buying their crops and selling them inputs. You can help these farmers by buying the better foods they raise and encouraging more farmers to join in. Doing so is critical not just for the current system of farmers but also for the next generation of farmers we need to care for the land and grow our better foods.

GROWING THE NEXT GENERATION OF AMERICA'S FARMERS

A strong argument can be made no issue is more important to the future of US agriculture than identifying the next generation of farmers. Who will produce our food, steward the land, and carry on the work of building a sustainable and resilient food system? The good news is the nation is experiencing a surge in interest of people who want to farm and who want to be involved in our food system. This includes farm kids, like the children of Niman Ranch farmers who want to carry on the family tradition of raising hogs, and like Chris Gaesser the young neighbor to whom we sold our land. It includes young people like the returning veterans taking part in the Combat Boots to Cowboy Boots initiative in Nebraska and the student interns at the UC-Santa Cruz farm, learning how to make careers raising better foods and caring for the land. One of those interns was Danelle Myers, who moved home to her parent's farm near Logan, to join the next generation of Iowa farmers and landowners. She represents an exciting dimension of the new farmer movement, women creating new farms and food businesses. This is the subject of Temra Costa's 2010 book, *Farmer Jane: Women Changing the Way We Eat*. Our nation and rural communities need the energy and creativity young people and new families bring to the land and to building a stronger rural economy. My 2011 article, "America's New Agrarians: Policy Opportunities and Legal Innovations to Support New Farmers" focused on new farmers and policies to support them. Our challenge is developing a comprehensive approach and national commitment to this next generation. There are ways this can be done: assisting them with training and education, offering financing to acquire land, tailoring government programs to their needs and the foods they produce, and encouraging the current generation of farmers and landowners to make room so land and farms can be smoothly transferred to the next generation.

A new generation of farmers offers opportunities for the land. It may be simplistic to generalize about the New Agrarians' motivations, but they appear to share more enlightened attitudes toward conservation, sustainability, and environmental stewardship. Many have been weaned on books by Michael Pollan and are inspired to be part of a brighter food future. This next generation views environmental issues like addressing water quality and confronting the challenges of climate change as social and moral responsibilities, as opportunities not economic burdens. New Agrarians see involvement in food production and agriculture as imbued with a dimension of public service. This ideal led Curt Ellis and others to create the Food Corps, a public service initiative giving young leaders the opportunity to work in the nation's schools, teaching children about gardening, food, and nutrition. Discussions leading to creation of the Food Corps, began when several of us met in Washington DC to explore how the federal government might support new farmer training as a form of public service. Farming bears elements of public service, but the business and profit motivations made it difficult to bring farming within government guidelines for public service. Training school kids about nutrition and food production however were acceptable and the Food Corps was launched. To date, hundreds of service members have been trained and many are joining the ranks of America's food policy activists and community leaders.

As with many issues involving food and agriculture, land plays a critical and foundational role. Issues of land access and affordability are major obstacles many new farmers have difficulty surmounting. Finding innovative ways to own and manage land is a mission of many land trusts. Some are exploring how land can be made available for new farmers to use. Examining the work of land trusts in creating new opportunities for owning and stewarding America's land in the subject of the next chapter.

Selling the farm to Chris.

Chapter Eight – Land Trusts to the Rescue

After staying put at Sunstead for several months a road trip to see Iowa's beautiful land seemed in order. The visit to Storm Lake for the watershed meeting discussed in Chapter Six had been a nice diversion and way to see Iowa in full bloom. The plan for this trip was to visit several examples of Iowa lands being given back to nature in more original forms. I started with my friend Paul Willis of Niman Ranch fame, to see what he calls the Dream Farm – and dream it is. After navigating to his farmhouse northwest of Thornton in the prairie pothole region of north central Iowa, we hopped on a four-wheeler to see what he and nature have been collaborating on. He bought the 160 acres in the early 1990s and farmed it for several years, raising the Iowa twins, corn and soybeans. Paul is a long-time bird watcher and nature lover, and after a few years of farming the wet bottoms and dry slopes he recognized the need to do something different with this land. The transformation began when he put most of the farm into the Conservation Reserve Program or CRP, retiring it from production under a ten-year contract with USDA. Then Paul learned about USDA's Wetland Reserve Program where he could sell a permanent easement on the land in exchange for creating wetlands and upland prairie. In 2002 he took the plunge and signed the first WRP easement in the county and the Dream Farm was born. The result is a complex of five wetlands and ponds spread across the bottomlands, surrounded by one of the finest examples of restored prairie in his part of the state. Touring the property, you learn Paul is a keen observer of plant life and proud of the native species he is bringing back to the land. Frequent stops to point out a new planting or to inspect a faded tiling flag used previously to mark a special species confirm you are in the company of a true "prairie enthusiast." Proof of his effort shows up in the count, today over 135 different native forbs, grasses, and prairie flowers grow on this site.

A stop at the wetland to watch the birds offered a similar window into Iowa's natural world. A swirling flight of Blue-wing Teal and the distinctive ratchet-like cry of the Belted Kingfisher greeted us. It wasn't the right time of year but Paul was proud to report he had seen Sandhill Cranes on the big marsh, and was pleased a pair of Trumpeter Swans had hatched a clutch of cygnets that spring. Paul's love for the land, working in tandem with progressive USDA conservation programs, have turned a hilly Iowa farm with marshy bottoms into a haven for nature, one that will exist long after we are gone. There is a lesson in this story. Paul didn't set out on his farming career with plans to turn his land into a showplace for nature. But the funding opportunities offered by the USDA programs made it possible for him to make the transition and bring his vision to life. The Dream Farm is a perfect example of the resilience of nature. All it took was breaking out the tile lines draining the land. Once the water was back, the willows came, followed by the rushes and the waterfowl. The story isn't much different on the prairie slopes. Once cultivation stopped and prairie seeds were spread, time, patience, and sunshine brought history back to life. It is clear Paul, now in his early 70s, finds more joy getting on his 4-wheeler to tour the prairie than he did clambering up on a tractor to try pulling one more corn crop off the land. By helping farmers and landowners find their inner naturalist, federal conservation programs are important keys for protecting fragile lands and restoring balance to the landscape. The Dream Farm is an oasis of nature, an island in a sea of cornfields. Like anyone alone on an island, Paul and other landowners who restore natural lands face a question, what comes next? What will happen to the land when they are gone, will the children continue working with nature or will the land go back under the plow with new owners?

It was nice to hear Paul talk about the trumpeter swans nesting on his wetland. Their return to Iowa is a great story, one even reaching Sunstead. On winter evenings walking across the meadow and along Sugar Creek in the bottom, I sometimes hear swans overhead. About three years ago a group of swans, perhaps as many as 150, began ganging up to spend the winter on the open water at Maffet Reservoir, eight miles to the south. I remember the first time hearing their distinctive notes. I was rolling the trash bins out to be collected one bitterly cold afternoon, and suddenly I heard what sounded like someone practicing the trumpet. Who would be out in this weather doing that? Then my eyes were drawn upward and not far overhead a dozen swans were flying low, fighting a head wind, and the source of the trumpeting was clear. What a glorious sound they make, even more musical than Leopold's goose music, and what a feeling to know they are back in Iowa.

The main goal of land trusts like the Iowa Natural Heritage Foundation is to work with landowners like Paul to help them care for their land, to make room for nature like the swans, and to find ways to be sure their efforts continue into the future. Paul recently joined me on the board of the Foundation and it is possible his land may come to INHF at some future time, if he so decides. Or his land might end up with the county or state, adding to the extensive network of publicly owned prairies and wetlands being restored in his region. The future of his land is for him to decide, along with his family. Who ends up with the title is not as important as what is being done on the land. The restoration and protection Paul began will continue because the conservation easement he signed with the USDA is permanent, meaning the Dream Farm will live on as his legacy to nature.

WHAT LAND TRUSTS MEAN FOR AMERICA'S LAND

I have spent over thirty years on the INHF board, and have gained a firsthand education in how land trusts work and how projects get funded. The role it plays as a bridge with federal, state, and county governments, and with individual landowners motivated to protect their land is a critical ingredient in our land future. The type of landowners INHF works with run the gamut but many are motivated by a Leopoldian land ethic – a desire to protect unique natural features they own on lands they have restored, such as prairies or oak savannas. It is important to appreciate how land trusts serve as a source of creative ideas for carrying out land protection. One example is INHF's historic work turning the WRP into a source of public land. INHF does this by working with farmers like Paul, to acquire the property rights remaining after permanent easements are placed on the land restored as wetlands. Landowners get paid a large portion of the land's fair market value but retain the actual title. The easements require the land be maintained as a wetland, be fenced, and the property taxes paid, obligations most owners are not interested in meeting once the land can no longer be farmed. As a result, many WRP participants have been glad to sell their residual legal interests or fee title to the land under easements to the INHF or to other public agencies. Subsequently, INHF has transferred title to thousands of acres of these restored wetlands to public authorities, like county conservation boards, meaning the once private lands are now open for public use, often as wildlife management areas with public hunting. The effect is to turn what began as a federal conservation program into a source of funding for acquiring new public lands, increasing wildlife habitat and recreational opportunities, and improving water quality.

Land trusts are at the tip of the fight against land abusers and property rights advocates who work against the public interest. Prime examples are the efforts of the Iowa Farm Bureau Federation to prevent non-profit conservation organizations and their public partners from acquiring more public land. Even some county boards of supervisors, like in Palo Alto County, have opposed INHF acquiring land for public entities to improve water quality. Land trusts play a critical role in "advocating" for public lands policy in ways state and local agencies are unable to, and can be flexible in financing and acquiring property for future sale to public agencies. Land trusts play key policy making roles as well. INHF members spent years leading the efforts to gain voter approval for a constitutional amendment to create the natural resources and outdoor recreation trust fund. In 2010, over 62% of Iowans voted to approve the fund, to be filled with the next 3/8 cent increase in the sales tax. Sadly, in the twelve years since then the Iowa legislature has failed to increase the tax or fund the trust.

Mark Ackelson, a friend from our days in Forestry School, served as the INHF president for eighteen years, helping the Foundation innovate with many new forms of land protection funding. Mark worked with interested officials in several Iowa counties to place bond issue referenda before the voters to increase property taxes to fund land protection and outdoor recreation. The efforts have been successful and local bonding in several Iowa counties—Polk, Linn, and Johnson—have added tens of millions of dollars to the public funds for natural resource protection and public land acquisition in the last decade. Bonding for nature is not just the province of more populous counties. I am proud to report voters in my home county Adams, the most sparsely populated county in Iowa with fewer than 4,000 residents, overwhelming approved a $2 million bond effort to fund improvements for camping and recreation at Lake Icaria. The Foundation's current president, Joe McGovern, continues this legacy of innovative leadership, working with landowners and others to expand the Foundation's reach. Creative approaches to project funding and a willingness to take risks to protect unique Iowa lands and natural resources are hallmarks of the INHF. It is showing how land trusts can organize coalitions of interested people to promote land projects with long-term community focus.

Collectively the land trust movement includes hundreds of organizations, thousands of staff and board members, and millions of citizens as donors, supporters, and members. At the national level, their issues are represented through membership in the Land Trust Alliance. It includes small land trusts focused on very local issues, like Iowa's Bur Oak Land Trust and the Whiterock Conservancy, as well as statewide land trusts like INHF. Larger organizations with national roles, like the Nature Conservancy, the Trust for Public Lands, and American Farmland Trust are important parts of the LTA. If people can be motivated to protect land, they can become powerful players in political issues. One challenge citizens face working on conservation is how their concerns may appear to be fragmented by region or locale, or even by the type of natural resource being protecting, such as farmland or wildlife habitat. Even with these different objectives, the common themes of land trusts are nature, land, citizen engagement, private action, and partnering with local governments and the public when needed. One critical role played by land trusts, sometimes by necessity rather than intention, has been in developing new types and models of land ownership and management. Promoting and refining the use of conservation easements tailored to the needs of the land and individual landowners is the best evidence of how land trusts have led innovations in property law.

A key issue for many in the land trust movement's future is exploring ways to increase public access and use of privately-owned property. Land trusts play a critical role in broadening the idea of "public lands" and public benefits, by working on behalf of the public interest and common good. Sometimes the efforts are to protect resources or values, such as scenic views, not traditionally recognized as "public." Land trusts are broadening how the public can be involved with nature, helping welcome the public back onto public lands. Creating ways for citizens to engage with the land, through volunteer events like prairie seed harvests and river clean up days, are important examples. Emphasizing the role of youth and future leaders in outdoor education and nature experiences, such as internship programs, is another. Land trusts expand the idea of how the public interest is promoted on the land, and are evolutionary in expanding options for property ownership and management. They are able to have a laser like focus on unique resource issues, such as "rails to trails" conversion. The Rails-to Trails Conservancy developed expertise and unique legal tools, such as rail banking soon to be abandoned corridors. It has been able to reach donors, members, and trail users in adding thousands of miles of recreational trails for the nation. Its success shows how land trusts can make great additions to the opportunities for citizens to be outside on the land.

The Back Forty Talks about Wildlife

For some reason people don't think of me as a living organism. Anyone who puts their hands in my soil knows I am full of life. The earthworms wiggling through me are just one sign. Others, like the microbes, diatoms, and fungi, some creatures you can't even see without a microscope, all give me life, make me fertile, and healthier. Many living things call me home. The clutch of young pheasant chicks in the fencerow, the vixen with her fox kits playing at the den entrance, even a badger every now and then, find places to live on me. Some wildlife friends only stop by for brief visits at certain times of year. It amazes me how each spring when the farmer comes to till my surface, exposing the rich black soil full of worms and bugs, a flock of gulls and terns appear as if by magic, swooping low as the fresh black stripes turn over. Where do they come from and how do they know this is the day to arrive, with me being miles from the nearest water?

Each spring and fall the evening air is filled with honking from the passing skeins of geese flying high headed north for a new breeding season or south for a winter rest. Leopold called this goose music and lamented how diminished must be the lives of those who never hear it play. My favorite sound from decades ago, was the bugling call of the majestic Trumpeter

278

Swan. Weighing over 30 pounds with a wingspan of 8 feet, these giants ruled the marshes and wetlands covering millions of acres of Iowa before what you like to call settlement, took place. Like their wildlife friends, the elk and bison, swans were soon eradicated from Iowa as wetlands were drained and hunters worked their will. The last nesting pair in Iowa was on Twin Lakes in Hancock County in 1883. It would be over 120 years before they returned. The Trumpeters almost joined the bison in the fate that befell the Passenger Pigeon, the doom of extinction, the darkest end possible in the scorecard of the land and nature. By the early 1930s only a few dozen Trumpeters remained tucked away in Yellowstone, but like the American bison who had also been saved by their isolation there, Trumpeters began the journey to recovery. Over the years the dedicated efforts of state wildlife officials and individuals devoted to raising swans helped rebuild the population, creating a supply of young birds to place on wetlands and lakes across the nation.

One of my great joys in recent years has been to hear the Trumpeters call again. State wildlife officials in Iowa are carrying out the most ambitious swan re-introduction effort in the nation. Beginning in the early 1990s, the state has placed over 1,200 young swans aged between one and two at over 80 locations in Iowa. Another 1,600 cygnets were hatched in Iowa's wetlands by nesting pairs of swans. Today, Iowa is home to hundreds of these magnificent birds and I am proud to report this includes Lake Icaria just 10 miles north of me. I remember in the late 1950s when the project was first proposed. Then it was called the Walters Creek Watershed, planned under the 1954 Watershed Protection and Flood Prevention Act, P.L. 83-566. USDA used this law all across the nation to work with state and local governments to fund installing thousands of small dams, creating lakes and ponds used for flood control, livestock, recreation, irrigation, and related uses. It took years of planning and effort to secure the federal funds needed to buy the farmland and build the dam, but today the Walters Creek Watershed project has morphed into Lake Icaria. This 650-acre lake built in 1978, is surrounded by 1,000-acres of grass, trees, and campgrounds. It is the gem of the Adams County Conservation Board Park system and popular with anglers from across the region. In May 2019, state wildlife officials and local school kids gathered there to welcome a new pair of swans to call Lake Icaria home. Who knows, one day I may hear their offspring bugling overhead searching for new feeding grounds.

Iowa has quite a record reintroducing wildlife to the land. The best example is the wild turkey. The last native turkey was killed in Lucas County around 1910 but in the 1960s Iowa began acquiring turkeys from game officials in Missouri. The reintroduction program started in the state forests of southern Iowa but over the years expanded to cover nearly the entire state. Today turkeys thrive in Iowa and now number in the tens of thousands, making them one of Iowa's most popular game birds pursued by hunters in fall and spring seasons. Their success created the opportunity for state officials to capture and trade wild Iowa turkeys for other game, like river otters from Louisiana, and ruffed and sharp tail grouse for reintroduction. Otters are another success story and today they are found in most of Iowa's river systems. The state's "They Otter be in Iowa" campaign built public enthusiasm for otters, and spotting one is an exciting thrill for paddlers and anglers. Not all the state's efforts at reintroducing wild game have been as successful as the swans, otters, and turkeys. Prairie chickens once covered prairies like me in southern Iowa, but efforts to re-establish them have been challenging, due to the limited supply of large open grasslands they need. Even so, the state keeps trying and dozens of birds are finding a toehold on public and private grasslands near Kellerton. Just the chance to see them attracts bird watchers on early spring mornings in hopes of watching the males dance their mating ritual on flattened grass leks or booming grounds.

I am happy the state has not given up on the prairie chicken and know Iowa conservation heroes like Aldo Leopold, who started the academic study of game management, and Ding Darling, who set the course for our nation's wildlife refuges, would approve as well. When I think of all the life coursing through and over me, my hope is you too will come to understand how the land is a living thing and give us the respect and opportunity for the life we and all who dwell in and on us deserve.

INHF PROJECTS – PROTECTING IOWA'S LAND AND FUTURE

After stopping at Paul's Dream Farm, I headed to Decorah in northeast Iowa to meet Brian Fankhauser, INHF's Bluffland and Senior Land Stewardship director, who manages our projects in the region. Our plan was to visit several INHF projects illustrating the versatility of our work, showing how it contributes to Iowa's land future. I spent the night in the RV parked on the northeast edge of Twin Valley farm, home of Seed Savers Exchange (SSE). I know this property well from my twenty-five years on the SSE board and there is an INHF angle to the property as well. Fifteen years ago, the SSE board was finalizing the purchase of the over 800 acres. It seized on the opportunity to apply for USDA's farmland protection funding. Because SSE has no plans to develop the land or do anything but farm it the program was a perfect fit. The challenge was figuring out who could pay the required matching portion of the easement price, not covered by the

USDA. This is where INHF stepped in to provide the needed matching funds. It now serves in holding the conservation easement on the 720 acres SSE entered in the program. Helping two of my favorite organizations triangulate this valuable USDA program was very satisfying. SSE got the funding it needed to purchase the land and INHF obtained a conservation easement protecting over 700 acres of unique land with rare plants like marsh marigolds, fens, and miles of coldwater streams in the Upper Iowa River watershed. US taxpayers did their part to make possible the permanent land protection. Today Twin Valleys is privately owned by SSE but the miles of trails are open for use by the public. In fact, several years ago the SSE board granted a fishing easement to the Iowa DNR, officially opening several miles of the trout streams for public fishing.

After meeting Brian in Decorah, we headed northeast, in separate cars to satisfy COVID-19 employee safety guidelines, toward a location a few miles from the Minnesota border. Our first stop wasn't on the original schedule but after about twenty miles Brian slowed his truck and turned north on a gravel road. I followed and after a mile, we came to the destination, the former Girl Scout Camp called Tahigwa. The INHF had acquired the campgrounds several years before when the Girl Scouts determined the camp no longer fit their plans and faced what to do with the property. INHF stepped in to purchase the 400-acres of timbered hills and creek bottoms with the plan to eventually transfer it to public ownership and use. We worked with the state to sell it the property and today it is an Iowa DNR wildlife management area, with several of the former Girl Scout buildings used by DNR staff. After a short hike to see the stream and bluffs, we resumed our trip and finally stopped two miles northwest of Dorchester at what INHF calls the Osterholm-Marti property. The beautiful valley holds what is believed to be the only site in Iowa where three cold-water streams braid together.

The purpose of our visit was to meet INHF's summer land stewardship crew hard at work cutting invasive species like Russian olive out of the bottomlands. Each year INHF hires interns recruited from Iowa colleges and universities and immerses them in land conservation work with landowners and INHF staff. Most interns, some forestry students like I had been years ago, work on the land stewardship crew performing conservation duties. Other interns with different backgrounds work with INHF staff to gain professional experience in areas like communications, grant writing, and policy. Most of the summer land work is done on properties owned by either the Foundation or by county conservation boards. The Foundation is happy to work with private landowners who undertake conservation efforts, like restoring prairies, day lighting oak savannas, or protecting banks along pristine cold-water trout streams, like the Osterholm-Marti property.

If the name Osterholm sounds familiar, it is another COVID-19 coincidence. Dr. Michael Osterholm, who directs the Center for Infectious Disease Research and Policy at the University of Minnesota, was a frequent guest on nightly news shows. For months he described the magnitude of threat posed by the pandemic and now serves the Biden Administration on the issue. He is a native of northeast Iowa and was responsible for restoring the streams and oak covered hillsides we visited. Helping private landowners like him is a key part of the INHF mission. INHF leaders know it is impossible for the public to acquire all the natural lands in Iowa needing protection, so INHF is happy to work with private landowners and other organizations engaged in land protection.

After visiting the interns and hiking the streamside trails, my next stop was fifty miles southeast in the Mississippi bluff lands near Marquette, home to Effigy Mounds National Monument. The Back Forty explained the unique history of the Mounds in Chapter Two and whenever I am close by, a climb to the ridge tops is a welcomed excursion. The parking lot was full that morning with vehicles from around the nation but the National Park Service Welcome Center was closed due to the pandemic. Walking around the building, I was pleased to see a wall plaque thanking INHF for leading the acquisition of the 1,000-acres of timberland added to the monument in 2001. I remember well the board meeting when we approved purchasing the land because it was the first time we approved spending over $1 million on a property. It was a few years before the National Park Service obtained the funds to buy the land but now Effigy Mounds and the adjacent Yellow River State Forest have grown to become one of the largest tracts of contiguous public forests in the Upper Mississippi region.

In the twenty years since the project, Foundation board approval to spend $1 million or more to protect Iowa land has become routine as land prices increase and our confidence in being able to fund large projects has grown. I was reminded of the changes in land prices and the scale of our efforts in spring 2020 when INHF agreed to purchase a 960-acre tract of farmland and timber from a farm family in Davis County in southern Iowa. The size of the purchase price, over $3 million, made it one of our more expensive projects but the opportunity to secure a property of that size from one owner is rare given Iowa's fractionated land ownership. Another feature made the acquisition a sobering footnote in Iowa's land history. My research included reading early volumes of *The Land*, and on page 322 in Volume One, published in 1941, is an article by Russell Lord about Ding Darling and "The Bleeding Hills of Iowa." The article describes what Lord called "Ding's plan" to have the government purchase 300,000 acres of eroded and abused land in three Davis County townships–Soap Creek, Salt Creek, and Licking. Ding's idea was for the USDA to buy the land for around $9 per acre and resettle the hundreds of tenant farm families onto better farmland under its land resettlement program. The government would hire the local people to install conservation practices and restore the bleeding hills for use in the proposed Hawkeye National Forest, then on the Forest Service drawing board. The project would protect the abused land and support jobs in conservation, outdoor recreation, and wildlife management.

You can guess what happened next. Nothing came of Ding's plan for the Bleeding Hills. By 1940 the Congressional appetite for buying eroded farmland from private owners had waned and with it, the push to create new national forests in the East, like those added in Illinois, Ohio, and Indiana. The political shift and early preparations for the coming war, combined to doom ambitious land restoration projects like what Ding had in mind for Davis County. After the Hawkeye National Forest plan was set aside, the federal government eventually transferred thousands of acres of the eroded farmland it had already acquired to the state of Iowa. The tracts are now some of the largest units in the Iowa State Forest system. What happened to the degraded farmland in the Bleeding Hills of Davis County? It remained in private hands and was farmed for the next eighty years after Ding's plan. That is, until now. You guessed it again, the 960 acres INHF agreed to purchase in 2020 for fair market value of over $3,000 an acre is in

Soap Creek Township. The owners and the land both experienced a rather healthy increase in value from the $9 per acre price tag owners were happy to accept in the late 30s to what INHF willingly paid in 2020. The lesson is clear, just like with planting trees, the best time to protect land or acquire it for pubic use is today rather than twenty years from now.

SECOND LIFE FOR SUMMER CAMPS

One of the many changes in American society is the declining participation in many traditional youth organizations, in particular for experiences like weeklong stays at summer camps. As membership in organizations such as the Boys Scouts, Girl Scouts, and 4-H have declined, their affiliated summer camps have been placed in jeopardy. This trend threatens the future of many historic summer camps, impacting hundreds of acres of forests, lakesides, and natural lands. Parent organizations face declining participation, lower revenue, and increasing costs to staff and maintain aging facilities. This makes managing extensive land holdings and retaining a camp more difficult to afford or justify. In the last twenty years dozens of summer camps have been shuttered in Iowa alone. Because the land often represents a valuable asset, financially strained organizations face the difficult decision of selling the land. Placing the land on the market is not easy given the history and identification people have with the camps and decisions to sell often face strong opposition from former campers and leaders with youthful memories of camping experiences. Because camp lands usually contain natural features like lakes and wooded hills, often located near growing populations, the properties can be prime locations for housing developments or other threats to the natural features.

The great news is what might otherwise be a loss for nature and wildlife can become a win for land and the public. In many states land trusts and conservation organizations have worked with local citizens to buy the camps and give their defenders the opportunity to write a new chapter in their use. In Iowa, the INHF has led efforts to protect former camps and in the last twenty years it has helped purchase and protect over a dozen youth summer camps. The INHF then works with local government agencies, such as the county conservations boards to transform camps into county owned parks open to the public. INHF has also acquired and transferred camp land to the state Department of Natural Resources for use as state parks or wildlife management areas, like Camp Tahigwa we visited. In 2019 INHF pulled off its most significant rescue of a former camp, when it paid over $3 million to acquire the 1,000-acre Clover Hills camp along the Des Moines River, twenty miles from Des Moines. The unique wooded bluffs and upland prairies site had been operated by the 4-H Foundation for seventy years and had hosted thousands of farm kids from every corner of the state. Now the future of the land is secure as the INHF and the state DNR craft a shared plan to protect the land for public use and enjoyment.

In addition to acquiring land like this for later transfer to a public entity, the INHF is directly engaged in land stewardship. It owns several thousand acres, like Heritage Valley on the Upper Iowa River, and holds over two hundred conservation easements covering more than 25,000 acres all obtained through voluntary negotiations with landowners.

Taking a Long Walk

If you want to connect with the land there is no better way than going for a nice long walk. If you can get out of town, off the sidewalks onto a trail, it is even better. Then you will have a chance to see nature and experience some of what the land can offer. If you happen to be near Decorah in far northeast Iowa there is a perfect trail for connecting with the land, rivers, upland timber, and even fertile rolling fields and dairy farms. The Trout Run Trail is an eleven-mile loop circling the town. At least five miles run alongside the beautiful Upper Iowa River or streams flowing into it. One unique highlight is a segment in the middle of farm fields. Depending on the season you might be swallowed up by towering rows of corn or flow through a sea of soybeans or alfalfa. The trail is more than just eleven miles of ups and downs. About half way along you come to the Decorah Fish Hatchery, where the Iowa Department of Natural Resources produces the millions of young trout used for stocking the cold-water streams found in that part of the state. The hatchery's open ponds are full of adult trout used for breeding, and by putting a quarter in a repurposed peanut machine you can buy a handful of trout food. Toss it in a pond and you can watch trout swirl to the top to devour the pellets. It is a real show but trout aren't the only ones feeding there. If you have ever seen footage from an Eagle Cam, and watched an eagle pair raise their young, you most likely were watching the famous Decorah eagles. Their nest is in a grove of trees just north of the trout hatchery, meaning their next meal is only a long swoop away. You have to give them credit for picking a home site, it is as if Yogi and Boo-Boo built their den behind the picnic basket factory!

INVESTING IN LAND – PROFITS OR NON-PROFITS?

On July 30, 2020, Dan Charles presented a story on National Public Radio titled, "Big Money Investors Gear Up for a Trillion Dollar Bet on Farmland." It was a sobering story illustrating many issues and fault lines in our current thinking and policies toward farming and owning farmland. The main storyline concerned how a wealthy lawyer turned farmer, and his brother, had decided to sell their land in Oregon in part due to their increasing age. Now with over $20 plus million to invest one brother had spent $3 million on two tracts of farmland 1000 miles away in northwest Iowa. The Iowa farmer and landowner who sold the land also made his decision partly due to age and because the land was some distance from his home farm operation. A key part of the story focused on People's Company, the farm management and real estate firm which brokered the sales, and was assisting the new owners with plans for operating the farm, including a focus on conservation practices. The idea of helping clients develop more "sustainable" approaches to farm management is one of People's selling points as it seeks new investors interested not just in owning farmland but in doing the right thing for the land.

As you might imagine, national coverage of a story implicating issues touching on the future of family farms, increasing investor farmland purchases, and "new" approaches to conservation, drew the attention of many farm policy and conservation activists, setting off alarm bells about "what can be done." Shortly after the story aired, Ferd Hoefner, the widely respected and long-time conservation policy guru with the National Sustainable Agriculture Coalition in DC, sent a note to other progressive leaders working on land and conservation issues to organize a Zoom call to discuss the story and its implications.

I joined the call with about twenty other conservationists, most of whom I knew. Several had served on the land tenure study committee I co-chaired for USDA six years before and others had spoken at Drake SOIL conferences over the years.

It was a wide-ranging discussion, though fairly predictable as each speaker struck their main themes about farmland moving to investor owners and the challenges of aiding new and beginning farmers. A new wrinkle in the conversation was the growing concern about how a new generation of start up for profit companies, like Indigo Ag, are actively promoting "climate change" protocols and signing up farmers with the promise of future carbon payments. This issue seemed of particular concern to many people on the call who appeared to doubt the sincerity of the new players and their ability to assist farmers. The common belief was the companies are more interested in monetizing access to the data they can collect from farm clients and marketing it for use by agro-chemical companies and other businesses, than in helping farmers improve soil health.

By the end of the call, everyone had shared their policy ideas or examples, such as for innovative farm transition efforts. However, the collective impression seemed to be there isn't a whole lot anyone on the call, or their groups, can do to confront or alter the economic forces influencing either farmland investors or the new carbon cowboys. After getting off the call, and going for a walk, I reflected on what had transpired. Even with the decades of experience and sincerity of all those on the call, the group was no match for the financially driven forces shaping the issues, and this impotency most likely means little can or will be done to slow the trends. The reality is large institutional investors, like TIAA, the teacher's annuity fund holding my retirement account, will continue to buy farmland adding to the millions of acres it already owns. Thinking about what explains the contrasts in the power of these institutions, the answer dawned on me - it is all about the money.

People investing in farmland have the financial ability to do so and are motivated by the opportunity for profits, the ability to diversify their portfolios, and perhaps a desire to "help" nature by farming better. The farm management companies and realtors involved are motivated by the opportunity to "do deals" and in doing so, increase the pool of investors with large farmland holdings who hire them to manage the land. This is their business model and purpose. The new "carbon cowboys," players like Indigo Ag, in the news on August 3, 2020, for raising $360 million in new funding, are staking their future on the premise of developing markets for carbon and monetizing the data coming off the millions of acres of farmland they hope to assemble.

The farmers and landowners deciding to sell their land to investors are responding to a myriad of personal and family issues. The very emotional decisions to sell land have historically been driven by: pending retirement, health or death, financial pressures from low prices, the opportunity to reap a significant profit, or lack of a successor. For the farmers and new investor landowners signing contracts with Indigo Ag and the other companies entering this space, the offer of a potential new stream of payments, even though undetermined, is still attractive. Better yet it may essentially be "money for nothing" if it means you just need to keep farming using the same conservation practices used for years. Where is the downside in that?

As a result, at all points along the story, money and the potential for new returns are driving the decisions. Weighed against these forces what do the folks gathered on the Zoom call and our well-meaning organizations have to offer? Financially speaking, almost nothing. We do have many good policy ideas and are experts at articulating how the public will benefit over the long term from having more – not less – farmer-owned land. We can explain how we need to plant the next generation of farmers and farmland owners if we want agriculture and rural communities to thrive. We are expert at explaining the need for greater commitments to soil and water conservation and putting farmers in the lead on addressing climate change. But none of these ideas yield profits for the intended audiences, at least in the near term. This contrast is a classic illustration of the difference between being a non-profit organization working for "better public policy" and being a for profit company created around a business model focused on financial returns. If the major issue with land is, as Leopold warned, how we consider it only in economic terms, Dan Charles' story and the trends it reveals are vivid proof.

This realization does not mean there is no hope for better treatment of the land. One reality it may help reveal concerns the land trust model and why this approach to conservation and land protection may offer more successful answers to the issues. From my experience, when the INHF comes to the table to talk with landowners about opportunities to protect land we do so with financial issues in mind and can suggest alternative approaches to make the economics work for those involved. Sometimes the lands are donated or acquired at reduced prices through bargain sales but the decisions are up to the landowners. We do use federal and state tax deductions and credits when available for public donations of interests in land, such as conservation easements, if landowners can benefit by doing so. But in all situations, there is recognition of the financial aspects of the land, as well as its natural features, and of the importance economics can play in landowner decisions. And the transactions are always voluntary. This is why the land trust model may play an increasingly important role in questions of farmland protection, conservation management, and even addressing climate change.

PROTECTING AND SAVING LAND

Driving west from Waukee, the town nearest Sunstead, you pass new developments on the north side of Highway 6, where a new Apple server farm facility is to be built. This is some of the most fertile farmland – not just in Iowa, but in the world – and we can't seem to pave it over fast enough. Last year just a mile to our east, a new exit off Interstate 80 and thoroughfare, Grand Prairie Parkway, opened thousands of acres for development. A new high school north of Waukee is already surrounded by housing developments, spreading north west along the Raccoon River Valley bike trail. All this development adds up to over 5,000 acres of prime farmland being converted in just the last decade! Once the improvements are in place and the buildings completed, there will be demand for more businesses to fill the vacant land skipped over in the first wave of development. Soon thousands more acres of farmland will harvest their last crop, converted permanently to concrete and car-based development. Is this progress?

I always told my students in Environmental Regulation of Agriculture and Land Use, a little nearby land conversion is like "Mr. Tooth Decay." If it is not constrained or prevented then it is only a matter of time before it spreads to neighboring lands. The issue of "farmland protection" has been a focus for much of my career. Even as an undergraduate forestry student, my honors thesis was on "Restrictive Use Agreements for Farmland Protection." It was a unique subject to examine forty-five years ago, when local governments first began using special property tax treatment to control development and conversion of farmland. Farmland protection was always an interest so when I started teaching at the University of Arkansas in 1981 the topic was central to my new class Environmental Regulation of Agriculture, the first class of its type in the nation.

This was a fruitful time in the history of farmland protection. The national lands study led by Bob Gray at USDA, *A Time to Choose* had focused on the issue of the loss of farmland. A new national organization, American Farmland Trust was finding its stride with key board members like Rich Rominger from Yolo County, former director of the California Department of Agriculture and soon to be the Deputy Secretary of Agriculture in the Clinton Administration. There was great interest and experimentation at the local level, especially with counties using zoning and regulatory powers to try new approaches, such as the 160-acre minimum lot size used in McHenry County Illinois. These innovative county and state efforts to protect farmland generated a great deal of pushback from landowners and developers who didn't want restrictions on being able to turn farm ground into housing lots and strip malls. In many ways, these early fights over farmland protection helped plant the seeds for the more organized, vocal, and radical "property rights" movement that emerged. Today any restriction on unbridled property use is quickly painted as unconstitutional and attacked as a regulatory taking that must either give way or result in compensation being paid the owners for the "lost" value. In most "takings" cases, courts may eventually side with the public authorities if the owner is left with a reasonable use of the land – but not always.

I enjoyed teaching students about farmland protection because it helps illustrate the difference (and distance) between an issue considered in the abstract as opposed to at the personal and local level. No one doubts farmland protection is important and given our demand for food and the growing world population it is reasonable to want to protect land so we have an adequate supply to grow food. If we are going to protect farmland it makes sense to protect the most productive land like the flat and fertile farmland found in central Iowa around Waukee and Des Moines. Yet ask anyone, especially a landowner, if they will forgo selling 40-acres to a developer for houses – because we will need their farmland to feed our future – and the answer will invariably be "are you kidding me!" The assumption is we have plenty of land, perhaps even too much given our historic crop surpluses and low commodity prices. This point is hard to argue with when for the last thirty years the US has averaged over 25 million acres of farmland taken out of production and idled under long-term contracts through the Conservation Reserve Program (CRP). If we have so much crop ground we have to pay owners not to farm it then where is the worry? Of course, the folks at American Farmland Trust, and in many local governments can quickly explain, not all acres of farmland are created equal.

Saving the last farm on the edge of town from development is different than protecting a forty in the middle of a rural Iowa county. The landowner's next question, if they are still talking to you, will be to ask, "if I am going to save the farmland who is going to pay me for its value?" If the answer they hear is there will be no compensation because the restriction is a local land use regulation and for the good of society, you can imagine how it will be received. This is the same reaction you will get from the local city planner or city council if they learn plans to annex "undeveloped" farmland to add new houses, citizens, school kids, and tax base to their town should be restrained because of the need to "protect farmland." The truth is most annexation laws and city development plans make no room or accommodation for "protecting farmland." If land is annexed it is going to be developed eventually. This is why farmland protection is such a hard sell and typically a non-starter, especially in states like Iowa and much of the Midwest. For politicians and developers, the issue isn't too little farmland, it is too little development and too little tax base.

We may "lose" over a million acres of farmland every year, as the periodic reports from the AFT say, but it is hard to generate public concern especially at the national level. Part of the problem is we don't lose the land all at once. It is not like a thief comes in the night and takes it. We lose it forty acres at a time through rational economic decisions made by families and landowners – decisions often set in motion decades earlier. The decisions happen for many reasons. The family may need the money, just as we did to pay the nursing home bills. Or perhaps the family is tired of trying to farm in an increasingly developed area surrounded by homeowners who don't appreciate the sounds of tractors in the morning or the smell of livestock in the fields. Perhaps it is just an offer they can't refuse. People have many reasons why they might choose to sell farmland for development. When land is your main asset, perhaps your only retirement account, the idea others can tell you what you can do with it, or even "take" it away without paying you for it, is understandably offensive. Farmers may love their land and want to hold on to it forever, but a cynic will tell you they just haven't received the right offer, perhaps one they fear their kids will find too appealing when their time comes.

The Back Forty on Being a Prairie

At one time I was a prairie. Prairies are all the rage now. In nature circles discussions about climate change and sequestering carbon in the soil much of the conversation focuses on prairies and how valuable they can be. Unfortunately, not much of the focus is on saving ones we still have, at least not in Midwestern states like Iowa and Illinois, because there is hardly anything left to save! The settlers and pioneers couldn't get rid of us fast enough! It was like there was a national contest to see who could plow up the most prairie the fastest – and in so doing you destroyed the native grasslands and many of the plants and critters living here. Come to think of it in many ways it was a national contest to clear the land and plow the prairie. "Improving land" was the term promoted by national policy and it soon became the lodestar of farmers and landowners. Turning the prairie under and planting crops was the road to wealth, profits, and prosperity, and it was providentially blessed as a religious duty. It worked for many people and for most of the time, even though the history of American agriculture is patterned with periodic economic booms and busts. The good times brought new barns and more "improvements" like tiling and bigger machines, while the busts left broken dreams, deserted houses, bankrupt farmers – and in many cases degraded and abused lands. We already plowed that ground in our discussion of soil conservation, here I want to talk about the prairie.

I enjoyed that life – who wouldn't, uninterrupted centuries of sun, rain, growth, wildlife, and nature with a periodic wildfire or blizzard to spice things up. All that came to a crashing end 150 years ago, not just for me but for over 25 million acres like me just in Iowa. Now that is change on a landscape scale! It is hard to argue with the farmers and landowners who plowed me under along with the other prairie lands. Their motivations were understandable, even noble. In some ways, we were like the bison and the Native tribes who lived here who were also plowed under in their own way – almost to oblivion. We were all in the way. As for me, the prairie, perhaps it was understandable how your ancestors could think there is plenty more where I came from by just going further west. When it came to value and economics, the return I could provide was meager compared to the wheat, corn, and hay they could grow in my rich fertile soils. We prairies had done our job, we had made the soils and offered them up with little resistance. Our demise was in many ways a blameless achievement and one that will never be easily undone.

There is good news on the prairie front though and it comes in several ways. First, although you did a great job of clearing us out, you didn't get everything. In the well-fenced railroad right-of-way, in the pioneer cemetery, and even in small tracts tucked away in long-grazed Iowa pastures, remnants of native prairie are still being found. These scraps and pieces are vital links to what once grew on me. They still contain dozens of native plants, the grasses, forbs, and flowers once blanketing the state. Today prairie remnants have a new audience of enthusiasts who treasure their discovery. Individuals and organizations clamor for the opportunity to "save" the prairie pieces and harness them to supply seeds to use restoring and creating new prairies and grasslands. Hundreds of landowners all across Iowa are working to bring prairies back to life. I bite my tongue and resist the urge to cry out "where were you 150 years ago when the teams and gangplow took my prairie away!" Then I remember how my time frame is so different than yours.

The most exciting prairie news for me is about a new one being recreated just one mile north, where I can even see it. The story is even more personal because of who is responsible for this deed. You will hardly believe me when I tell you where it is. It is in Section 2 of Grant Township, the original home place purchased by Mankin Wray in 1871. Yes, this is the same Mankin Wray who gave me to his daughter Anna. The story gets even better because the person responsible for having the prairie restored is the boy professor who grew up on me! The short and sweet version of what is now "Hamilton Prairie," owned by the Adams County Conservation Board, started about thirty-five years ago when he purchased a 40-acre portion of the original Wray home farm from the widow of Mankin's grandson Leo. After pasturing cows for fifteen years, the burden of long-distance management became too great so he decided to sell the land and invest in the farm where he and his wife live. He sold the cattle and then the farmstead to a couple who have restored it. He was left with twelve acres, land his father believed had never been plowed, at least not since the 1920s. At this point the serendipity of interests, sentiment, good deeds, and vision all came together.

As a long-time board member of the INHF the boy had helped the Foundation protect land all across the state, but there were still five Iowa counties without INHF projects and Adams County was one. At the time Adams County had a grand total of one tract of public land available for use by its citizens, the park at Lake Icaria. As he likes to tell it, "Adams County needed a restored prairie more than it needed another corn field." He and his wife worked with the county conservation board and INHF to donate the land and to get the papers signed. Today if you happen to be driving on Highway 34, one mile east of the Prescott corner or one mile west of Stringtown, follow the sign a half mile south on Redwood Ave and you will come to Hamilton Prairie. It is only 12 acres but it seems larger when you get out and walk it, a beautiful prairie in an ocean of cornfields. If you are interested and have time, a mile farther south you can visit Mankin's grave at the former Salem church. That is Iowa land history in a nutshell!

WHEN IS THE RIGHT TIME TO ASK ABOUT THE LAND?

Getting home from my northeast Iowa visit to the INHF projects and to SSE, I was greeted with the aftermath of the Derecho – a freak windstorm that struck central Iowa on August 10th during my visit to Paul's Dream Farm. All we got while walking the prairie was a few sprinkles but the story was much different 100 miles south at Sunstead. First came the dark clouds, then the rain and winds reaching over 80 mph filling the yard with limbs and leaves and toppling a 100-year old oak behind the house. Thankfully it fell south rather than crash down on the deck. Things were much worse in central and eastern Iowa where winds reached 140 mph. Officials later described it as an inland hurricane, and the storm wreaked havoc on millions of acres of Iowa crops and destroyed half the trees in Cedar Rapids. By harvest time over 800,000 acres of crops were considered a total loss and millions more acres suffered yield losses from downed corn. That type of damage made sawing limbs off the oak and hauling them away pale in comparison. The storm did renew a nagging question concerning the land though, when is the right time to criticize how we care for it?

This question of when is the right time to ask if we can't do a better job with our land, soil, and water is a perennial issue in farm country policy debates about conservation and water quality. If farmers are dealing with a devastating windstorm, or low prices, or markets lost to COVID-19, or whatever new plight has recently befallen them, is it fair to ask are they being good stewards? This begs the more important question, if not now, then when is it the right time? If the answer to efforts to push for better soil conservation and improved water quality is always "yes we believe it is a problem but now is not a good time to ask" when will it ever be a good time? The water doesn't know a storm has struck, the land doesn't know the price of corn, any more than it knows who owns it. What it does know is how it is being treated. Why should important societal goals like protecting soil and water be determined by market conditions, either for the farm sector or for individual farmers and landowners? Our answer can't be society should only expect clean water when agriculture can afford it or if landowners believe in it. Who decides what is affordable and what if their answer is never? One reason society needs and uses regulations is to set expected standards of conduct. Developers don't put fire alarms in the apartments they build only when they feel like paying for them, they install them as an obligation to society and because the law requires it.

In 2020 the nation dealt with unfolding conflicts and tensions from the bitter Presidential race, demands for racial justice, the dogged prevalence of COVID-19, the lunacy of Q-anon, and the death of beloved Justice Ginsburg. Viewed from the perspective of society, these cascading crises seemed to challenge if we could move forward as a strong, united people. Viewed from the perspective of the land the scene was different, the land is stable and unknowing about the affairs of people. It will continue doing its job, performing the many functions we expect it to play. If our answer to the question when, is always "not now, it is not a good time to expect us to be good stewards," doesn't this really show our true attitude to the land? If our attitude to the land is it can always wait, this assumes the issues are not pressing and there will always be more time? Do we have more time? Will it ever be calm enough or the political climate right so farmers and landowners can be asked to do more? The truth is the time when most owners will voluntarily act to protect water and soil will never come. There will always be some new distraction – a trade war, a new farm bill, a flood, or a disaster to make taking steps to protect nature inconvenient or "too" expensive. We can always kick the can down the road, in fact we are experts at doing so, even if this is how we ended up with polluted water, sick land, and a farming system locked into abusive and illogical practices. Purdy reminded us, we can always lie about the land, that is until we no longer can. When will the merry-go-round slow, the lies stop, and we get off? The answer is when we, the public, decide to make the change and face a new future. The new future on the land is unfolding all around us. Our challenge is whether we are bright enough or courageous enough to seize it. The last chapter examines what it promises.

Farmland south of Sunstead to be paved for houses.

Chapter Nine – Finding Hope and Resilience in the Land

Visiting the Seeds at Svalbard

When the guard unlocked the fourth and final door, thickly covered with frost and ice, we were 140 yards into the mountainside and 75 yards below the surface in a former coal mine in the Arctic. As the metal gate swung open to reveal the contents of Vault #2, the magnitude of what we saw was nearly overwhelming. Rows and rows of shelves, stacked high with boxes deposited by gene banks from all around the world. At the time of our visit in February 2018 the Global Seed Vault held over 500 million seeds, representing nearly one million of the plant species humans depend on for survival. It is hard to describe what one feels being in the presence of such a collection, gathered into a space no larger than a modest classroom. Potential, responsibility, and human frailty, are all captured there.

We were in a mountainside above the airport on the outskirts of Longyearbyen, on Spitsbergen, one of Norway's Svalbard islands 600 miles north of the Arctic Circle. At 78'12" North the SAS flight in was the farthest north of any regularly scheduled flight. We made the journey to visit the Global Seed Vault, known by some as the Doomsday Vault, the world's storehouse of "backup" copies for seed collections held in gene banks around the globe. Creators envisioned the vault as insurance against the risks, both natural and man-made, threatening the seed collections. Some threats are natural like the Philippine typhoon that struck the rice collection at IRRI, the International Rice Research Institute in Manila. Other risks are man-made, like the civil war that decimated the dryland agriculture institute seed collection in Aleppo, Syria. In either case the Global Seed Vault is an invaluable investment in the future of humanity. Our long journey from Iowa was on the occasion of the 10th anniversary celebration of the vault's dedication. Then the doors were opened to accept new deposits of seeds, including the third shipment from Seed Savers Exchange in Decorah. Having served on the SSE board since the 1990s, I was proud to know it is the only private non-profit seed bank placing seeds in Svalbard.

The trip was at the invitation of our friends Amy Goldman and Cary Fowler. Amy is famous for her series of beautifully photographed books on heirloom vegetables, like her recent *The Melon*. We served for years together on the SSE board and her philanthropy has supported SSE and many other organizations working on land conservation and sustainable agriculture. She was a long-time funder of my work at Drake as well. Cary is the creative force behind development of the Global Seed Vault, work he began as an advisor to the Nordic gene banks, and continued while head of the Global Crop Diversity Trust in Rome, part of the UN. The vault is managed and funded by NordGen, a collaboration of the Nordic gene banks, and the remarkable story of its creation is told in Cary's beautiful 2016 book, *Seeds on Ice*.

I have known Cary since the mid-1990s. Our friendship found its roots in my law review article, "Who Owns Dinner? Evolving Legal Mechanism for the Ownership of Plant Genetic Resources." The article was my attempt to present an objective appraisal of the risks and benefits in the global proliferation of intellectual property rights in plant genetics. The article led to consulting projects in Peru, the UK, Columbia, and to travels around the world, even to a term chairing USDA's National Genetic Resource Advisory Committee advising the national seed storage collections like the main facility in Ft. Collins.

All that was in the future, what I did know when writing the article was how the international conflicts over ownership and control of plant genetics were resolved would shape the future of agriculture and of those who farm. The work took me to Rome where I met Cary. His soft-spoken manner and accent reveal his Memphis roots. Years earlier he had been thrust into the world of international seed diplomacy by co-authoring with Pat Mooney a groundbreaking 1990 book, *Shattering: Food, Politics and the Loss of Genetic Diversity*. Cary also served for a time on the SSE board, helping advise the organization about how to manage the burgeoning collection of nearly 20,000 varieties of heirloom vegetables. As fate can do, Amy and Cary became acquainted, and found love through their shared fascination with plants and concern for world food challenges. They were married in 2012 in Central Park across from Amy's 5th Avenue home.

Our flight to Oslo on SAS took us first to Copenhagen, and presented an opportunity to reflect on my last visit to my grandmother's homeland. It was in December 2009 when two Drake agricultural law students joined me for a week to observe proceedings of the COP-15 Climate Summit, the UN global talks promising to set the world's path for addressing climate change. Secretary Vilsack and his wife Christie were there, representing USDA in support of the Obama Administration's ambitious cap and trade carbon tax proposal. Cary was there, promoting the Global Vault, opened the year before, and I made sure to introduce them. Anyone who follows the nation's attempts to address climate change knows COP 15 ended with little to show, fizzled out might be a better description. At home the US Senate refused to consider the carbon tax, so efforts to develop a robust cap and trade program, even paying farmers to store carbon in the soil, went dormant. Domestic politics in the US meant we have spent much of the last decade dithering and back sliding on any national plan to address climate change – or even worse, come to agreement it is even happening. Nature did not take the decade off and science didn't wait either. Today we are harvesting the poisoned fruit of our delay in forest fires, rising sea levels, more frequent hurricanes, and the other climactic injuries predictable and associated with a warming planet. On Svalbard, the seeds are safe because in choosing the location, Cary and the others planned for the eventuality if all the ice caps melt and a tsunami strikes, the vault's entrance will still be high enough on the mountain to keep the seeds safe, cold, and dry. This is nice to know but offers cold comfort, considering the litany of calamities the design foretells.

Now ten years down the road, we face increasing proof of a warming climate. If COP-15 was too soon, is 2021 too late? Perhaps this is like asking the best time to plant a tree. The answer is twenty years ago, but failing that, the next best time is today. That is where we are with climate change and in recognizing the critical challenges it presents. If the last decade has given us anything it was time to reach a better understanding of the critical role the land will play in addressing the changing climate. It also gave us time to identify people and practices we can look to for solutions. Prospects for progress became brighter with the election of a president committed to addressing climate issues. The theme of this book is finding reasons for hope in the land. There is resiliency in the land, if we are wise enough to unlock it. We turn now to the answers to our future in the land.

HOPE FROM THE LAND

I spent the last year writing about the Land – our history with it, how it shaped my life, and why we as a people need to be more attentive in thinking about its care. During this time, our nation was – and still is – facing what seemed like more existential and profound challenges. The on-going COVID-19 crisis, as this goes to press, was approaching one million Americans even as hopes for a vaccine came true. The social unrest unleashed by the murder of George Floyd called out for continued action and attention focused on racial justice and wealth inequality. The economic crisis unleashed by the pandemic forced 40 million Americans out of work, shuttered large parts of the economy, and left millions unsure of their next meal in our bountiful nation. We are slowly and steadily pulling our selves out of this hole and thankfully have a new enlightened Administration to lead the efforts. But the nation's grip on a sustainable future seems tenuous. The climate crisis is on us, presenting global threats cutting across not just the built environment, but going to the very nature of everyday choices we make – transportation and travel, what we eat, and how we live.

Contemplating these challenges made me wonder did it even make sense for me to spend my time thinking and writing about something as prosaic as the Land and our relation to it? Is this a good time to ask readers and the public to think about the Land? Is this a good time for us to hear from the Back Forty and think about how the land may see our actions? Then it dawned on me – this is the perfect time to focus attention on the Land because the land will provide the vehicle to address all these crises and more. Let me explain.

Nicholas Kristoff's July 19, 2020, column in *The New York Times*, was titled, "We Interrupt This Gloom to Offer … Hope." He discussed our past history to note how the current crush of challenges offers the Nation the opportunity to pivot to a new future not unlike how FDR seized the Depression as the opening for the New Deal. Our ability to pivot depends on many things, not the least of which is the dreaming and planning needed to provide its base. This raises at least two questions about where the Land fits into the picture. First is the matter of priority. Given the significance of the other major issues we face, how and why should we focus on the land? Second, if this new era Kristoff writes about is to happen, how will the Land issues raised in this book be embraced and where is the new thinking? Which path is more likely – that any changes will be incremental or that shifts in our actions and attitudes will be large and innovative?

Answering the first question of why we must focus on the land has been the premise of the book. The answer is the fundamental and foundational role the Land plays in life and to society. Building on this premise, now consider how the Land is connected to all four of the major crisis we face.

First, the COVID crisis has demonstrated the role of nature and the importance of being outdoors. It has increased the demand for public lands and recreational opportunities, and demonstrated the relation of a clean environment to the economic benefits it brings.

Second, the fight for racial justice links directly to the history of economic inequality and lack of access to land. The land history detailed in Chapter Five has stunted the ability of minority families to build wealth in land, and to pass the wealth across generations. This history continues to haunt us today in issues as widespread as access to quality housing, ownership of farmland, and access to other productive resources.

Third, the economic fragilities exposed by the COVID pandemic, go beyond the lack of an adequate safety net to feed people and the brittle nature of the food supply system. The dislocation of our lives from where we work to if we will ever hold meetings again has torn at the fabric of social connections. The pandemic illustrated how a healthy economy is linked to a healthy environment, safe spaces, and access to nature. As the economy rebuilds and we move to more mobile and decentralized work places, the potential for an exodus of people from cities to more rural and dispersed locations will depend on available land, economic opportunities, and internet connectivity.

Fourth, addressing climate change is a background issue for all of these challenges. It requires enlightened public policy on such matters as our energy supply, methods of transportation, markets to value carbon, and building more resilient infrastructure. Millions of new "green jobs" will open as the economy and society retool and we shift our orientation to new approaches and more sustainable lifestyles. This is the future Van Jones wrote about in 2008 in *Green Collar Economy: How One Solution Can Fix Our Two Biggest Problems*. Frederic Rich addressed these themes in 2016, in *Getting to Green: Saving Nature – A Bipartisan Solution*. Today the futures they envisioned may finally be here in part brought on by a pandemic that challenged our complacency and shook us from the inertia of tradition.

In all of the issues and uncertainties we face there are several things we can know for certain. The future will require new and different approaches. The Land will remain a source of strength and serve as the foundation for whatever work may come. People need access to clean water and food to survive, and Land will be needed to grow the food. It may be hard in stressful times to think about the Land as a priority, and about its strengths and weaknesses. Land has strength because it is always there. It has a permanence we can, and in many ways do, take for granted, while addressing issues we find more pressing, timely, and immediate. But land holds weakness for the same reasons. Does the land become a priority only in a time of crisis? Does it take a Dust Bowl for us to care about soil erosion or a Flint to care about water quality? In my view there is never going to be a best time to focus on Land or a right time when we are not otherwise occupied. The truth is now is an excellent time to focus on Land because it is enduring and because it provides a source of hope and a reason for the optimism we need to pull us through the dilemmas we face.

The Back Forty on Patience

I hear you had one of your periodic elections, this one for who will be President of the United States. There is always much at stake when it relates to the land and the environment any time there is an election, so the outcome was important to me. Elections are an opportunity for learning lessons and one from this election is what a hard time you people have with the idea of patience and waiting for things to happen. The election was on a Tuesday and folks went to bed without a clear winner, due to tens of millions who voted by mail. By Wednesday there was no result, nor on Thursday and not even on Friday. People were becoming frantic, waiting and watching the cable news to see if any new vote tallies would tip the race. Time is such a different matter for me, I don't wear a watch or own a calendar but do feel the sun and the chill of night. The seasons change, as they always have and will continue to do. One day or one week – even one year are pretty much the same to me. I guess it is because I don't really have a lifetime, at least not like you. You will be considered fortunate if you live for 70 or 80 years. Few of you will make it to 100 like Mankin almost did, falling two days short. Many of you will spark out in your fifties or sixties. If I knew my days were numbered I might be impatient too. People finally got the answer on Saturday, and as you know the answer pleased half the nation, sending them into the streets with spontaneous outpourings of joy as if a war had ended. As for the other half, they were left embittered and angry, believing the election had been rigged. That worried me because if I have learned anything in my centuries, nothing good can come from an angry people, either for the land or themselves. My worries proved true on January 6th, 2021 when the soon to be ex-President fanned the flames of hatred and mistrust to unleash a tragic insurrection threatening the very fate of your democracy.

The election is over and the insurrectionist's dust has settled even as their willingness to believe the lies told by their so-called leaders slowly evaporates. The good news is you were able to get vaccinated and turn attention back to living your lives, enjoying nature's bounty. It will even be an opportunity to think about me – about what the land does for you and for what you can do for me, the land. You know my view of life is fairly timeless and eternal, in many ways, unitary. The farmer may come out with a tractor and then a combine a few times each year, but the rest of the time it is just me. Don't get the impression I'm lonely, that is more a trait for you, but we all want to be loved and cared for. I guess it means we all want to have friends. Yes, I said it, the land can use and needs friends. My friends can come in many forms – the owner sensitive to my needs who doesn't abuse me or alter me or push me too hard. It can be the farmer who cares about conservation and my health – my soil's health. My friends can be the local officials like the soil and water conservation commissioners and USDA conservationists who keep an eye out to make sure my erosion is under control. In many ways, the public can show they are my friends by supporting the environmental rules designed to benefit me, and all the other wild things calling me home.

I am happy there are people who join together to care for the land to be my friends, and who educate and encourage others to do so. Folks like the Izaak Walton League or Ikes and land trust members like in the Iowa Natural Heritage Foundation. It has a staff and board and thousands of Iowa supporters working to protect the land. All those years ago when Russell Lord and Louis Bromfield and others got together to create a new organization dedicated to conservation they had it just about perfect when they chose the name Friends of the Land, as their rallying banner. The vision and hopes they shared still resonate today long after they all have passed and FOL is just a footnote in land conservation history. It doesn't take a new name or letterhead, or even belonging to a group to be my friend. All it takes is looking, listening, and caring. When you are out on the land next time, walking over me, take the time to listen and open your heart and mind to me, then you might find you have made a new friend too.

LAND WASN'T ON THE BALLOT, OR WAS IT?

Election Day 2020 has come and gone, and as the Back Forty notes, land wasn't on the ballot, at least not directly. But in many ways land *was* on the ballot, at least the people who will set the policy for how land is used. With the Presidential race now over, the question is how quickly can the Biden-Harris Administration reverse the many disastrous policies of the last four years *and* move forward with a new vision of hope for the land? A vision embracing science and addressing the challenge of climate change by improving soil health, harnessing the public lands, and empowering farmers and landowners to lead. Control of Congress will tip the balance and shape the ability of the new Administration to implement the ambitious $2 trillion climate initiative proposed during the campaign, as well as shape the next farm bill and many other land related issues. In Iowa, the General Assembly remained firmly in Republican control, meaning efforts to address water quality, reform drainage laws, or acquire more public lands are unlikely. The Governor abandoned her support for increasing the sales tax to fill the natural resources trust fund Iowa voters created a decade ago so only time will tell if this ever happens.

Land was even on the ballot in local elections, most notably in electing commissioners for county soil and water conservation districts. I had a vested interest in that outcome. We voted on the first day of early voting and were surprised to see the ballot listed only one candidate for the Dallas County SWCD position, even though three spots were available. We both wrote my name in as a candidate and over the next weeks I solicited former students, friends, neighbors, and others in the local conservation community to do the same. The outcome was a surprising twist of fate. Results showed over 1,750 votes were cast for "write in" candidates. It took several days for election officials to wade through the votes but a call revealed I came in third in "write in" votes with 51, behind the 257 and 57 votes of the two "winners." In a surprising development, the election official informed me the candidate on the ballot had been determined ineligible for the position. A provision in Iowa law limits commissioners to two per township, and the two remaining commissioners lived in her township. It took some time to sort out but the ruling stood, and I joined the ranks of Iowa's five hundred elected SWCD officials. The position and experience will be an opportunity to test my ideas for what local conservation districts can do to protect the soil and water.

MIGHT THIS BE AMERICA'S MOST FAMOUS FARM?

You probably haven't heard of Matt Russell or Coyote Run Farm but you might someday. Matt and his husband Patrick operate a 110-acre farm near Lacona, selling good food they grow to people they know, what Matt calls relationship marketing. Whether the pasture-raised hens that supplied their egg business for many years, the produce they sell to local restaurants, or their grass-fed "freezer beef", the goal is the same – raise great food and find customers happy to pay what it is worth. Coyote Run Farm is not just well known to its customers, it may be the most important farm in Iowa.

During the 2019-20 Presidential campaign, before the Iowa Caucuses, Coyote Run Farm was a "must do" stop for many Democratic candidates and staff who wanted to see and experience a more progressive take on the future of agriculture – especially how farmers can address the challenge of climate change. Those who visited got to hear Matt explain how conservation practices are rebuilding the soil and restoring the health of their farm. They got to learn about his vision for how Iowa farmers can and should be the leaders, the people in the driver's seat, demonstrating the role agriculture must play in our Nation's approach to climate change. The subject is of great interest to the big food companies and national environmental groups who hope to control that agenda. Matt and Patrick showed the visiting would-be Presidents how practices like planting cover crops and using grass-based farming to sequester carbon can provide some of the answers we need.

I was honored to have Matt work with me at Drake for a dozen years, but he has spent the last few years encouraging neighbors and Iowa farmers to join the climate fight. His new job is leading Iowa Interfaith Power & Light, a faith-based organization committed to addressing climate change. The Presidential campaign provided him the opportunity to spread his message to a national audience and did he ever!

What makes Matt's work so important? Why might Coyote Run Farm possibly be the most famous farm in America? Here are two reasons. During the 2019 campaign in Iowa now President Joe Biden and his wife Jill stopped there. They spent a morning with Matt and neighboring farmers, walking the fields and hearing Matt's message. You guessed it, another candidate who visited was Kamala Harris, now our Vice-President! She and her staff got to hear the message too and see resilient farming in action.

I don't know of another farm or farmer in the US, certainly none in Iowa, who "hosted" visits by both the new President and the new Vice President, to see how farmers, if given the chance can help create a brighter climate future. This isn't your typical sad farm story about failed trade policies, the latest natural disaster, or how farmers need another financial bailout. Most of the billions in subsidies the last Administration showered on farmers these past years went to folks who most likely didn't vote for Joe Biden and probably wouldn't have even if he had written the checks from his own account. But that's OK, he will be a president for all farmers and all citizens no matter their politics. President Biden has proposed a $2 trillion plan to address climate change, and farmers like the ones he and Vice-President Harris met visiting Matt will be front and center in the effort. Their climate plan has a role for farmers of all types, who want to be conservation farmers, committed to improving the land by working with nature – not against it. Doing so can restore the joy to farming, to growing food, and to addressing an important national need.

The Back Forty Explains How Imagination Will Find Hope in the Land

It will take imagination to do the things you know need done, for your health and the health of the land. Imagination will be the secret sauce Matt Russell and his friends use to help farmers lead efforts to address climate change by using the land to store and build carbon. David Montgomery and his colleagues like Drs. Hatfield and Cruse, dream of a revolution in agriculture embracing conservation farming and focused on soil health, a revolution only possible with imagination. Terry Tempest Williams writes in *Erosion*, "Conservation begins with a crisis" and your crisis is at hand. In the fall of 2020, one of Montgomery's mentors, Dr. Rattan Lal from Ohio State received the World Food Prize in recognition of his career helping farmers restore soil by building carbon and improving soil health. After a lifetime spent working with farmers in what you call "developing countries" his work is finally receiving the attention it deserves in the US. Some see it as the foundation for the resilient agriculture many believe is necessary to address the changing climate. In comments about the award Dr. Lal noted how the US has a Clean Water Act and a Clean Air Act, but still needs a Healthy Soils Act as well. If we ask the boy professor his opinion on the suggestion he would no doubt explain how water and air are free flowing goods and inherently public in nature. In contrast the soil and land don't typically move, current farming practices aside, and instead are treated as private property subject to state and local laws. The point is unless you use imagination, a federal law on soil health will face challenges just like the rights for Lake Erie.

This is where history provides a valuable lesson. At the turn of last century, the nation faced a crisis protecting the beautiful waterfowl of Florida being decimated for their feathers to use as plumes in the millinery trade. The problem was a lack of federal authority to protect wildlife. An Iowan, our friend Congressman John Lacey with his long history in regulating railroads, stepped in to suggest the interstate commerce clause could be the basis for a federal law preventing movement of wildlife killed in violation of local laws. Congress passed the Lacey Act and with it, the whole realm of not just federal wildlife protection laws, but environmental laws was born. Lacey's gift was the legal imagination to see how the interstate commerce rules used to resolve railroad issues could be the basis for protecting the natural world.

Is it too great a leap to believe the same spark of imagination cannot provide the legal basis for Dr. Lal's dream of a Healthy Soils Act? Don't the living organisms in my soil, the ones who make your food and health possible deserve protection? Perhaps the public trust doctrine, the constitutional duty officials have to protect natural resources imbued with public traits, will provide the basis. Or it might be new scientific understandings of the link between soil health and human health. When smoking was considered only a matter of personal health risks for the smokers, little was done to enact laws restricting smoking in public. But once scientific evidence proved the connection between second hand smoke and health risks for others, the floodgates opened wide and new anti-smoking laws became so prevalent smokers today have trouble finding a place to indulge, and society has benefited. Could the same happen if scientists show human health and climate are shaped by the health of the soil and water? If this happens do you believe your lawmakers will leave the question of how you choose to treat me solely to the economic needs of my owners? I like to think not. My hope is you will find the genius in the law and the imagination in your hearts to protect me and make it possible the land remains.

FINDING A VISION IN OUR CONNECTION WITH THE LAND

On a September walk with Matt Russell, we discussed his work helping farmers become leaders addressing climate change and my work examining the land and our attitudes to it. We talked about various initiatives underway to encourage farmers to embrace carbon sequestration and prepare for possible markets for carbon credits. We reflected on the many Zoom meetings we have been on concerning the land and climate connection, and agreed something is missing. Matt criticized our fellow progressives noting how we focus on policy and getting the "how we do it" right but often miss describing the larger vision, the reasons why it is the right thing to do. In his thinking, the larger vision is the source of political energy and funding to motivate progressive changes is addressing climate change. If we can articulate a vision, the policy will follow to help integrate and support the larger goal.

Our conversation came at a good time because in working to finish this book, I faced trying to summarize these ideas and articulate ways for moving forward. The book has covered many discrete issues with land as their common connection. The challenge is seeing how the issues *are all* connected: public lands, soil conservation, landowner attitudes, and the work of land trusts, as well as related concerns of water quality, climate change, and better food. It is obvious these topics are all parts of the same challenge - how society will deal with the threat of climate change. If you picture the issues as a circular interlocking chain, all the issues are present and interconnected. When you grab the chain, one link is between your fingers but all the links are connected. Now picture the chain as representing climate change - the over-riding, existential challenge facing our nation – and world. Is it the organizing issue we can use to consider what needs to be done with Land and what land can do for us?

Thinking about the range of issues we have covered in this book they can be seen as being in two sets. The first set focuses on six environmental and social outcomes we can hope for:

Better Food;

Better Farming;

Better Land;

Healthier Eaters;

Happier Farmers; and

Stronger Social Ties

All six are key elements in a vision for a better food and farming system and for a more sustainable social future. The second set of issues focus on the land and its attributes:

Healthier Soils;

Grasslands, Forests, and Wildlife Habitat;

Improved Water Quality;

Renewable Energy;

Protected Public Lands; and

Regenerative and Sustainable Agriculture

All six are key elements in a vision for a more livable, more environmentally sustainable natural world. The questions then are how are these two sets of issues related and how can one help drive the other or vice versa?

Think about the farmers we have met – folks like Matt, Ray, Paul, Khanh, and Seth. Their work on the land shows the many ways these issues are interconnected. Practices we can consider "better farming" such as planting cover crops or better nutrient management, lead directly to improved water quality. Having cleaner water helps improve farm productivity especially in regard to water management. Protecting water quality will improve society's image of farmers as being good stewards and deserving of public support. You get the idea – the issues all link together. Now think about the exciting developments happening on the land, being led by farmers and their organizations, and the exciting better foods being created by food artisans working with farmers and the land.

People like Sarah Carlson and her colleagues at Practical Farmers of Iowa, encourage planting cover crops and growing more small grains to help diversify Iowa agriculture. PFI has championed cover crops for years under the slogan "Don't Farm Naked." The exciting news is in 2020 PFI received a $1.1 million Conservation Innovation Grant from the USDA to promote this work and is partnering with food companies like Cargill to create markets for its members.

Food artisans like our friends Herb and Kathy Eckhouse own La Quercia, and make some of the finest prosciutto in the world. What began in their basement many years ago has grown into a nationally known company employing dozens who create some of the finest cured pork products on the market. They are working with farmers to raise hogs, often old-fashioned heirloom breeds, using practices like feeding them a diet of acorns, to create delicious foods consumers and chefs appreciate. The high-quality meat they produce is tied directly to the land and how the hogs are raised.

When Seth Watkins wanted to expand Pinhook Farm, his family's grass based cattle operation in southwest Iowa, he was interested in making his better land management practices permanent. Seth has a storied legacy in the history of American agriculture, being a grandson of Jessie Field Shambaugh, known as the "Mother of 4-H". To secure the future of Pinhook Farm, Seth worked with INHF and USDA to put over four hundred acres of his grasslands under a permanent farmland protection easement. The easement payment will help finance his operation and allow him to convert additional crop ground back to grass, bringing wildlife and nature back to his land.

These are just some examples of how food, farmers, and land are coming together. They illustrate how better farming can help address climate change and much more. One value of seeing these connections is considering how they offer a way to evaluate proposed policies, such as offering farmers public financial incentives to plant cover crops, and as a way to characterize developments taking place in the farm and food community involving land. For example, how do efforts by new companies like Indigo Ag asking farmers to sign contracts to take advantage of potential carbon markets, or efforts to create better science around carbon sequestration, relate to addressing climate change? How does answering these questions influence the future of the land involved?

A key factor missing in the discussion so far is obvious, there has been little mention of money, markets, or economics! If economics are what drives society and determines the way we farm, eat, and treat the land then how can it be ignored? What if better food isn't affordable or doesn't motivate consumers? What if farmers don't believe they need to change practices to have "better farming?" The question is where do money, markets, and economics fit into this vision, if these forces drive and shape what we do now on the land?

One part of the answer is recognizing how each of the twelve issues listed above can also be seen as identifying something needing to be changed or improved in our current food and farming system. Why do we need better food, what is wrong with our current farming practices, and what do we mean by better land? Why aren't eaters healthier, farmers happier, or rural communities stronger? Don't we have to answer these questions to get to the reasons why we need to change and then consider how to do it?

The answer is yes but we must begin by recognizing how each of these current problems or "challenges" is presently supported by the current market system, and how economics and money are behind each one. The drive for cheaper food and greater efficiency helps explain poor diets and cash strapped farmers. The constant push for increased crop yields fuels demand for more agro-chemicals and fertilizers, as well as the drive to consolidate farms into larger industrial scale operations for livestock, dairy, and even grain production. These forces drive soil erosion, degraded water, fewer farms, and depleted rural communities as well as eroding the quality of the food we eat.

You can't ignore economics and still hope to make a better world. Instead, the answer is you have to recognize and harness economic forces to support the needed changes. This is where the societal and economic necessity of addressing climate change becomes so significant. Taking positive steps on the land to address climate change provides the vehicle for integrating markets, money, and economics into all the various efforts to create a better food and farming system. The topics we have identified represent twelve opportunities, each important in its own right. Each issue has a constituency of organizations, activists, advocates, farmers, and entrepreneurs working to promote the goal. Consider the synergistic power we can unleash if all of these topics – better food, better farming, better land – and more can be harnessed together!

How does producing better food support climate efforts, how does building healthier soils do the same? These are the questions we need to ask – because the answers are real and empowering. Our focus shouldn't be on our problems but instead the focus should be on what are our solutions. Once you take this step – reversing the image to look at the food and land economy from the other side of the window, as solutions and opportunities rather than problems, then a new world of opportunities opens.

It doesn't matter what the community or societal goal might be: better wildlife habitat, more protected lands, better food, or happier farmers. Each can be achieved, in part, through programs, policies, products, and practices designed in some way to address climate issues. Want more wildlife habitat, then preserve and plant more grasslands and protect our forests. Want better food, then raise cattle on grass and chickens on pasture. Want happier farmers then pay them for the better food their practices produce and for protecting the soil, water, and land. Want more protected public lands, then use conservation easements to protect the land so the conservation stays done and compensate landowners for their efforts. Want to reduce greenhouse gases and sequester more carbon in the land, then use grasslands, plant cover crops, reduce reliance on agro-chemical fertilizers, put livestock back on the land, and retire the unprofitable crop acres to plant prairies and pollinator habitat. These steps and practices are being taken by innovative farmers and landowners alike, and are being promoted by forward looking food and agriculture companies, institutions, and organizations working for a better future. The tools and policies to help achieve a better climate future exist and new markets can and are being created to support them. What we need to understand is how all these issues and practices aren't just interesting individual examples but instead how they reflect a collective image of a larger quilt, and a grander vision for a brighter future.

THE BIG OAK

My evening walks pass under the Big Oak and often lead to my thinking about what it could tell us about the land. To own a big tree, or more accurately to own the land where a big tree resides, is to hold a passport to history and your imagination. At the very northwest corner of our ten acres here at Sunstead we are caretakers for just such a tree. It is an ancient white oak with a circumference at chest height of fourteen-and-a-half feet. Guidelines from the state forestry department for estimating the age of trees indicate our oak is over 320 years old! It is hard to imagine this lone tree on the west edge of a long ridge above Sugar Creek surviving so many years. It is about fifty yards from our house but looking out the windows, you can tell it is a huge tree with massive spreading limbs. Not until you stand under it do you realize just how large it is. The first lateral branches are as big around as the hundred year old oaks shading our house.

At 320 years, our oak sprouted around 1700, about the same time Father Joliet waded onto the northeastern shore of Iowa along the big river he "discovered." At 320 years our oak was already a substantial tree in 1790 when the American states ratified the Constitution uniting us as a nation bound by laws. When the 6th battalion of the Iowa

1st Regiment mustered in Adel, county-seat of new Dallas County, and marched to join the other Union forces fighting the southern rebellion, our oak was 160 years old.

A sense of history leads me to believe our oak served as a witness tree for surveyors in 1852 marking the section lines in Boone Township. Witness trees were the visual landmarks surveyors used to identify corners as they mapped the 640-acre sections to give the land "official" legal status. Blazes were cut into trees to indicate directions to the actual corners. An oak as large as ours would have been in the 1850s, made an ideal marker located on the southern edge of the flat, almost treeless prairie stretching miles to the northwest. You see what I mean about a big tree being an invitation to imagination! Now we have the honor of possessing the big tree – or is it the other way around? Our twenty-five years here on Sunstead mark us as beginners in the relation. Hopefully it will continue for another twenty-five years but of this we have no guarantee. Regardless when our time here ends, the Big Oak will remain, beckoning new owners and visitors to stand under its arms, inviting them to imagine the history it knows and to think about how the land sustains us.

The Back Forty Talks about the Future

This is a good time to talk about my future. I can't do that without talking about the farm family who own me, because my future, at least for the next few decades, is intertwined with theirs. If you live in Iowa you may have heard of Ray Gaesser, a well-known and respected figure in the agricultural community. For the last 20 years or so Ray and his wife Elaine have been my owners and going back years before Ray farmed me under a lease with the Hamiltons. Ray and Elaine blew into the area – as the locals would say – over thirty years ago from their native Indiana. A young farm couple, they were looking for the opportunity to buy some fertile southwest Iowa land, lower priced than back home. Since arriving in Mercer Township their farming operation has unfurled like an umbrella. What started on a modest scale has grown to include over 800 acres of owned land and another 3,000 plus acres farmed under leases with other non-operator owners.

Ray Gaesser

The Hamiltons were fortunate when the Gaessers bought the old Rundlett farm a mile south next to the country school. When Lowell, or Ham as some called him, began to age an important question was who would farm his land next? After recovering from open heart surgery at 78, and suiting up for one more year farming, Lowell hung it up and rented the farm. Ray stepped in and over the years became a friend, neighbor, and loyal tenant. He took great care of the land and boosted the yields on the fertile soil far beyond what Lowell ever dreamed possible. Lowell had always been a reluctant farmer more interested in a good book than farming. Ray's lease payments were fair and generous and he looked after Lowell and Zella, making sure the driveway was plowed and they were well. Their boys appreciated his attention, so when conversations turned, as they inevitably do, to who might buy the land if the day came to sell, agreement was easy – Ray would have first dibs. The sale came sooner than planned when Lowell's health forced him into the Lenox nursing home and the monthly bills piled up. That is when they decided to sell me. Ray and Elaine were happy to have the chance to buy me, remember I am a flat black and fertile forty! The money changed hands, a fair price at the time, and the nursing home bills were paid. Zella died the next year breaking her neck in a fall down the stairs. A tragic end for an 80-year old dynamo, though she seemed worried about the senility she sensed coming. Lowell died the next year, shortly after turning 91, never knowing she was gone. In some ways he, or at least his spirit, had departed several years before. He died before more land had to be sold to meet the tiller's toll. The 160 acres left went in halves to the boys and the older one soon sold the south 80 acres to Ray. Now the Gaessers owned me, and the 80 to my west. A few years later when the boy professor and his wife had a house fire, they sold another twenty acres to Ray to help rebuild their home at Sunstead. You see the pattern here, so it was no surprise a decade later when they decided to sell the last sixty acres to Chris, their son.

Gaesser's farm is different than the Hamilton's, measuring in thousands of acres not 200, and on the business end, adding more zeroes for the yields produced, expenses paid, and grain checks cashed. Yet in many ways the farms were the same, Iowa family farms where the income and opportunities all came from me, the land. The scale and technology may differ but in many ways their spirit and soul were the same.

The Hamiltons were happy to sell the land to Ray because they knew he was a great farmer and cared for the land. I am happy they sold me to Ray for the same reasons. In some ways, Ray is a typical Iowa farmer who wants to produce big crops, but in other ways he is quite different. One difference is how committed Ray is to the future and to demonstrating how farmers can steward the land, care for the soil and water, and still be productive and profitable. That is why he plants thousands of his acres to cover crops, not because a federal program pays him to, but because it is a good practice improving soil health and enhancing yields, all while protecting water quality. Ray has spent decades devoting time and energy as a farm leader through the soybean associations. He served as President of the Iowa Soybean Association and nationally led the United Soybean Board. He even ran to be Iowa Secretary of Agriculture, coming close to securing the Republican nomination.

His choice of the Iowa Soybean Association was no accident. Unlike most other commodity groups, the ISA takes a more progressive view on environmental issues and the need for farmers to lead in addressing them. Rather than deny the problems or resist reasonable efforts to address water quality, the ISA has stepped forward to help its members show what can be done in their fields to address the issue. For over twenty years the ISA has played a leading role on water quality in the Raccoon River watershed. Roger Wolfe, a long time ISA staff member, is in charge of the ISA environmental initiatives. The ISA's work on water quality has put them at cross purposes with other Iowa agricultural groups more willing to deny the issues, but the ISA board is resolved to support innovative efforts on the land. As politicians and environmentalists come to recognize the opportunities for farmers to market what are known as "environmental services," ISA's leadership is proving invaluable. They developed a program called Agricultural Solutions, working with farmers on thousands of acres of land to improve water quality, store carbon in the soil, and reduce fertilizer inputs. The program is funded by corporate partners like Cargill, who "purchase" the environmental benefits and pay farmers as much as $50 an acre for the improvements. ISA is creating exactly the type of "farmer-led" effort to address climate change Matt Russell talks about. It is putting farmers in the driver's seat and stacking the environmental benefits to market. This is exactly the type of new thinking your President and Vice-President heard about when visiting Russell's farm. It is exactly what the ISA is showing can be done, if farmers put their minds to it. I am in good hands with the Gaessers owning me. It makes me optimistic for my future, here in the middle of section 13 in Mercer Township, Adams County, Iowa.

WHAT YOU CAN DO FOR THE LAND

As we come to our conclusion for this book about the Land, you may be wondering what you can do to help move these issues forward. Here are eight simple steps you can take to engage with the land:

1. Learn more about the land issues in your area. What are the key disputes and opportunities being addressed and which governmental bodies are responsible for making the decisions?

2. Look for opportunities to be on the land. Explore your local public lands like county parks and find maps and schedules to know the activities available. Buying a kayak or canoe and getting out on the local water is a great way to see and experience what is going on.

3. If you are a landowner think about what you are doing with your land and how it is being managed. What opportunities do you have to enhance nature, like plant-

ing pollinators and installing bird houses, restoring a prairie, or putting a buffer along a stream?

4. If you own land think about its future. If you preserved a natural feature or restored an oak savanna what is your plan to pass it on? If you are interested in making your protections permanent think about what agency, land trust, or group can help you do so.

5. Buy some land and become a landowner. There is no better way to connect with the land than owning some and having the opportunity to leave your portrait on the land you steward.

6. Become involved in organizations working with the land, especially land trusts like the INHF. There are over 1,400 land trusts in the nation, from national groups like the Nature Conservancy to local land trusts. They offer many ways to be involved as a member or donor, or as a volunteer for a prairie seed harvest or stream clean-up.

7. Support politicians and local officials who share your values and feelings toward the land and nature. It might be the legislator working to acquire public lands or the city council member or soil commissioner protecting water quality. Democracy works when engaged citizens aid our elected and appointed officials. Find out who is responsible for the lands you enjoy and let them know your views and expectations.

8. Become a land leader so you are in the position to make decisions for the land. You can run for elected office like county soil commissioner or seek appointment to

the city park board. There are many great ways to exercise your civic rights to make sure your voice and views about the land are heard.

These are all steps you can take to be involved with the land – and there are many more you can discover. The land is a wellspring of wealth and wellness, and of a lifetime of satisfaction, enjoyment, and fulfillment - so get out on the land and get started.

Acknowledgments

This book grew from decades of teaching, writing, lecturing, and thinking about what has happened during my lifetime to the land and to our rural society. Many people played a role in shaping my thinking on these issues and helped give me opportunities to gain new insights and understanding. The process of listing those who deserve special thanks is fraught with the peril of leaving someone off the list who feels they too deserve credit. So by way of a blanket waiver let me say if you feel you played a role shaping my career and thinking – I appreciate your help and my apologies if you do not find your name here.

First thank you to my agricultural law colleagues who labor in these fields and whose advice and support I have sought on many occasions, notably Susan Schneider, Michael Roberts, Janie Hipp, Christopher Kelly, and Anthony Schutz. My law school colleagues and friends at Drake University have for almost forty years tolerated my presence and given me a place and space to engage in wide ranging work on almost any topic I found of interest – always free of political or institutional restraint. In particular my Deans – Richard Calkins, David Walker, Peter Gopelrud, and Jerry Anderson deserve special thanks for providing me with the support and autonomy to seek the opportunities and projects giving life to the work of the Center. A special thank you to the hundreds of students who came through my classes and our program on agricultural and food law over the decades - for sharing their energy, backgrounds and enthusiasm. A special thank you to the several who stayed to work at the Center - Greg Andrews, Ed Cox, and Anna Jordan Gray. A special thank you to my former student Jennifer Zwagerman who became not just a protégé but my successor as the Center Director, giving me the confidence to retire knowing the Center is in good hands. The person I worked with most closely for over 12 years, Matt Russell, is featured in the book and deserves special thanks for his friendship, loyalty, and love for rural culture and the people who farm, like those we grew up knowing in southwest Iowa.

My colleagues in "Harry's Book Club" – Jim Autry, Harry Bookey, Dr. Dick Deming, Jeff Fleming, the late Dick Gibson, Bob Riley, and Mike Schaeffer were the first readers of the working draft and I thank them for their insights, suggestions, and even criticisms – and for letting me impose on their kindness. Our friends Bill and Susan Knapp deserve special thanks for sharing their lives with us and for providing the opportunity to enjoy the beauty of Siesta Key as a place to write and think – as well as enjoy the pleasures and company of true friends. Many other friends and professional colleagues deserve mention, like: Amy Goldman Fowler whose decades of friendship and support have been a touchstone of stability; Paul Willis and Bill Niman for inviting me in to experience the growth and evolution of the Niman Ranch Pork Company and to see first hand how good farming, good food, and caring for the land are linked; and my three mentors - Jake Looney, Louis Lorvellec, and Gus Schumacher whose friendship and contributions to my life are discussed in the book. Thank you also to the good farmers like Ray and Elaine Gaesser, Seth Watkins, and Liz Garst who by caring for their land are showing others what good land stewardship means. Thanks also to my many friends in the land trust community, in particular the board and staff of the Iowa Natural Heritage Foundation – and its two leaders – Mark Ackelson and Joe McGovern for giving me the opportunity – now for over 30 years – and a front seat to observe how private land conservation can work to protect nature and the land, even in a farming dominated state like my Iowa.

A special thank you to Steve Semken at Ice Cube Press for his faith in this project and for giving me the opportunity to give voice to the land.

Finally a special thank you to my wife Khanh for her love, support, inspiration, and example in creating a home and garden where we find peace and beauty - and offer hospitality to our many well-fed friends. To conclude, a book about the land and my life on it would not be complete without recognizing the hard work and sacrifices of my parents and the other family members who made it possible the land remains.

THE LAND REMAINS
suggested reading list and bibliography:

Wendell Berry, *Culture and Agriculture: The Unsettling of America*, (1977)

Bosselman, Callies, and Banta, *The Taking Issue: An Analysis of the Constitutional Limits of Land Use Control*, White House Council on Environmental Quality (1973)

Douglas Brinkley, *The Wilderness Warrior: Theodore Roosevelt and the Crusade for America* (Harper 2009) and *Rightful Heritage: Franklin D. Roosevelt and the Land of America* (Harper 2016)

Louis Bromfield, *Pleasant Valley (1943), Malabar Farm (1947), and Out of the Earth (1948)*

Novella Carpenter, *Farm City: The Education of an Urban Farmer*, (2009)

Rachel Carson's *Silent Spring* (1962)

Temra Costa, *Farmer Jane: Women Changing the Way We Eat*, (2010)

Art Cullen, *Storm Lake: A Chronicle of Change, Resilience, and Hope from a Heartland Newspaper*, (Viking 2018)

John C. Culver and John Hyde, *American Dreamer: A Life of Henry A. Wallace*, (Norton 2000)

Bernard DeVoto, *The Easy Chair*, (1955)

Tim Egan, *The Worst Hard Times*, (2006)

Edward Faulkner, *"plowman's folly,"* (1943)

Cary Fowler, *Seeds on Ice*, (2016)

Cary Fowler and Pat Mooney, *Shattering: Food, Politics and the Loss of Genetic Diversity*, (1990)

David Gessner, *Leave It as It Is: A Journey Through Theodore Roosevelt's American Wilderness*, (Simon and Shuster 2020)

Eddie Glaude Jr., *Begin Again*, (2020)

Amy Goldman, *The Melon*, (2019)

Hagenstein, Gregg, and Donahue, ed., *American Georgics: Writings on Farming, Culture and the Land*, (2011 Yale)

Gove Hambidge, *Enchanted Acre: Adventures in Backyard Farming*, (1935)

Miles Harvey, *King of Confidence: A Tale of Utopian Dreamers, Frontier Schemers, True Believers, False Prophets, and the Murder of an American Monarch*, (2020)

Stephen Heyman, *The Planter of Modern Life*, (2020)

Ken Ilguanas, *This Land is Our Land: How We Lost the Right to Roam and How to Take it Back* (Plume 2018)

Van Jones, *Green Collar Economy: How One Solution Can Fix Our Two Biggest Problems*, (2008)

Christopher Ketcham, *This Land: How Cowboys, Capitalism, and Corruption are Ruining the American West*, (Viking 2019)

David Korten, *The Great Turning; From Empire to Earth Community*, (2006)

Harold Lee, *Roswell Garst: A Biography*, (Iowa State Press 1984)

David L. Lendt, *Ding: The Life of Jay Norwood Darling* (1979)

Aldo Leopold, *A Sand County Almanac*, (1949)

Andro Linklater, *Measuring America: How an Untamed Wilderness Shaped the United States and Fulfilled the Promise of Democracy* (2002)

James Loewen, *Lies My Teacher Told Me*, (1995)

Russell and Kate Lord, ed., *Forever The Land: A Country Chronicle and Anthology*, (1950)

Neal M. Maher, *Nature's New Deal: The Civilian Conservation Corps and the Roots of the American Environmental Movement*, (2007)

David Mas Matsumoto, *Epitaph for a Peach* (1995)

Anthony McCain, *Shadowlands: Fear and Freedom at the Oregon Standoff*, (Bloomsbury 2019)

H.L. Mencken, *Treatise on the Gods*, (1930)

David Montgomery, *Growing a Revolution: Bringing Our Soil Back to Life*, (2017)

John Wesley Powell, *1878 Report on the Lands of the Arid Region.*

Jedediah Purdy, *After Nature: A Politics for the Anthropocene* (2015)

Jedediah Purdy, *This Land is Our Land: The Struggle for a New Commonwealth*, (Princeton University Press 2019)

Frederic Rich, *Getting to Green: Saving Nature – A Bipartisan Solution*, (2016)

Richard Rothstein, *The Color of Law: A Forgotten History of How Our Government Segregated America*, (2017)

Neil Sampson, *Farmland or Wasteland: A Time to Choose*, (1981)

William Souder, *Mad at the World: A Life of John Steinbeck* (2020)

William Souder, *On a Farther Shore: The Life and Legacy of Rachel Carson* (2012 Crown)

Wallace Stegner, *Beyond the Hundredth Meridian: John Wesley Powell and the Second Opening of the West* (1954)

Wallace Stegner, *The Gathering of Zion*, (1964)

Wallace Stegner, *The Uneasy Chair* (1974)

John Steinbeck, *Grapes of Wrath* (1939)

Steven Stoll, *Ramp Hollow: The Ordeal of Appalachia* (2017)

John Taliaferrois, *Grinnell: America's Environmental Pioneer and His Restless Drive to Save the West* (2019)

Terry Tempest Williams, E*rosion: Essays on Undoing (Sarah Crichton Books 2020)*

Donald Worster in *A Passion for Nature: The Life of John Muir*, (Oxford 2008)

USDA, 1938 Yearbook of Agriculture, *Soils and Men*

USDA 1958 Yearbook of Agriculture, *Land*

USDA Report on the Structure of Agriculture: A Time to Choose, (1980)

Neil Hamilton is an emeritus professor of law and the former director of the Agricultural Law Center at Drake University in Des Moines. He retired from full-time teaching in 2019 after thirty-eight years focusing on agriculture and food law. Raised on his family farm in Adams County, he attended Iowa State University for Forestry and the University of Iowa for Law. Teaching, writing, and consulting work led to travels around the globe and across the state and nation. His advice is sought by Presidential candidates, cabinet secretaries, reporters, and others looking for insight on issues involving farming, rural society, conservation, and land tenure. He has served for decades on a variety of non-profit boards including the Iowa Natural Heritage Foundation and Seed Savers Exchange. He lives with his wife Khanh at Sunstead Farm, a market garden oasis they created on Sugar Creek, near Waukee, just west of Des Moines.

The Ice Cube Press began publishing in 1991 to focus on how to live with the natural world and to better understand how people can best live together in the communities they share and inhabit. Using the literary arts to explore life and experiences in the heartland of the United States we have been recognized by a number of well-known writers including: Bill Bradley, Gary Snyder, Gene Logsdon, Wes Jackson, Patricia Hampl, Greg Brown, Jim Harrison, Annie Dillard, Ken Burns, Roz Chast, Jane Hamilton, Daniel Menaker, Kathleen Norris, Janisse Ray, Craig Lesley, Alison Deming, Harriet Lerner, Richard Lynn Stegner, Richard Rhodes, Michael Pollan, David Abram, David Orr, and Barry Lopez. We've published a number of well-known authors including: Mary Swander, Jim Heynen, Mary Pipher, Bill Holm, Connie Mutel, John T. Price, Carol Bly, Marvin Bell, Debra Marquart, Ted Kooser, Stephanie Mills, Bill McKibben, Craig Lesley, Elizabeth McCracken, Derrick Jensen, Dean Bakopoulos, Rick Bass, Linda Hogan, Pam Houston, Paul Gruchow, and Bill Moyers. Check out Ice Cube Press books on our web site, join our email list, Facebook group, or follow us on Twitter. Visit booksellers, museum shops, or any place you can find good books and support our truly honest to goodness independent publishing projects in order to discover why we continue striving to "hear the other side."

Ice Cube Press, LLC (Est. 1991)
North Liberty, Iowa, Midwest, USA
Resting above the Silurian and Jordan aquifers
steve@icecubepress.com
Check us out on Twitter and Facebook.
www.icecubepress.com

Celebrating Thirty-One Years of Independent Publishing.

To Fenna Marie—
one of the beautiful reasons
I know that the land and love
shall remain everlasting.